TOPPLING QADDAFI

Toppling Qaddafi is a carefully researched, highly readable look at the role of the United States and NATO in Libya's war of liberation and its lessons for future military interventions. On the basis of extensive interviews within the U.S. government, this book recounts the story of how the United States and its European allies went to war against Muammar Qaddafi in 2011, why they won the war, and what the implications for NATO, Europe, and Libya will be. This was a war that few saw coming, and many worried would go badly awry, but in the end the Qaddafi regime fell and a new era in Libya's history dawned. Whether this is the kind of intervention that can be repeated, however, remains an open question – as does Libya's future and that of its neighbors.

Christopher S. Chivvis is a senior political scientist at the RAND Corporation and teaches International History at the Paul H. Nitze School of Advanced International Studies at Johns Hopkins University. Chivvis has served in the Office of the Secretary of Defense for Policy and worked for more than a decade on international security and political economic issues in the United States and Europe. He has written for several top policy and scholarly journals, including *Current History, International Affairs, Journal of Contemporary History, Foreign Policy, The National Interest, Survival, The Washington Quarterly, International Herald Tribune, The Washington Times, U.S. News and World Report, The Christian Science Monitor*, and CNN.com.

WITHDRAWN
UTSA LIBRARIES

Toppling Qaddafi

LIBYA AND THE LIMITS OF LIBERAL INTERVENTION

Christopher S. Chivvis

RAND Corporation

CAMBRIDGE
UNIVERSITY PRESS

32 Avenue of the Americas, New York, NY 10013-2473, USA

Cambridge University Press is part of the University of Cambridge.

It furthers the University's mission by disseminating knowledge in the pursuit of education, learning, and research at the highest international levels of excellence.

www.cambridge.org
Information on this title: www.cambridge.org/9781107613867

© Christopher S. Chivvis 2014

This publication is in copyright. Subject to statutory exception and to the provisions of relevant collective licensing agreements, no reproduction of any part may take place without the written permission of Cambridge University Press.

First published 2014

Printed in the United States of America

A catalog record for this publication is available from the British Library.

Library of Congress Cataloging in Publication Data
Chivvis, Christopher.
Toppling Qaddafi: Libya and the limits of liberal intervention / Christopher S. Chivvis.
   pages cm
ISBN 978-1-107-04147-9 (hardback)
1. Libya – History – Civil War, 2011– Participation, American.   2. Libya – History – Civil War, 2011 – Participation, European.   3. North Atlantic Treaty Organization – Armed Forces – Libya.   4. Military assistance, American – Libya.   5. Military assistance, European – Libya.   6. Regime change – Libya.   I. Title.
DT236.C44   2013
961.205–dc23   2013029439

ISBN 978-1-107-04147-9 Hardback
ISBN 978-1-107-61386-7 Paperback

Cambridge University Press has no responsibility for the persistence or accuracy of URLs for external or third-party Internet Web sites referred to in this publication and does not guarantee that any content on such Web sites is, or will remain, accurate or appropriate.

Library
University of Texas
at San Antonio

For my parents

Contents

List of Figures	page x
List of Table	xii
Foreword by Ambassador James F. Dobbins	xiii
Preface	xv
Abbreviations	xvii

Chapter 1	**Libya and the Light Footprint**	1
	Libya's Relevance for the Future	3
	Controversies over Libya	6
	Libya as Contemporary History	13
	How Can Intervention Work?	15
Chapter 2	**Precipitous Crisis**	18
	Libya in the Arab Spring	19
	The Libyan Arab Jamahiriya	21
	Libya Revolts	25
	Pressure for Action Mounts	31
	The NATO Defense Ministerial	37
Chapter 3	**The Pivots of War**	43
	The Defense Department and Other Skeptics	44
	The Administration Debate	48
	The Decision to Intervene	53
	United Nations Security Council Resolution 1973	59

	Enabling the International Community "To Act in Concert"	64
	Why the United States Changed Course	67
Chapter 4	**Crippling Qaddafi and Infighting over NATO**	69
	The Debate over NATO	71
	Coalition Operations under Odyssey Dawn	79
	Rearticulating the Strategy and Objectives	90
	A Country Divided	93
Chapter 5	**Stalemate**	96
	Handoff and Operational Structure	97
	"NATO Is Disappointing Us"	101
	Relative Weakness of the *Thuwwar*	104
	Allied Capability Shortfalls	110
	The Naval Dimension	119
	Return of the Predators	121
Chapter 6	**Grinding Away**	123
	Attacking with Helicopters	126
	Upping the Political Pressure: The Contact Group	131
	The Coalition Starts to Creak	134
	Troubles with Congress	139
	Postconflict Conundrums	143
Chapter 7	**Sudden Success**	147
	Negotiating a Way Out	148
	Special Forces and Glimmers of Progress	154
	Divisions in the Rebel Camp	159
	The Fall of Tripoli	160
	When to End It	164
Chapter 8	**The Impact of the War and Its Implications**	169
	Libya after Qaddafi	169
	How Successful Was the Intervention?	173

	Implications for the Future	187
	Libya and the Future of Liberal Intervention	200
Appendix A	*Operation Unified Protector Participating Nations*	207
Appendix B	*Operation Unified Protector Basing*	209
Appendix C	*Regime Defections*	214
Appendix D	*Contact Group*	223
Bibliography		225
Index		245

Figures

1.1	Rubble at Bab al Aziziya, Tripoli	page 2
2.1	The Mediterranean Basin	19
2.2	Libya	24
2.3	Protests in Benghazi, February 2011	26
2.4	Weekly cross-border movements from Libya during the conflict	28
3.1	President Obama and Secretary Clinton confer in the Oval Office, March 18	48
3.2	United Nations Security Council votes on Resolution, March 17, 1973	64
4.1	French Air Force Rafale flies in Operation Harmattan	70
4.2	Arleigh Burke–class guided-missile destroyer USS *Barry* (DDG 52) launches a Tomahawk missile in support of Operation Odyssey Dawn	82
4.3	President Obama delivers his addresses on Libya at the National Defense University, March 28	92
5.1	The early phase of the operation focused heavily on Tripoli and Misrata (targets April 11–May 15)	105
5.2	A Rebel technical	109
5.3	Operation Unified Protector average daily sorties per week	115
5.4	Evolution from static to dynamic targets (weekly totals: April 17–October 23)	115

LIST OF FIGURES

6.1	A French Tigre flying from the amphibious assault ship *Tonnerre*	127
6.2	Northwestern Libya was the most targeted region, followed by the northeast, May 16–July 17	130
6.3	Operation Unified Protector European basing	138
7.1	Libya's mid-northern coast/mid-western region was the most heavily targeted in the latter phase of Operation Unified Protector, July 18–October 23	163
7.2	Secretary Clinton meets Libyan soldiers at the steps of her C-17 military transport upon her arrival in Tripoli in Libya, October 18, 2011	166
8.1	Libyans celebrate their newfound freedom in Martyr's Square in Tripoli	170
8.2	Free Libya graffiti on a wall in Tripoli, February 2013	201

Table

8.1 Libya and Kosovo in comparative perspective *page* 177

Foreword

Toppling Qaddafi is a detailed, carefully researched look at U.S. and NATO roles in Libya's war of liberation. It is also an attempt to draw lessons from that experience. This can only be done by relating this operation to past events and future contingencies. Chris Chivvis thus places NATO's war in Libya squarely in the line of post–Cold War humanitarian interventions that began in Somalia in 1991 and continued throughout that decade in Haiti, Bosnia, and Kosovo. He also so notes its continuity with the U.S. air campaigns conducted in Afghanistan as well as in Bosnia and Kosovo. Rather remarkably, all four of those air wars achieved their objectives without the need for substantial U.S. ground forces or the loss of a single American pilot.

While the Libya intervention thus has many antecedents, it is also unique in one respect. In contrast to nearly every U.S. intervention since at least 1945, it involved no postcombat U.S. military presence – no occupation force, no peacekeepers, no trainers, no advisors, nothing. In this regard the Libyan operation was not a product of the relatively benign 1990s experience with humanitarian peacekeeping operations (the last three of which also occasioned no American casualties), but rather the more sobering consequences of the U.S. invasions of Iraq and Afghanistan, where thousands of American service members were lost and maimed. In this sense the "no boots on the ground" Libya operation is unprecedented, and as Chivvis indicates, this lack of any postvictory follow-through may yet prove its most controversial legacy.

Chivvis opens his account of NATO's war in Libya with an amusing survey of the Monday morning quarterbacking from across the American political and ideological spectrum that accompanied and followed these operations. In his concluding chapter he provides a much more comprehensive and thoughtful reflection on what the Libyan experience may mean for future U.S. policy, NATO cooperation, humanitarian intervention, the employment of airpower, the nature of postconflict stabilization, and, of course, for Libya.

The war in Syria has already occasioned more civilian casualties than the conflict in Libya. The Libyan precedent is already being cited by both those who favor a Western intervention in Syria and those who oppose it, most notably Russia, which clearly regrets having joined in authorizing the former intervention. If that earlier air operation was one step forward for liberal interventionism, Syria would seem two steps back. *Toppling Qaddafi* provides both a highly readable account of NATO's war in Libya and a carefully analytical basis for evaluating the relevance of this precedent for current and future conflicts.

Ambassador James F. Dobbins
Director, International Security and Defense Policy Center
RAND Corporation
Washington, DC

Preface

When it began, I was among those skeptical about the 2011 intervention in Libya. To me, working in the Pentagon at the time, evidence of the many burdens the Iraq and Afghanistan wars had placed on our country was ever present. On the surface, another war hardly seemed wise. But further research, reflection, and many discussions with friends, colleagues, and those who were involved in the conduct of this intervention encouraged me to take a more positive view of what had been accomplished and why. This book does report some deficiencies in the conception and conduct of the war, but the picture presented is, on the whole, far more positive than I had envisioned at the outset.

The need to design cost-effective solutions to crises such as the one that occurred in Libya in March 2011 will be with us for many years. The study of what was and was not accomplished in Libya gives insight into both the limits and the potential for liberal intervention – the use of force to protect the basic liberal values of human rights, the rule of law, and constitutional government.

Funding for this book was provided in part through the RAND Corporation's continuing program of self-initiated independent research. Support for such research is provided, in part, by donors and by the independent research and development provisions of RAND's contracts for the operation of its U.S. Department of Defense federally funded research and development centers. The research was conducted within the National Security Research Division (NSRD). NSRD conducts research and analysis on defense and national security topics for the United States and allied defense, foreign policy, homeland security, and intelligence communities and foundations and other nongovernmental organizations that support defense and national security analysis.

Many people supported the research for this book by offering advice, support, or interviews about the intervention, including Mustapha Abushagur, Assad Aljerbi, Abdulmonem Alyaseer, Ali Aujali, Christina Bartol, Warren Bass, Robert Bell, John Berger, Jim Bergeron, Sam Berkowitz, David Calleo, Derek Chollet, Ivo Daalder, Etienne de Durand, Liz Dibble, Jim Dobbins, Jim Goldgeier, Phil Gordon, Mark Jones, Seth Jones, Athena Katsoulos, Melissa Ko, Wolfram Lacher, Jeff Martini, Joe McMillan, Karim Mezran, Khaled Mezran, Bradley Mitchell, Karl Mueller, Michael O'Hanlon, Mark Ramsay, Lisa Samp, Camille Sawak, Will Schlickenmaier, Julie Smith, Joe Stein, Dirk Vandewalle, Marten van Heuven, Justin Vaïsse, Sandy Vershbow, Andrew Weiss, Fred Wehrey, Catherine Weisner, George Willcoxon, and Damon Wilson. Several others in Washington, Brussels, Paris, and Tripoli also supported the effort, and I have also benefited from discussions with my students at the Johns Hopkins University School of Advanced International Studies.

Abbreviations

AFRICOM	U.S. Africa Command
AQIM	Al Qaeda in the Islamic Maghreb
AWACS	Airborne Warning and Control System
CAOC	Combined Air Operations Center
CENTCOM	U.S. Central Command
DFID	Department for International Development (UK)
DPKO	Department of Peacekeeping Operations (UN)
EU	European Union
EUCOM	U.S. European Command
FMS	Foreign Military Sales
ICC	International Criminal Court
ISR	intelligence, surveillance, and reconnaissance
LIFG	Libyan Islamic Fighting Group
NAC	North Atlantic Council
NATO	North Atlantic Treaty Organization
NDU	National Defense University
NTC	National Transitional Council
OUP	Operation Unified Protector
RAF	Royal Air Force
SACEUR	Supreme Allied Commander Europe
SAR	search and rescue
SEAD	Suppression of Enemy Air Defense
SHAPE	Supreme Headquarters Allied Powers Europe

STRATCOM	U.S. Strategic Command
TRANSCOM	U.S. Transportation Command
UAE	United Arab Emirates
UN	United Nations
UNSCR	United Nations Security Council Resolution
WTO	World Trade Organization

1 Libya and the Light Footprint

On August 23, 2011, rebels armed with Kalashnikov assault rifles and backed by NATO warplanes overran Muammar al-Qaddafi's Tripoli compound, Bab al-Aziziya, ending the North African dictator's nearly forty-two-year reign. Within days, ordinary Libyans were visiting Bab al-Azizya en masse, wide-eyed tourists in the seat of power of their own land. Signs reading "Down, Down U.S.A" and "We love our Leader Muammar Qaddafi forever" greeted them at the door – perhaps posted during the revolt, perhaps of older provenance. Inside the rubble-strewn compound, visitors found the iconic House of Resistance, which was bombed by the United States in 1986 in retaliation for Qaddafi's terrorism and then preserved in its ruined state by Libya's self-proclaimed "Brother-Leader" as a symbolic reminder of his country's oppression by the "great powers."[1]

Six months earlier, almost to the day, Qaddafi had stood there, in front of the very same House of Resistance, and delivered a bloodcurdling speech promising to crush a week-old revolt in Libya's second largest city and eastern hub, Benghazi. With rebel forces on the verge of victory, the end was now near. Qaddafi would flee to his hometown of Sirte, and the fighting against him would drag on through October, but for all intents

---

[1] Jon Lee Anderson, "King of Kings: The Last Days of Muammar Qaddafi" *New Yorker*, November 7, 2011, vol. 87, no. 35.

Figure 1.1 Rubble at Bab al Aziziya, Tripoli. Photo by author.

and purposes, with his compound now in rebel hands, his four decades of dictatorship were over.[2]

When the revolution had first erupted in February, on the heels of uprisings in neighboring Tunisia and Egypt, the United States and its allies had seemed unwilling to do much to stop Qaddafi from brutally repressing it. The financial and political toll of the previous decade's interventions in Iraq and Afghanistan was still high, and Europe was in the throes of a major economic crisis that threatened to upend its post–Cold War political and economic structures, buffet the world economy back into recession, and possibly cost President Obama a second term.

[2] Other books that discuss the war in detail include Ethan Chorin, *Exit the Colonel: The Hidden History of the Libyan Revolution*. New York: Public Affairs, 2012; Alison Pargeter, *Libya: The Rise and Fall of Qaddafi*. New Haven: Yale University Press, 2012; Jason Pack, ed., *The 2011 Libyan Uprisings and the Struggle for the Post-Qaddafi Future*. New York: Palgrave, 2013; Karl Mueller, ed., *Precision and Purpose: Airpower in the Libyan Civil War*. Santa Monica, CA: RAND, forthcoming.

Moreover, the crisis in Libya was only one of numerous issues dominating headlines from across the turbulent Arab world, and some of the rationales for military intervention in Libya might also have been applied to other states in the region and beyond.

But as the violence in Libya intensified in the weeks that followed, and Qaddafi's forces threatened to terrorize the civilian population further, the pressure to act mounted. In early March, Qaddafi recovered his footing, ordering his tanks to recapture Benghazi, and threatened to slaughter anyone who stood in his way. French and British leaders pushed the UN to endorse military action that would stop the regime forces from leveling the city. Unexpectedly, the Arab League voted in favor of a no-fly zone over Libya, and, within days, the Obama administration changed course from reticence about military action to a full-court press for a UN Security Council Resolution authorizing military action to protect Libyan civilians from the regime's attacks.

On March 17, that resolution, UN Security Council Resolution 1973, passed, authorizing "all necessary means" to this end. Two days later, cruise missile and bomber strikes from a U.S.-led coalition destroyed Qaddafi's air-defense systems, forced his armored columns to retreat, and established a no-fly zone over most of the country. An international contact group with a broad-based membership was created to manage the politics of the intervention, support the rebels (*thuwwar*), and pressure Qaddafi to step down. A seven-month, NATO-led military intervention that would end in Qaddafi's capture and death had begun.

Libya's Relevance for the Future

This intervention was a high-tech, combined, joint mission operating from Europe, the United States, and elsewhere in the Middle East and North Africa. Military operations relied heavily on precision airpower, striking some 6,000 targets, mostly along Libya's Mediterranean coast. All told, the operation would draw on more than 8,000 personnel, 21 warships, and some 250 aircraft flying more than 26,000 sorties. Nineteen countries contributed military forces, including four from the Middle East. By contrast with interventions in Kosovo, Afghanistan, and Iraq, the Libya intervention started with a mandate from the United Nations for the use of force to protect civilians – although the interpretation of that mandate would become a central controversy of the war.

If military intervention in the broadest sense is defined as the use of force to affect the internal affairs of another country, Libya was the seventh significant U.S. military intervention since the end of the Cold War.[3] In the 1990s, the Clinton administration had intervened in Somalia, Haiti, Bosnia-Herzegovina, and Kosovo. The following decade, the George W. Bush administration intervened in Afghanistan and Iraq. The intervention in Libya was heavily influenced by the lessons of these earlier experiences, but it also departed from them in novel ways that will shape the American and allied approach both to NATO and to military intervention in the future.

To begin with, in Libya, the United States encouraged European allies, and France and Britain in particular, to take the lead and bear the heaviest burden they could. Prior to Libya it was widely assumed on both sides of the Atlantic that the United States would always take the lead in any significant allied military intervention. This, however, was often a cause of consternation among U.S. allies. They argued that America had a track record of refusing to agree to military operations unless it was fully in command, yet when given command it too often conducted operations in ways that accounted poorly for allied interests. In the early years of the Bosnia war, for example, the Clinton administration was uneasy about getting pulled back into military commitments in Europe just as the Cold War had ended, and resisted allied overtures for greater U.S. political and military support. At that time, many allies saw U.S. reluctance as problematic. A few years later, however, when

---

[3] If one accepts that the 1991 Gulf War was primarily international. Technically Panama was post–Cold War, but it was closer to the Cold War mode of U.S. unilateral intervention in Latin America.

NATO intervened in Kosovo, European allies sometimes complained that the United States was dictating strategic and operational choices without due consideration for European needs. Fairly or not, Europeans felt marginalized in important military decisions, where their interests were arguably more intensely in play than those of the United States. European concerns that the United States would not intervene unless it had a dominant role eventually became an impetus for the European Union's (EU) push to build a military capability independent of NATO.

In Libya, however, the U.S. offered broad support but adopted a limited military role and did not seek to dictate terms to the allies. Many analysts and politicians in the United States disapproved of this approach and criticized it roundly. In general, however, it worked. Why it worked, and whether it can be used again – or whether this was a unique case where the stars aligned in favour of a European lead – is one of the central issues of this book. The French surprised many by following up their action in Libya by spearheading an intervention against Al Qaeda linked rebels in northern Mali, thus suggesting the U.S. approach to Libya may be replicable. But before U.S. defense planners start to base their assumptions on the Libya model, they will also have to consider the difficulties European militaries faced in Libya, as well as nagging questions about Europe's broader financial and defense outlook.

Beyond the novel U.S. approach to NATO, the Libya intervention was also a test case for a less ambitious concept of operations, sometimes referred to as the "light footprint." Although it drew on an impressive array of advanced weaponry, the intensity of allied operations over Libya was low in comparison with previous post–Cold War U.S. interventions. The Libya intervention contrasted sharply both in size and scope of ambition not only from the two interventions of the George W. Bush administration, but also from those of the late Clinton era in the Balkans. In Libya, the initial objective was limited to stopping violence against innocent civilians. Although this objective would eventually entail others that were more ambitious than many critics would have liked, allied objectives in Libya were on an altogether different scale from Iraq and

Afghanistan. Likewise, operations in Libya were largely restricted to airpower, which itself was used in a very limited way in keeping with the UN Security Council Resolution and need to avoid civilian casualties.

How well this approach worked, how it might be improved in the future, and the overall implications for the future of military intervention are also central issues in this book. As the United States emerges from the wars of the post-9/11 decade deeply reticent about extended foreign military deployments and focused on fiscal and economic restoration, the possibility of a lower-cost approach to the challenge of state failure and other forms of violent international crisis is much needed. U.S. political leaders will surely be more reserved about interventions after Iraq and Afghanistan, but it would be naïve to think the United States could eschew interventions altogether; the moral, political, and national security costs of permitting the spread of chaos in today's highly integrated world are simply too high. A more cost-effective approach to meeting this challenge than the one currently in place is nevertheless sorely needed. Libya serves as a partial guide to how the circle can be squared.

Controversies over Libya

In Washington, heated debates over intervention started as soon as the revolution broke out in February. Many esteemed observers argued sharply against taking any action to help Libya's suffering population. "We don't need Libya to offer us a refresher course in past mistakes," wrote General Wesley Clark, who commanded NATO's 1999 intervention in Kosovo.[4] U.S. interests in Libya were simply too weak to warrant another war, he argued. This was not Egypt, with its access to the Suez, much less Saudi Arabia, with a major share of the world's petroleum, or Iran, with its aspirations to nuclear weapons (which Qaddafi had renounced several years earlier). Opponents such as Clark argued that a military intervention would do more harm than good, since NATO

---

[4] Wesley K. Clark, "Gen. Wesley Clark Says Libya Doesn't Meet the Test for U.S. Military Action" *Washington Post*, March 11, 2011.

would never commit the military might required to succeed; if it did, they argued, blowback from another U.S. invasion of a Muslim country would be worse than any possible gains from ousting Qaddafi (who everyone at least agreed was odious).[5]

But neoconservative hawks, progressive interventionists, and others contended the revolt in Libya gave the United States an opportunity to save lives, support democracy, and improve America's reputation in a region where it was exceptionally bad and had suffered greatly over the past decade. Former George W. Bush administration officials called for immediate U.S. military action, as did liberal European interventionists such as Paddy Ashdown, who had led international state-building efforts in Bosnia in the previous decade.[6] A leading progressive proponent of intervention, was Princeton University Professor Anne-Marie Slaughter, who had recently departed from a post as director of the Policy Planning Staff in the Obama State Department. Slaughter argued that doing nothing while Qaddafi killed innocent civilians would make U.S. rhetorical support for the uprisings elsewhere in the Arab world look like so much worthless posturing, and potentially undermine pro-democracy movements in neighboring Tunisia and Egypt. She also claimed Qaddafi was not as tough as he looked and predicted that if he were confronted with a UN Security Council Resolution he would quickly cave and seek a negotiated settlement, thereby limiting the need for an extended military action in the first place.[7]

The debate would evolve as the war did. A few weeks into it, former U.S. secretaries of state Jim Baker and Henry Kissinger penned a joint article arguing that although the United States should normally only use

---

[5] See, e.g., Richard Haas, "The U.S. Should Keep Out of Libya" *The Wall Street Journal*, March 8, 2011; Leslie H. Gelb, "Don't Use U.S. Force in Libya" Daily Beast, March 8, 2011.

[6] Jim Lobe, "US Neo-Cons Urge Libya Intervention" Al Jazeera, February 27, 2011; Paddy Ashdown, "It Is Time for Europe to Back a No-Fly Zone in Libya" *Financial Times*, March 13, 2011.

[7] Anne-Marie Slaughter, "Fiddling While Libya Burns" *The New York Times*, March 13, 2011.

military force when a national interest is at stake, Libya was an exception to the rule, a case where "a limited military intervention solely on humanitarian grounds could be justified" by the fact that Qaddafi's forces had already done so much harm, were about to do much more, and the regime was so weak. The Carter administration's national security advisor Zbigniew Brzezinski voiced support, albeit tepid, on MSNBC, saying that the intervention "really isn't war," but rather "something between war and military intervention." He ultimately backed the decision to go to war.[8]

Once underway, there was no shortage of skepticism about the chances the intervention would work. Observers such as Princeton Professor Gary Bass and *New York Times* columnist Ross Douthat warned that the United States would never commit the resources needed to win. Relying on rebel forces on the ground was a risky strategy, these critics argued, not only because the rebels might lose, but also because they would likely have very different objectives from the United States and be much less sensitive to western concerns about human rights and the rules of war.[9]

Other critics charged that the administration was confused about its objectives and needed to prosecute the war much more aggressively. Initial support for the intervention notwithstanding, Kissinger soon censured the White House for an alleged lack of clear objectives on *Fox News*. The *Washington Post* charged the administration of being "confused in Libya" and pushed for more aggressive action.[10] Archconservative John Bolton fumed that the "Nobel Peace Prize-winning president has gotten things badly wrong by demanding Muammar Gadhafi's ouster while restricting U.S. military force to the more limited objective of protecting civilians." He predicted the intervention would be a "massive strategic

---

[8] Hiram Reisner, "Brzezinski: Libya Action Isn't War, But Necessary Intervention" Newsmax, March 24, 2011.

[9] Gary J. Bass, "How Doing the Right Thing Can Go So Wrong" *Washington Post*, April 10, 2011.

[10] "Confused in Libya" *Washington Post*, March 23, 2011. See also, "Mr. Obama Speaks on Libya" *Washington Post*, March 29, 2011; "Saving Lives in Libya" *Washington Post*, April 28, 2011.

failure."[11] For the GOP presidential candidate Mitt Romney, Bolton had it right: the United States was in "mission muddle in Libya."[12]

More partisan political attacks on the U.S. strategy mounted in May, as initial military success gave way to stalemate and an unnamed administration official dubbed the White House strategy "leading from behind" in an interview in the *New Yorker*. Although the article in which the phrase appeared, written by Ryan Lizza and titled "The Consequentialist," was very positive overall about the Obama administration's first three years in office, the phrase "leading from behind" opened the floodgates of reproach for many on the right.[13] "Leading from behind is not leading. It is abdicating. It is also an oxymoron," wrote Charles Krauthammer in the *Post*.[14] For Jim Dubik, a retired U.S. Army three-star general, leadership was "not exercised from the rear by those who seek to risk as little as possible." Like it or not, Dubik prognosticated, "America's leadership has been crucial to most of NATO's successes. The same will be true in Libya. … Airpower alone does not produce victory."[15] Administration officials would rue the day the Lizza article appeared, as their efforts to get the genie back in the bottle by disowning the comment only seemed to make matters worse.

Yet just as the neocons and others pushed for more aggressive action in the face of difficulty, other analysts complained about alleged hypocrisy and called for NATO to pull out. Richard Haass, president of the Council on Foreign Relations, argued in testimony to the U.S. Senate that the administration had greatly exaggerated the potential scale of the humanitarian crisis that was brewing, and overstated the significance of

---

[11] John Bolton, "Obama Wobbly on Libya" BostonHerald.com, April 21, 2011.
[12] Mitt Romney, "Mission Muddle in Libya" National Review Online, April 21, 2011.
[13] Ryan Lizza, "The Consequentialist: How the Arab Spring Remade Obama's Foreign Policy" *The New Yorker*, May 2, 2011.
[14] Charles Krauthammer, "The Obama Doctrine: Leading from Behind" *Washington Post*, April 28, 2011.
[15] James M. Dubik, "Finish the Job" *New York Times*, April 26, 2011.

Qaddafi's repression for the rest of the region. He urged a cease-fire that allowed Qaddafi to remain in office.[16] In an anonymous article in *Slate* titled "A Solution from Hell" – in reference to White House National Security Staff Senior Director Samantha Power's Pulitzer Prize–winning book, *A Problem from Hell* – a group that went by the pseudonym "n+1" pronounced that "wars waged by the U.S. are inevitably imperialist" while simultaneously charging the United States with hypocrisy for acting in Libya but not Syria, Bahrain, or elsewhere.[17] In a similar vein, Steven Erlanger of the *New York Times* lamented the doctrine of the "responsibility to protect" which he thought dubious given its uneven application around the world.[18] Still other critics foresaw a repeat of the Iraq and Afghanistan wars,[19] while, Leslie Gelb, former president of the Council on Foreign Relations, lectured the administration for allegedly weakening NATO,[20] and several observers attacked the White House for allegedly conducting an "illegal war."[21]

When Tripoli fell to the rebel forces in August, some of these critics changed their tune, but many did not.[22] "But oh what a war!" wrote Erlanger with apparent sarcasm. "More than six budget-busting months against one of the weakest militaries in the world, with shortages of planes, weapons and ammunition."[23] Neo-isolationists and libertarians insisted that the political and economic costs of intervention were too

---

[16] "Prepared statement by Richard N. Haass" *United States Senate Committee on Foreign Relations*, First Session, 112th Congress, April 6, 2011.

[17] n+1, "A Solution From Hell" *Slate Magazine*, August 17, 2011.

[18] Steven Erlanger, "Libya's Dark Lesson for NATO" *New York Times*, September 4, 2011.

[19] Rajan Menon, "Breaking the State" *The National Interest*, (May-June 2011).

[20] Leslie Gelb, "How Libya Saps America's Power" Daily Beast, April 17, 2011.

[21] George F. Will, "Obama's illegal war" *Washington Post*, May 29, 2011; Bruce Ackerman, "Obama's Unconstitutional War" ForeignPolicy.com, March 24, 2011; Eric A. Posner, "Outside the Law" ForeignPolicy.com, October 25, 2011.

[22] For example, Richard Haass, "But Plan to Put Boots on the Ground" *Financial Times*, August 23, 2011; Ross Douthat, "Libya: The End and the Beginning" New York Times Blogs, August 24, 2011.

[23] Steven Erlanger, "Libya's Dark Lesson for NATO" *New York Times*, September 4, 2011.

high, even if Libya emerged as a more just society where humans lived with greater dignity and security,[24] complaining of an "aimless foreign policy supported by a purposeless alliance [i.e., NATO]" in which the "benefits paled in comparison to the costs."[25]

But praise for the intervention was also widespread and sometimes fulsome. Supporters hailed a "Huge Win for Libyans, a Win for Obama" even while noting that there was still a lot of work to be done.[26] Anne Marie Slaughter said the case had shown that "it clearly can be in the U.S. and the west's strategic interest to help social revolutions fighting for the values we espouse and proclaim."[27] Neoconservatives were also upbeat, though more cautiously. Robert Kagan cast the operation as an "imperfect triumph ... a big victory for the ongoing pan-Arab revolution" as well as NATO. But NATO had triumphed in spite of itself – the administration had been too slow to take action and then too timid to use military power, he argued.[28] George W. Bush's deputy secretary of defense Paul Wolfowitz credited President Obama for intervening, but also lamented that the United States had not played a bigger role.[29]

For commentators such as Fareed Zakaria, these complaints were way off the mark: the Libya model offered a whole new way for the United States to work with allies, at least under certain conditions. A "new era in U.S. foreign policy" had dawned. In the future, the United States could hope to restrict itself to a supporting role in some wars. "The old model of American leadership – where we took all the decisions, bore all the burdens,

---

[24] Benjamin A. Valentino, "The True Costs of Humanitarian Intervention" *Foreign Affairs*, (November-December 2011), vol. 90, no. 6.
[25] Doug Bandow, "Libya: Costs Outweigh Benefits" *The National Interest*, October 21, 2011.
[26] Steve Clemons, "Libya: Huge Win for Libyans, a Win for Obama, Challenges Next" *The Atlantic*, August 22, 2011.
[27] Anne-Marie Slaughter, "Why the Libya Sceptics Were Proven Wrong" *Financial Times*, August 25, 2011.
[28] Robert Kagan, "To the Shores of Tripoli" *The Weekly Standard*, Vol. 16, No. 47, September 5, 2011.
[29] Paul Wolfowitz, "America's Opportunity in Libya" *The Wall Street Journal*, November 3, 2011.

paid all the costs and took all the glory – has to change," Zakaria said.[30] Others agreed, but were doubtful the conditions that had made it possible for the United States to play a lesser role would ever materialize again.[31] For national security expert Michael O'Hanlon of the Brookings Institution, for example, "Libya was a success but a provisional and limited one to date."[32]

Throughout the conflict and after, the Obama administration's approach to the intervention also fuelled Washington dinner party/think tank/blogosphere debate about the principles that underlay President Obama's foreign policy, whether or not Obama had a doctrine and, if so, what that doctrine was and where it fit within traditional U.S. Wilsonian and realist foreign policy currents. The Lizza article characterized the president's policy in Libya as grounded in a pragmatic, case-by-case analysis that focused heavily on the consequences of action instead of ideological considerations. Writing in the Daily Beast, Michael Tomasky compared Obama's handling of Libya to George H. W. Bush's cautious engagement in the face of the breakup of the Warsaw Pact, arguing that Libya was evidence of the administration's self-conscious "no-doctrine doctrine."[33]

Other observers saw Libya as a major inflection point in the administration's record. Daniel Drezner argued that the Obama team had arrived in the White House intending to curtail U.S. commitments overseas, restore U.S. global standing, and shift the U.S. international burdens onto others, but the Libya intervention revealed a revival of American exceptionalism and an overall shift in strategy toward "counterpunching" by asserting U.S. ideals, reassuring allies, and showing resolve with adversaries.[34] Seeking perhaps to irritate Obama's supporters, Walter Russell

---

[30] Fareed Zakaria, "A New Era in U.S. Foreign Policy" CNN.com, August 23, 2011.
[31] Daniel W. Drezner, "Why Libya Is Not a Template for Future Military Statecraft" foreignpolicy.com, August 25, 2011.
[32] Michael O'Hanlon, "Libya and the Obama Doctrine" foreignaffairs.com, August 31, 2011.
[33] Michael Tomasky, "Obama's True Claim to Fame" Daily Beast, August 23, 2011.
[34] Daniel W. Drezner, "Does Obama Have a Grand Strategy?" *Foreign Affairs*, vol. 30, no. 3 (May–June 2011).

Mead took this line of argument a step further, rendering Obama's foreign policy as a more effective incarnation of Bush-era neoconservatism. Obama was a "more effective neoconservative than President Bush," declared Mead, noting that the Obama democracy agenda in the Middle East was as aggressive as Bush's, that this president was "not afraid to bomb." The difference was more of tone, he said – Bush was a tough guy, Obama a "reluctant warrior."[35]

Zakaria tried to kill the whole discussion of the Obama doctrine, quipping that the search itself was misguided because "the doctrinal approach to foreign policy doesn't make much sense anymore." But even he could not resist the urge to speculate about Obama's worldview, which he also said was akin to the pragmatic realism of George H. W. Bush and his tough-minded internationalist predecessors, Harry Truman, Dean Acheson, and George Kennan.[36]

Libya as Contemporary History

One purpose of this book is to offer an account of the intervention from the perspective of Washington and other key capitals so that readers can begin to parse the validity of these various claims about the war. Given that the research for this book began during the war and continued through its immediate aftermath, it may be worth acknowledging at least three limitations inherent in the writing of contemporary history. The first of these is the lack of publicly releasable information regarding the internal U.S. and allied thinking about the intervention. In keeping with standard declassification procedures, most of the important classified documentation on the Libya intervention will not

---

[35] Walter Russell Mead, "W Gets a Third Term in the Middle East" National Interest.com, August 22, 2011.

[36] Fareed Zakaria, "A Doctrine We Don't Need" *Washington Post*, July 7, 2011. See also Clay Risen, "Obama's Non-Doctrine Doctrine" New York Times Blogs, August 26, 2011.

be available for at least a quarter century. The basis of this study is largely off the record, but unclassified interviews with high-level U.S. policy makers from the White House, State and Defense departments, and foreign officials closely involved with the intervention. Those interviews are combined with the broadest range of available public-source information about the intervention, including newspapers, television reports and interviews, multimedia sources, and social networking such as Twitter. Although field research was conducted on the ground in Libya, what follows focuses on the strategies and debates in the capitals that contributed forces to the intervention, in particular the United States.

A second challenge is that we do not yet know the whole story about the Libya intervention. On one level, this is a problem with any historical writing – hence Chou En Lai's famous quip to Henry Kissinger about it being too soon to judge the historical significance of the French Revolution. Yet if historical writing is to have any real value, it must draw some conclusions about the events that it depicts. Hence, historians must always decide where to end the story and take a stand. Here, the story ends with the death of Qaddafi in October 2011. But from a certain perspective, Qaddafi's death was only the end of the beginning. The intervention will certainly look different if Libya collapses back into a lengthy civil war, another dictator emerges from the fray, or a virulently anti-Western form of quasi-democracy develops. None of these is the most likely outcome for Libya, but they are all possible, so some analysts might wish to reserve comment pending further information about the long-term implications of the intervention. Nevertheless, while judging events so soon after they have transpired carries inherent risks, these risks can be diminished by an effort to distinguish between known outcomes, outcomes that appear likely, and those where more speculation is required.

A third challenge is the risk that the closeness to events will impair the historian's responsibility to judge events with due objectivity. One of the benefits of contemporary history is that the emotional and psychological character of the events under examination is more accessible, even if other more traditional data points are not. It is true that too much proximity can make objectivity difficult, but it hardly makes it impossible. An effort in this book has at least been made to be objective about the implications of the intervention for the United States and its allies.

How Can Intervention Work?

The extraordinary costs of the Iraq and Afghanistan wars have generated outsized skepticism about the wisdom of intervention. Some critics have emphasized the negative impact intervention can have on the national purse.[37] Others fear a tendency to destabilize the constitutional balance of power between the executive and legislative branches of the U.S. government.[38] Still others believe intervention simply cannot work, no matter how much money is spent and how wise intervening powers may be, given inevitable cultural and nationalist resistance. For them, the U.S. foreign policy apparatus is culturally, politically, and constitutionally incapable of understanding let alone having any significant effect on the wilderness they encounter when they intervene. They argue that the post–Cold War belief in intervention is indicative of the hubris of Western foreign policy elites. One such critic writes about Afghanistan, "The international community was confident that it understood the nature of Afghanistan's problems, and despite its short tours, security restrictions, and lack of experience and knowledge, it was [wrongly] confident that it was in a position to transform the situation."[39]

---

[37] For a leading contemporary neoliberal view of the Libya intervention, see Ted Galen Carpenter, "Another War of Choice" *National Interest*, March 18, 2011. For background, see Friedrich Hayek, *The Road to Serfdom* (Chicago: University of Chicago Press, 1944); Christopher S. Chivvis, *The Monetary Conservative: Jacques Rueff and Twentieth Century Free Market Thought* (De Kalb: Northern Illinois University Press, 2010), chapter 4.

[38] For a classic statement of this view, see Robert Taft, *A Foreign Policy for Americans* (New York: Doubleday, 1951), p. 23.

[39] Rory Stewart and Gerald Knaus, *Can Intervention Work?* (New York: Norton, 2011), p. 31.

Critiques of military intervention such as these are important to bear in mind, but eschewing intervention altogether will simply not be possible.[40] Intervention will remain one of the most difficult and vexing international security issues U.S. and allied policy makers face.

The Libya example is helpful in meeting this challenge in part because it reminds us that there is also no one way to intervene, and that not all interventions need to follow the Iraq and Afghanistan model. Instead, there are a range of military options from armed drones to full-scale conventional war, as well as a variety of combinations in which the diplomatic and financial tools of national power can be deployed alongside the military. When faced with a crisis, the real challenge is how these tools can be assembled to increase the chances of an outcome favorable to our interests and compatible with our values. In practice, therefore, the question is not so much whether or not to intervene as how.

To help decisionmakers, some international security analysts have sought to develop rules, guidelines, and standards for intervention. They suggest, for example, the attributes of a violent crisis – the number of deaths, how gruesome they are, and so on – that can justify the use of force.[41] But there will never be a single rule that determines whether a particular crisis meets the bar for international intervention, just as there will never be a silver bullet that guarantees an intervention's success. A cost benefit analysis that considers the national security and humanitarian stakes, includes a realistic estimation of the likely costs and probabilities of success, and looks at multiple options will always be the best practice. It is not enough for there to be good reason to intervene; there also has to be a feasible strategy and a realistic hope that the use of force will make things better rather than worse for both those who intervene and those the intervention is meant to help. We may intervene decisively in less important cases simply because the costs are relatively low and the

---

[40] For the most concise and compelling argument to this effect, see Robert Cooper, "The New Liberal Imperialism" Observer.co.uk, April 7, 2002.

[41] For a recent example, see Robert A. Pape, "When Duty Calls: A Pragmatic Standard of Humanitarian Intervention" *International Security*, vol. 37, no. 1 (Summer 2012), 41–80.

chances of success are high, and cautiously – or not at all – in more important cases because the costs are too much.

Understanding even in general terms what the outcome of a particular formula will be in advance is, of course, an extremely difficult if not impossible task. Interventions frequently turn out to be more challenging and resource intensive than expected, especially when measured against optimistic promises often made at the outset. Moreover, some interventions that were popular at the start – Somalia, for example – turned out to be fiascoes. The difficulty of knowing how a strategy will work out would be high even if policy makers were not forced to operate and make decisions on tight timelines and with very ambiguous information about a complex and rapidly changing situation on the ground. A large degree of improvisation will therefore always be part of a successful intervention.

There is no single model, strategy, or capability that can serve as a silver bullet for intervention. The careful study of past cases, however, is the best – and really the only – option available for understanding how alternative intervention strategies might work in the future. The Libya case demonstrates the pros and the cons of a more limited form of intervention. Limited intervention in Libya worked but only in achieving the limited aims of stopping Qaddafi's violence against his people and showing support for the Arab uprisings. It could not, for example, in itself guarantee a flourishing postwar Libyan democracy, even if it opened the door to it. But the Libya example does offer insight into a different approach from that which the United States has pursued in recent years and, in that way, points one possible path toward the future.

2 Precipitous Crisis

The war came on fast. In early 2011, European leaders were struggling with an economic crisis that threatened the foundations of post–Cold War European unity. European parliaments and publics were anything but enthusiastic about NATO's protracted operations in Afghanistan, and many sharply disapproved of the U.S.-led coalition that toppled Saddam Hussein in 2003. Across the Atlantic, the United States was still struggling to overcome the effects of the 2008 financial crisis, and the U.S. public was sick of war after a decade of overseas deployments in Iraq and Afghanistan. As of early 2011, the chances NATO would go to war again thus seemed remote at best. Echoing this sentiment, U.S. Secretary of Defense Robert Gates gave a speech at West Point on February 24, citing President Dwight Eisenhower and warning that "any future defense secretary who advises the president to again send a big American land army into Asia or into the Middle East or Africa should have his head examined."[1] Only a few weeks later, however, the United States and its allies were again headed to war in the Middle East. There would be no land army, but the fact they intervened at all was, in retrospect, rather remarkable.

---

[1] Robert Gates, speech delivered at the United States Military Academy, West Point, NY, February 25, 2011. As of May 8, 2012: http://www.defense.gov/speeches/speech.aspx?speechid=1539.

Figure 2.1 The Mediterranean Basin.
Source: University of Texas Libraries.

Libya in the Arab Spring

The revolutions that began in Tunisia in late 2010 and spread across the Middle East in subsequent months posed a number of thorny problems for U.S. policy in the region. The United States had a long-standing tradition of supporting peaceful democratic change around the world, and U.S. support for conservative regional powers was viewed as having complicated U.S. efforts to undermine the appeal of militant Islamist extremists. At the same time, however, America's relationship with these conservative regimes, especially Egypt and Saudi Arabia, was a bulwark of U.S. strategy in a region that still had major strategic significance on account of its energy resources, and it was clear the revolts underway in early 2011 might produce Islamist regimes with policies inimical to the United States.

President Obama had entered office at a time when public opinion of the United States in the Middle East had fallen to historic lows. Despite efforts to restore America's reputation during the second term of the

Bush administration, the negative fallout from the 2003 Iraq War persisted. Obama's approach to the region had been pragmatic, seeking to improve America's standing with the Arab "street," while at the same time promoting gradual rather than revolutionary political reform. In a speech in Cairo in June 2009, Obama expressed a cautious universalism by noting on the one hand that "all people yearn for certain things: the ability to speak your mind and have a say in how you are governed; confidence in the rule of law and the equal administration of justice; government that is transparent and doesn't steal from the people; the freedom to live as you choose," while emphasizing on the other hand that change ought not to be imposed "from the outside."[2]

The Cairo speech had an immediate and positive impact on the U.S. standing in regional public opinion, but it also set high expectations. A year and a half later, those expectations had yet to be met, and opinion of the United States was dropping again to 2008 levels when the protests erupted in early 2011.

At first uncertain about the depth and resilience of these protests, the United States attempted to navigate with general, though careful, statements of support for democracy in Tunisia and the importance of reform in Egypt, while at the same time continuing to back Egyptian President Hosni Mubarak and tolerating crackdowns on protesters elsewhere. In January, however, Protests in Tunisia reached a boiling point and the authoritarian Tunisian president Zine al-Abidine Ben Ali fled the country. In February, the United States called on the Egyptian military to eschew violent repression and effectively cast off its long-standing ally, Mubarak. Mubarak's subsequent resignation raised hopes and energized protestors across the region. The protests now looked like revolts and were gaining momentum. The spotlight shifted to the United States and its allies for concrete signals of support.

---

[2] White House, Office of the Press Secretary, "Remarks by the President on a New Beginning" Cairo, June 4, 2009. On these issues, see Martin S. Indyk, Kenneth G. Liberthal, and Michael E. O'Hanlon, *Bending History: Barack Obama's Foreign Policy* (Washington, DC: Brookings Institution Press, 2012), pp. 112–184.

The Libyan Arab Jamahiriya

Libya is the seventeenth largest country in the world, with 1,759,540 sq km landmass, an area slightly larger than Alaska. There are 4,348 km of borders, including approximately 1,000 km each with Algeria, Chad, and Egypt, shorter borders with Tunisia, Sudan, and Niger, and 1,770 km of coastline on the Mediterranean. The Sahara Desert runs through its middle, and more than 90 percent of the territory is desert or semidesert, with only 1 percent arable land. As a result, most of the population lives along the Mediterranean coastline. Libya's three provinces – Cyrenaica in the east, Tripolitania in the west, and Fazzan in the south – were separate under Ottoman rule, brought together under the Italians, and held together only reluctantly under King Idriss. Fazzan is dislocated from the northern provinces by the Sahara, and while the connection between east and west is better, the distances are still long and thoroughfares are limited largely to a few roads along the coast. As a leading U.S. scholar of modern Libya put it, at liberation in 1951, Libya was "an accidental state: created by and at the behest of great power interests and agreed to by the local provinces who feared other alternatives."[3]

When Qaddafi came to power in a 1969 coup that overthrew the Senussi monarchy, he thus became the ruler of a state that had gained its independence from colonial rule just eighteen years earlier, had no experience with democracy, was increasingly dependent on newly discovered oil reserves, and had long-standing differences between its three major regions. Qaddafi drew his inspiration from the anti-European Arab nationalism of his Egyptian neighbor Abdel Nasser, and used the Senussi monarchy's close ties to the West – the United States had given significant aid to the Libyans in the 1950s and enjoyed access to Wheelus and al-Adem airbases – as a justification for his coup.

---

[3] Diederik Vandewalle, *History of Modern Libya* (New York: Cambridge University Press, 2012), p. 40.

His *Green Book*, the first volume of which was introduced in 1975, emphasized popular rule, stateless society, and direct democracy, and called for populist economic policies. Playing on traditional Libyan suspicion of the state, Qaddafi claimed not to be part of it and set up a system of informal governing institutions alongside the formal instruments of power. He would use these institutions to control the political apparatus of the state while undermining and remaining formally detached from it. With these institutions, his own skill and charisma, intensifying confrontation with the West, and harsh repression of dissent, he managed to hold Libya's various regional, religious, and tribal groups at bay. Meanwhile, society was atomized by its historically apolitical nature and the lack of any of the intermediary bodies that would normally accompany the emergence of a modern economy. By 2011, energy production still accounted for 65 percent of GDP and 80 percent of government revenue. Although per capita income was fairly high at $14,100, an estimated one-third of the Libyan population was still very poor and lived below the poverty line.[4]

Libya had never held the same importance in U.S. regional security strategy as that of larger countries such as Egypt or Saudi Arabia. To the extent that Libya was important, it was not because of what Libya offered to the United States so much as what it threatened. Since the later 1970s, Qaddafi had been a bête noire of Western governments, a sponsor of terrorist attacks on a Berlin nightclub in 1986, a perpetrator of the 1988 bombing of Pan Am Flight 103, and an aspirant to nuclear arms.

More recently, however, Qaddafi's once hostile relationship with the United States and Europe seemed to have been transformed. In 2003, in the wake of the U.S. invasion of Iraq, Qaddafi dropped his nuclear program and renounced terrorism. His standing with Europe and the United States improved, and Libya was removed from the U.S. list of

---

[4] Vandevalle, *History of Modern Libya*, passim.; *CIA World Factbook*, 2012.

state sponsors of terrorism; Libya's ties with the European Union strengthened, and Qaddafi visited European capitals, including Paris, where he was received with pomp and circumstance in 2007, signed billions of Euros in business deals, and literally pitched his tent on the lawn of the neoclassical nineteenth-century Hotel de Marigny. In 2009, the United States and Libya exchanged ambassadors and normalized diplomatic relations. New bilateral trade and defense agreements were reached in 2009 and 2010.

Although some scholars would later argue that this diplomatic opening sowed the seeds of Qaddafi's eventual overthrow, the regime's renunciation of terrorism and nuclear weapons was not indicative of any noticeable change in the underlying nature of the regime, which remained one of the most repressive on earth, stuck at the bottom of global rankings of democracy-tracking organizations such as Freedom House.[5] The International Criminal Court, for example, reported that "people who opposed the regime, referred to by the regime as 'stray dogs,' as well as members of their families, were arrested, tortured and in some instances even disappeared."[6]

Shortly after the fall of Ben Ali in January, Qaddafi again put his tyrannical instincts on full display, blaming the revolt on Wikileaks and warning that Tunisians could be "raided and slaughtered in their bedrooms and the citizens in the street killed as if it were the Bolshevik or the American Revolution."[7] In retrospect, these statements are a clear sign of his insecurity and delusions. Leaders such as Qaddafi who have avoided such rhetoric – Syria's Bashar al-Assad, for example – have had greater

---

[5] Freedom House, *Freedom in the World*, 2010. As of May 8, 2012: http://www.freedomhouse.org/report/freedom-world/2010/libya. For a history of U.S. engagement with Libya in the years prior to the revolution, see Ethan Chorin, *Exit the Colonel: The Hidden History of the Libyan Revolution* (New York: Public Affairs, 2012).

[6] International Criminal Court, "Situation in the Libyan Arab Jamahiriya" ICC-01/11, June 27, 2011, para. 20.

[7] Matthew Weaver, "Muammar Gaddafi Condemns Tunisia Uprising" *Guardian*, January 16, 2011.

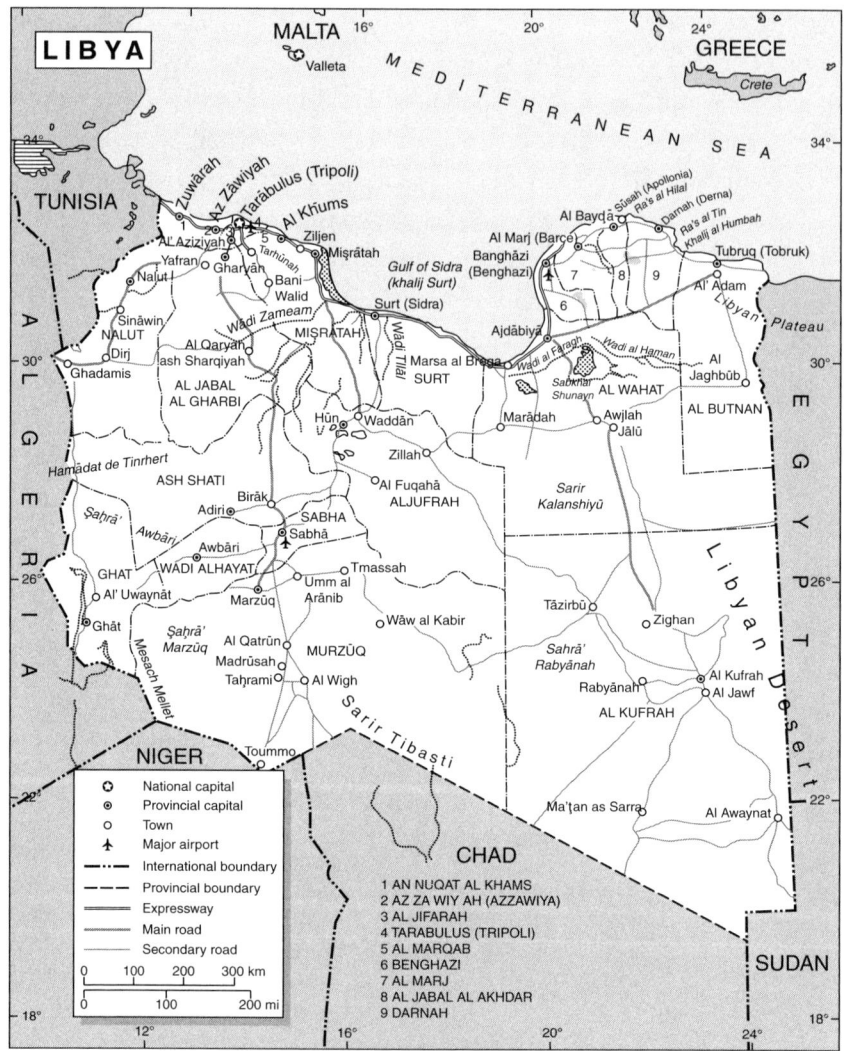

Figure 2.2 Libya.
Source: United Nations.

success in thwarting efforts to generate support for international interventions. In Qaddafi's case, their growing number and menacing tenor would soon draw the attention of the world, becoming a key factor in the decision to intervene and ultimately leading to his downfall.

Libya Revolts

Libyans normally date their revolution to February 17, a few days after the announcement of Mubarak's abdication. But, as in Tunisia and Egypt, the revolution really started a few days earlier as a virtual revolt, with protests posted on Facebook pages by small numbers of activists seeking changes to the Libyan constitution and other reforms. As elsewhere in the region, discontent with the iron fist of authoritarianism was not the only cause of disaffection. Corruption, inequality, bad employment prospects, and lack of housing were also driving factors, as was coverage of protests elsewhere in the region by television channels such as Al Jazeera.[8]

The virtual revolt turned physical on February 15 with a protest staged by a small group of lawyers outside the courthouse in the eastern city of Benghazi, where another lawyer named Fathi Terbil had been imprisoned earlier in the day. Terbil was representing the relatives of some 1,200 men who had been killed by Libyan security forces at Abu Salim prison in 1996. Soon others joined the protest, and by midnight the police were using water cannons against the crowd. The next day protestors gathered again, and the regime fought back with greater force. On February 17, a "day of rage" was proclaimed and protests exploded across the city (Figure 2.3). Libyan soldiers and police fired on unarmed crowds with machine guns. The death toll mounted, sparking further outrage. The full-on revolt against four decades of Qaddafi's rule had begun.[9]

Within a few days, Qaddafi's security forces in Benghazi had either retreated or defected, and the city was suddenly under full rebel control. Benghazi is Libya's second largest city and the main power center in the east. Its occupation by the rebels undermined Qaddafi's authority across the entire eastern province of Cyrenaica, which had long-standing

---

[8] Richard Northern and Jason Pack, "The Role of Outside Actors" in Jason Pack, ed., *The 2011 Libyan Uprisings and the Struggle for the Post-Qadhafi Future* (New York: Palgrave, 2013).

[9] Robert F. Worth, "On Libya's Revolutionary Road" *New York Times Magazine*, March 30, 2011.

Figure 2.3 Protests in Benghazi, February 2011.
Source: Al Jazeera English.

disputes with western Tripolitania, the location of both Tripoli, the capital, and Qaddafi's hometown of Sirte.[10]

Qaddafi's attempted repression encouraged rather than deterred imitation, and the revolt spread across the country. People's committees organized by exiles, human rights activists, local defense forces, and others sprung up organically from Benghazi to Misrata, Sirte, Tripoli, and other cities and towns. By February 20, the committees controlled the towns of Baida, Benghazi, and Tobruk.[11] More than 200 protesters were reported killed, with some 900 wounded.[12] The regime then deployed snipers, helicopter gunships, planes, and foreign mercenaries

---

[10] See Saskia van Genugten, "Libya after Gadhafi" *Survival*, vol. 53, no. 3 (June/July 2011), pp. 61–75; William Lewis, "Libya: Dream vs. Reality" *Mediterranean Quarterly*, vol. 22, no. 3, (Summer 2011), pp. 42–52.

[11] Evan Hill, "The Day the Katiba Fell" Al Jazeera, March 1, 2011. As of May 8, 2012: http://www.aljazeera.com/indepth/spotlight/libya/2011/08/20118219127303432.html.

[12] "Libya Unrest: Scores Killed in Benghazi 'Massacre'" BBC News, February 20, 2011. As of May 8, 2012: http://www.bbc.co.uk/news/world-africa-12517327.

against protestors across the country.[13] Within a few days, hundreds were dead and many more wounded.[14]

On February 21, Qaddafi's son Saif al-Islam, in whom many had once put their hopes for moderation and reform, gave a speech that, while somewhat conciliatory, failed to satisfy the protestors. It is rumored that Saif had actually presented his father with a text far more sympathetic to the protestors, but the aging dictator had rejected it and forced his son to take a much harder line. Saif's appearance on television, looking grim in a black suit, burst the bubble of hope that many held for a peaceful transition of power along the lines of the one that seemed to have just occurred in Egypt.[15]

A wave of defections followed. Libya's ambassadors to India, the United Kingdom, Indonesia, Bangladesh, Poland, the Arab League, and the United States resigned. Qaddafi's justice minister, Mustafa Abdel Jalil, defected to the rebel camp. Two senior pilots in the Libyan Air Force flew their jets to Malta rather than follow orders to fire on protestors. At the United Nations in New York, Qaddafi's diplomatic corps defected. Ibrahim al-Dabbashi, the Libyan deputy UN ambassador, abandoned Qaddafi, warned that thousands were at peril of death, and predicted the regime's rapid collapse. He pleaded for international powers to establish a no-fly zone over Libya to prevent Qaddafi from using his air force against the people of Benghazi, cut off the regime's military supplies, and keep foreign mercenaries out.

Qaddafi's response to the escalating crisis was a rambling television address in which he referenced Tiananmen Square, promised to stay in power to the end, and threatened to "cleanse Libya house to house" if the

---

[13] "Révoltes Arabes: Répression Brutale en Libye, à Bahreïn et au Yémen" *Le Monde*, February 20, 2011, p. 1; Anthony Shadid, "Clashes in Libya Worsen as Army Crushes Dissent" *New York Times*, February 18, 2011, p. A1; "Libya Jails Russia, Ukraine, Belarus 'Mercenaries'" *Agence France Press*, June 4, 2012.

[14] Peter Beaumont and Martin Chulov, "Libyan Protesters Risk 'Suicide' by Army Hands" *Guardian*, February 19, 2011. As of May 8, 2012: http://www.guardian.co.uk/world/2011/feb/19/libyan-protesters-gaddafi-suicide-army.

[15] Multiple interviews, Tripoli, February 2013.

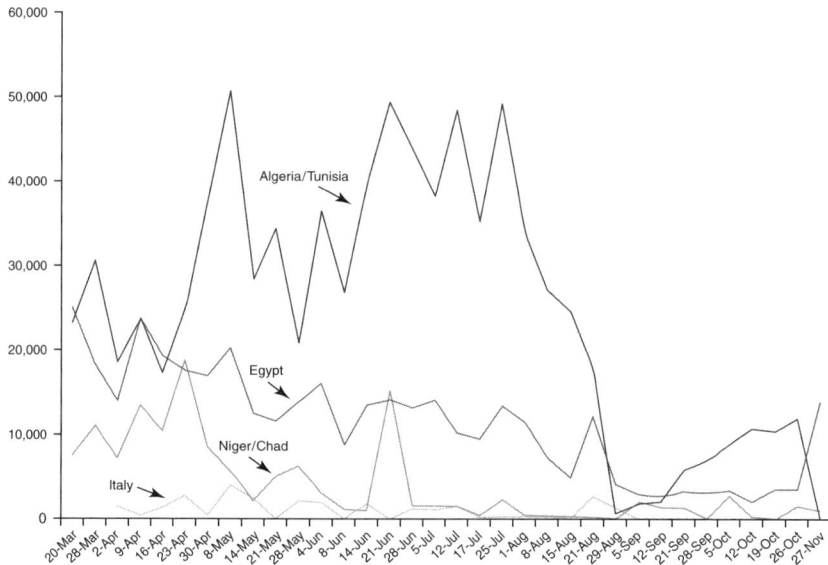

Figure 2.4 Weekly cross-border movements from Libya during the conflict.
Sources: International Organization for Migration, Daily Statistical Reports: Migration Crisis from Libya – IOM Middle East North Africa Operations, March 12–November 27, 2011. As of August 29, the chart does not include statistics on cross-border movements for Libyans.

protests continued.[16] The situation was unraveling rapidly. People started to flee (Figure 2.4).

On February 22, the United Nations Security Council held an emergency meeting, which produced a statement expressing "grave concern" with the situation in Libya and "deploring" the use of violence against

---

[16] Nicholas Watt and Patrick Wintour, "Libya No-Fly Zone Call by France Fails to Get David Cameron's Backing" *Guardian*, February 23, 2011, p. 6; "Live Blog – Libya Feb 22" Al Jazeera, February 22, 2011. As of May 8, 2012: http://blogs.aljazeera.net/africa/2011/02/22/live-blog-libya-feb-22; Kareen Fahim and David D. Kirkpatrick, "Qaddafi's Grip on the Capital Tightens as Revolt Grows" *New York Times*, February 23, 2011, p. A1; "Libye : Kadhafi prend le Risque d'Encourager une Guerre Civile" *Le Monde*, February 22, 2011.As of May 8, 2012: http://www.lemonde.fr/afrique/article/2011/02/22/libye-kadhafi-prend-le-risque-d-encourager-une-guerre-civile_1483828_3212.html.

civilians.[17] The following day in Washington, echoing the Cairo speech, President Obama voiced U.S. support for the "universal rights" of the Libyan people, including their right of peaceful assembly, free speech, and "ability to determine their own destiny." The President said these were non-negotiable human rights, that the Qaddafi regime had a responsibility to refrain from violence, and warned that if it did not, it would have to be held accountable.[18]

In hindsight, these remarks might be read as evidence that an intervention was afoot, but the reality was that the world was far from ready to use military force to stop what was happening in Libya. The very next day, Secretary Gates delivered his West Point speech calling for strategic restraint. The immediate concern of most governments as the violence mounted was the safety of their expatriate citizens on the ground.[19] There were no routes out of Tripoli, and the airport was closed. U.S. embassy staff and their families had to leave by ferry, which got held up in port for a day with three hundred nervous U.S. citizens aboard. In the process, they were forced to abandon their belongings – many of which were looted or destroyed later during the war. Several hundred British nationals had to be evacuated from deep in southern Libya, where they worked in the oil industry. Frenchmen, Italians, and others were also pulled out.

By the weekend of February 26–27, with their citizens out of harm's way, the United States, France, and Britain moved quickly to sanction the Qaddafi regime. President Obama had consulted with French president Nicolas Sarkozy, British prime minister David Cameron, and Italian prime minister Silvio Berlusconi in telephone calls on Thursday, February 24. Leaders agreed that the violence violated international norms and that they would support the Libyan people's demands for

---

[17] United Nations, "Security Council Press Statement on Libya" February 22, 2011. As of May 8, 2012: http://www.un.org/News/Press/docs/2011/sc10180.doc.htm.

[18] White House, Office of the Press Secretary, "President Obama Speaks on the Turmoil in Libya" February 23, 2011. As of May 8, 2012: http://www.whitehouse.gov/blog/2011/02/23/president-obama-speaks-turmoil-libya-violence-must-stop.

[19] Mark Lander, "U.S. Condemns Libyan Tumult but Makes No Threats" *New York Times*, February 23, 2011, p. A10.

free speech, freedom of assembly, and the right to "determine their own future."[20] The French and British then introduced a resolution to the Security Council, which passed on Saturday, February 26, as UN Security Council Resolution 1970. It imposed an arms embargo and travel ban on regime officials, froze the regime's assets, and referred Qaddafi to the International Criminal Court (ICC) – a move that would later prove a double-edged sword. The EU followed up with sanctions of its own, including an arms embargo, further asset freeze, and visa ban.[21] Other countries took additional measures.

The sanctions imposed by UN Security Council Resolution 1970 would eventually limit the resources the regime could draw on to prosecute the war, but their immediate impact was largely symbolic. There was no effect on the ground or any indication that Qaddafi would negotiate or consider a ceasefire. He continued his efforts to stifle the revolt while denying that civilians were in fact being killed and claiming the *thuwwar* were Western-backed Al-Qaeda operatives seeking to turn Libya into Somalia on the Mediterranean.[22]

---

[20] White House, Office of the Press Secretary, "Readout of President Obama's Calls with President Sarkozy of France, Prime Minister Cameron of the United Kingdom and Prime Minister Berlusconi of Italy" February 24, 2011.

[21] Hélène Mulholland, "Libya Crisis: EU Agrees Sanctions as UK Warns of 'Day of Reckoning' for Gaddafi" *Guardian*, February 28, 2011. As of May 8, 2012: http://www.guardian.co.uk/world/2011/feb/28/libya-crisis-eu-sanctions-day-reckoning-gaddafi; United Nations, *Security Council Resolution 1970 (2011)*, February 26, 2011; Irwin Colter and Jared Genser, "Libya and the Responsibility to Protect" *International Herald Tribune*, February 28, 2011. As of May 8, 2012: http://www.nytimes.com/2011/03/01/opinion/01iht-edcotler01.html?scp=205&sq=Libya&st=nyt; Helene Cooper and Mark Lander, "Following U.S. Sanctions, U.N. Security Council to Meet on Libya" *New York Times*, February 26, 2011. As of May 8, 2012: http://www.nytimes.com/2011/02/27/world/africa/27diplomacy.html?pagewanted=1&sq=Libya&st=nyt&scp=177; Helene Cooper and Mark Lander, "U.S. Imposes Sanctions on Libya in Wake of Crackdown" *New York Times*, February 25, 2011, p. A1; Natalie Nougayrède, "M. Sarkozy cherche à corriger l'image de la France en saluant la vague démocratique arabe" *Le Monde*, March 1, 2011, p. 11.

[22] Kareem Fahim and David D. Kirkpatrik, "Qaddafi's Forces Hit Back at Rebels" *New York Times*, March 1, p. A1.

By the first week of March, rebels still held Benghazi, other cities in the east, and a few key western cities such as the port town of Misrata and Zawiyah, which lies only 30 miles west of Tripoli. The strength of the rebel army was growing, albeit from a very small base. Makeshift camps for rudimentary military training had been set up in Benghazi. These camps took in some 300 soldiers per day for a three- to five-day course in how to use a Kalashnikov rifle. Reliable figures on the number of recruits are difficult to come by – record keeping being a low priority – but some were claiming to have trained 12,000 soldiers by early March. A rate of 300 per day, however, would yield a figure roughly half that by March 7, assuming that training began in the immediate aftermath of Benghazi's fall to the rebels.[23]

Pressure for Action Mounts

The flurry of activity in final week in February had brought Libya to the forefront of global headlines, with events in the Middle East dominating and Libya dominating within these, according to the Pew Research Center. Yet in Washington Libya was only one of several competing items on the agendas of senior government officials. Revolts and protests were also underway in Egypt, Tunisia, Yemen, Bahrain, and Jordan. Meanwhile, South Sudan's referendum on independence had also just passed and was eating up the time and attention of Africa experts in the U.S. government, some of whom were also responsible for Libya policy. Although temporarily off the front page, the EU's sovereign debt crisis still threatened to derail the fragile global economic recovery on which the Obama administration's hopes of reelection were widely thought to rest. Iraq, Afghanistan, and Iran were still the more pressing national security issues, and a budget impasse in Congress raised the specter of

---

[23] Ben Farmer, "Inside Benghazi's Training Camps" *Telegraph*, April 24, 2011. http://www.telegraph.co.uk/news/worldnews/africaandindianocean/libya/8469896/Libya-Inside-Benghazis-rebel-training-camps.html; Nicolas Bourcier, "Libre soldats de Libye" *Le Monde*, March 10, 2011, p. 3; Rémy Ourdan, "A Ras Lanouf, les rebelles en déroute" *Le Monde*, March 12, 2011, p. 1.

government furloughs that could have seriously constrained the ability of an already stretched Pentagon and State Department to react to unfolding events in Libya. Preparations underway for an informal meeting of NATO defense ministers in Brussels focused largely on issues related to Russia, missile defense, and especially Afghanistan – not Libya.

In the next few weeks the outlook would change rapidly as France and Britain began to push hard for military action, broad regional support emerged for a no-fly zone, the violence intensified, and a military strategy that had a high probability of making an impact at acceptable cost emerged and started looking feasible. The first development was the advent of rebel representation on the international scene. The revolutionary councils that had sprung up to govern the rebel-held areas coalesced in March under an umbrella group called the National Transitional Council (NTC) (sometimes also Transitional National Council (TNC)). There were thirty members, though only fourteen names were made public at the outset in order to protect the security of those living in Qaddafi-controlled areas. The group included a heterogeneous mix of regime defectors, representatives of key tribes, former prisoners, human rights activists, lawyers, intellectuals, and others.[24] It would also include a growing number of expats who had fled the regime decades earlier and now saw their opportunity to recover their homeland by providing technical expertise to the rebellion or with connections to the outside world, especially in Washington, London, or other key capitals. Recently defected Justice Minister Mustafa Abdel Jalil was made the council's president, while a lecturer on dental practice named Abdel Hafiz Ghoga became spokesman and the council's deputy head. In a declaration from their first meeting on March 5, the NTC proclaimed itself the sole representative of the Libyan people and named as its representatives to foreign governments Dr. Ali el-Asawi and Dr. Mahmoud Jibril. Both were reform-oriented technocrats that put a pro-business, pro-Western

---

[24] Youssef Mohammad Sawani, "Dynamics of Continuity and Change" in Jason Pack, ed., *The 2011 Libyan Uprisings and the Struggle for the Post-Qadhafi Future* (New York: Palgrave, 2013).

face on the council and by extension on the revolt. This was a helpful, if less than accurate, image.

The formation of the council put a face on the rebel movement and gave them a voice on the international stage with which they could exert pressure on governments and help keep public attention focused on the crisis. They immediately demanded recognition as the sole representatives of the Libyan people and pleaded for intervention in the form of a no-fly zone to stop the flow of arms and mercenaries to Qaddafi. At the same time, they rejected an apparent offer of negotiations from the regime (although they later denied that any real offer had been made) and simultaneously voiced objections to any deployment of foreign forces on Libyan soil.[25] The council would become the de facto government of eastern Libya in the absence of other political institutions and would need to work simultaneously to coordinate the fight against Qaddafi and press the world for attention to its cause, while maintaining some semblance of order in the liberated territories themselves. Within the council, however, the exiles, former Qaddafi officials, and revolutionaries (especially the Islamists) would coexist somewhat uneasily. Moreover, operating from Benghazi, where fighting was less intense than Misrata or other western areas, the NTC had an inherent legitimacy problem, of which it was keenly aware, and that would plague it during and after the war.

Pressure increased further as the regime regained its footing and began to advance aggressively against rebel positions. The week of March 8, Qaddafi's forces repulsed the rebel advance toward Tripoli with tanks, artillery, and a small but effective number of airstrikes against rebels and rebel-held towns in Brega, Ras Lanuf, and Zawiyah.[26] Any

---

[25] Nicolas Bourcier, "Benghazi: Les Insurgés se dotent d'un gouvernement" *Le Monde*, March 8, 2011, p. 6; Kareem Fahim and David D. Kirkpatrick, "Rebels Face Onslaught by Loyalists in Libya" *International Herald Tribune*, March 9, 2011, p. 1; Anthony Shadid and Kareem Fahim, "Rebels in Libya Strain to Forge a Unified Front" *New York Times*, March 9, 2011, p. 1.

[26] Rémy Ourdan, "Les raids aériens, terreur des 'chabab' insurgés" *Le Monde*, March 13, p. 7; Peter Beaumont and Chris McGreal, "Front: Libya: Military: Gaddafi's Jets Slow Rebel Advance on Sirte" *Guardian*, March 8, p. 5; Fahim and Kirkpatrick, "Rebels Face Onslaught by Loyalists in Libya."

initial hope that the rebels might topple the regime quickly or force it into negotiations started to evaporate.

French and British leaders now also began to enter the fray. Initially, France, like its allies, had preferred the sanctions strategy and supported Resolution 1970. In the second week of March, however, President Sarkozy changed course and took up the mantle of military intervention more forcefully than any other Western leader. On March 10, after meeting in Brussels with European diplomats, NTC representatives travelled to Paris for an audience with Sarkozy. In a move that astonished many and infuriated his European counterparts, especially German chancellor Angela Merkel, Sarkozy then called for targeted strikes against Qaddafi and recognized the NTC as the government of Libya – a move that surprised professional French diplomats, who would spend the next several months trying to "nuance" the recognition.[27]

For his part, Prime Minister Cameron had also begun to press for action, although somewhat less publicly than his French counterpart, perhaps out of concern for syncopation with Washington. Soon after Resolution 1970, Cameron had announced Britain was prepared to begin military planning for a no-fly zone in order to ensure the option was on the table.[28] The British were also looking to get discussion started at NATO about military options.[29] Defense Secretary Liam Fox had phoned NATO Secretary General Anders Fogh Rasmussen as early as February 24 to discuss the crisis. At the time, the two leaders agreed NATO had some capabilities – for example, for humanitarian relief – that might be useful, but they did not consider anything further.

Britain and France also started working together with Lebanon on a draft UN resolution that called for a no-fly zone in the second week of

---

[27] Rémy Ourdan, "A Ras Lanouf, les rebelles en déroute" *Le Monde*, March 12, 2011, p. 1; Arnaud Leparmentier and Philippe Ricard, "Libye: L'Europe écarte pour l'instant l'option militarie" *Le Monde*, March 13, 2011, p. 7.

[28] "UK Working on 'No-Fly Zone' Plan for Libya" BBC, February 28, 2011.

[29] Interviews with representatives to NATO, Brussels, February 7, 2012.

March.[30] On March 10, Cameron and Sarkozy signed a joint letter addressed to EU president Herman Van Rompuy urging the EU to push Qaddafi out and calling on NATO to begin planning for a no-fly zone coupled with strikes against military targets in Libya.[31]

This joint Franco-British pressure was essential in generating diplomatic momentum for intervention. Yet the rationale behind it has sometimes been misconstrued. After the decision to intervene, it was common to portray the leading French and British roles as stemming from the particular interests of European allies in Libya, but this is not altogether accurate. U.S. allies in Europe had an interest in stability on Europe's southern flank, but maintaining stability might have been achieved equally well by leaving Qaddafi in power. They also had an interest in ensuring the flow of oil and gas to Europe and protecting their investments in the Libyan economy, but here again, intervention was not the only way to sustain those flows, or even the most cost-effective one. Existing arms deals with Qaddafi were obviously a reason to support the regime, not overthrow it.

In retrospect, French and British pressure to intervene in Libya had at least as much to do with perceived threats to security and economic interests as with domestic and international power politics. With the uprisings in the Arab world, France, like the United States, confronted a dilemma between its self-image as a proponent of universal rights on the one hand and the fact of its cozy relationships with conservative regimes in the region on the other. France's colonial and postcolonial role in Africa, with which French conservatives were closely associated, further complicated the picture. At the outset of the revolts in Tunisia, the French government had taken a number of missteps, with French foreign minister Michèle Alliot-Marie offering to advise the beleaguered Tunisian

---

[30] "World Cannot Stand Aside from Libya, Says Cameron" BBC.com, March 8, 2011.

[31] "Letter from the PM and President Sarkozy to President Van Rompuy" March 11, 2011. http://www.number10.gov.uk/news/letter-from-the-pm-and-president-sarkozy-to-president-van-rompuy/.

president on police training in the midst of the revolt and French prime minister François Fillon accepting a Christmas holiday at Mubarak's expense. President Sarkozy was under fire from the left and the right for his government's inept response.[32] A tract published in *Le Monde* on February 23 by a number of former French ambassadors denounced his foreign policy as "amateurish" and "impulsive" and claimed that France's voice "had disappeared from the world."[33]

Sarkozy needed a change of course, and the crisis in Libya was a chance to do so. Sarkozy likely recalled his predecessor Jacques Chirac's success in pushing Bill Clinton into strikes in Bosnia in 1995 and the positive impact it had on Chirac's image. This is not to say his decision was driven entirely by political considerations. The French writer-philosopher Bernard Henri-Levy had met with Sarkozy and his top foreign policy advisory Jean David Levitte shortly after visiting Benghazi, and made the case for intervention on humanitarian grounds. Henri-Levy's appeal clearly had the same effect.

If Sarkozy wanted intervention, however, he was not keen on the idea of using NATO. The ideal format in his view would be joint Franco-British strikes, conducted if possible without the United States and preferably under the flag of the European Union. This was in part because Arab League Secretary General Amr Moussa had told French Foreign Minister Alain Juppé that NATO was unwelcome in the region, but it was also because keeping NATO out would underscore the role of French power and minimize the risk that the United States would get the lion's share of the credit for intervening. Also, in November 2010, France and Britain signed a far-reaching bilateral security cooperation treaty at Lancaster House in London, and Qaddafi had provided a chance to cement that

---

[32] Katrin Bennhold, "France Tries to Re-Seize Its Lost Momentum" *International Herald Tribune*, February 24, 2011, p. 4; "Sur fond de critiques, Nicolas Sarkozy demande des sanctions contre la Libye" *Le Monde*, February 23, 2011. http://www.lemonde.fr/politique/article/2011/02/23/sur-fond-de-critiques-nicolas-sarkozy-demande-des-sanctions-contre-la-libye_1484003_823448.html.

[33] "'On ne s'improvise pas diplomate'" *Le Monde*, February 23, 2011, p. 7.

relationship in practice and demonstrate the continued relevance of both powers on the international scene.

Like Sarkozy, Cameron also saw an opportunity to bolster his domestic position with forceful action on Libya. He personally drove the process in the United Kingdom, often over the objections of a professional bureaucracy that was skeptical about the strategic rationale for military action.[34] Cameron was under fire at home for the deep cuts outlined in his 2010 Strategic Defence Review, and a tough line on Libya could burnish his credentials on defense.

At first, however, the British government had expressed concern that the French demand for a no-fly zone would alienate not only the Russians and the Chinese but also Arab states and possibly Libyans themselves. MI6 and the British military, including Sir David Richards, chief of the Defence staff, had their doubts about whether action was worthwhile. Like Obama, Cameron had come to power with the intent of distancing himself from the wars of his predecessor. Nevertheless, Cameron soon came around to the French view. Several in the Conservative camp would eventually support tougher action, including Foreign Minister William Hague and National Security Advisor Sir Peter Rickets. Cameron asked the military for plans for a no-fly zone on February 28, after which he and Sarkozy worked together to keep attention focused on the crisis and generate momentum for international action.[35]

The NATO Defense Ministerial

As Qaddafi's forces started beating the rebels back, there was also renewed pressure for action in Washington. Senators Lieberman and McCain issued

---

[34] Michael Clarke, "The Making of Britain's Libya Strategy" in Adrian Johnson and Saqeb Mueen, eds., *Short War, Long Shadow: The Political and Military Legacies of the 2011 Libya Campaign*. London: Royal United Services Institute, 2012.

[35] Watt and Patrick, "Libya No-Fly Zone Call by France"; Sam Coates, "A Lonely War for Cameron . . . But Now He Knows His Comrades in Arms" *Times*, September 10, 2011; Patrick Wintour and Nicholas Watt, "Cameron's War: Why PM Felt Gaddafi Had to Be Stopped" *Guardian*, October 3, 2011, p. 13.

a joint statement calling for full consideration of a no-fly zone, recognition of the rebel government, and other potentially more aggressive measures. "From Bosnia to Rwanda," they wrote, "we know that the international community has in the past been too slow to react to situations like the one unfolding in Libya – with awful and unspeakable costs in human life. For both moral and strategic reasons, we must not repeat this mistake."[36] Senator Kerry made similar statements.[37]

Within the U.S. administration, however, resistance to military action was strong. In testimony to Congress on March 2, Secretary Gates voiced caution about what he thought was becoming loose talk about the need for a no-fly zone over Libya. The fact was, he said, this would be "a big operation in a big country," adding, "Let's just call a spade a spade … a no-fly zone begins with an attack on Libya to destroy the air defenses. That's the way you do a no-fly zone."[38] Moreover, the U.S. president's two top White House foreign policy advisors, National Security Advisor Tom Donilon and Deputy National Security Advisor Denis McDonough, shared Gates's skepticism, as did Vice President Biden.[39] The administration had enough on its plate already to start another war.

On March 3, Obama thus joined Sarkozy and others in deploring Qaddafi's actions and calling for him to step down, but this hardly implied that the U.S. president was ready to use the U.S. military to force Qaddafi out. U.S. Africa Command was tasked to provide airlift for Egyptian refugees stranded in Tunisia, but no other military measures were taken. The administration adhered to the strategy set out in Security Council Resolution 1970, relying on sanctions and diplomacy to bring Qaddafi to the negotiating table. The strategy would have limited impact

---

[36] Senator John McCain, Press Office, "Statement by Senators McCain and Lieberman Regarding the Situation in Libya" March 4, 2011.

[37] David E. Sanger and Thom Shanker, "Gates Warns of Risks of a No-Flight Zone" *New York Times*, March 3, 2011, p. A12.

[38] Budget Hearing, Department of Defense, "Hearing of the Defense Subcommittee of the House Appropriations Committee" March 2, 2011.

[39] Michael Hastings, "Inside Obama's War Room" *Rolling Stone*, October 27, 2011.

on the crisis other than to increase Qaddafi's international isolation, although it was better than nothing at all.

On March 8, President Obama called Prime Minister Cameron and they agreed their joint objective in Libya was an immediate end to brutality and violence, the departure of Qaddafi from power, and a political transition. They also agreed to move ahead with planning, including at NATO, on the full spectrum of possible military responses, including surveillance, humanitarian assistance, enforcement of the arms embargo, and a no-fly zone.[40] The next day, the president's top national security advisors met to discuss U.S. strategy, but the official U.S. position did not change.[41] The United States would support humanitarian action but nothing more.

NATO defense ministers convened in Brussels for a Defense Ministerial on March 10 against this backdrop. The week before, Secretary Rasmussen had called NATO ambassadors to an exceptional meeting of the North Atlantic Council (NAC) to discuss the crisis. Supreme Headquarters Allied Powers Europe (SHAPE) and the NATO International Military Staff had both been asked to develop preliminary options for NATO assistance. When these were briefed, the emphasis was on humanitarian relief, increasing situational awareness, and evacuation of civilians. The no-fly zone was discussed, but not as a serious option. Allied ambassadors nevertheless agreed to initiate so-called prudent planning for various other scenarios at the discretion of Supreme Allied Commander Europe (SACEUR) Admiral James Stavridis, but a more formal "crisis response" procedure would still be required to initiate any official NATO planning for intervention.[42]

---

[40] White House, Office of the Press Secretary, "Readout of the President's Call with Prime Minister Cameron of the United Kingdom" March 8, 2011.

[41] White House, Office of the Press Secretary, "Press Briefing by Press Secretary Jay Carney, 3/9/2011" March 9, 2011; interview with senior U.S. official, February 6, 2012.

[42] Interview with senior U.S. official, February 6, 2011; interview with member of International Staff, January 30, 2012; Helene Cooper and Mark Lander, "U.S. Imposes Sanctions on Libya in Wake of Crackdown" *New York Times*, February 25, 2011, p. A1.

The Monday prior to the ministerial, Rasmussen said that although NATO had begun prudent planning, it had "no intention to intervene in Libya."[43] Planning, in other words, "did not mean action," as one senior official at NATO put it.[44] Allies had increased aerial surveillance, dedicating AWACs around the clock to monitoring the situation, but otherwise they had taken no real steps toward military action.

Going into the March 10 ministerial meeting, therefore, allied views on how to respond to the crisis were disparate. France was out in front, with the most aggressive public position, followed closely by Britain. Germany, Poland, Turkey, and others, however, were opposed to any intervention, as was the United States. In reality – as so often before – neither Europe nor NATO was fully united. Differences would persist throughout the intervention.

When the defense ministers convened, there were several issues to address. First, there was the potential impact of any military operations on NATO operations elsewhere, especially in Afghanistan. The alliance was already stretched thin, and any assets made available for Libya would de facto reduce assets available for NATO operations elsewhere. Although NATO had slack in some areas, in critical areas such as surveillance, any new operation was bound to come at a cost.

Second, there was the question of what the political goals of any military action would be. As Secretary Gates had already indicated, there was reason for concern about what post-Qaddafi Libya would look like – not only how stable it would be but also what opportunities toppling Qaddafi might offer Al-Qaeda and its affiliates. Without a clear picture of an intervention's overarching political goals, military planning and strategy would be difficult.

Third, there were the second-order effects on the Arab Spring to consider. Proponents of intervention had been arguing that if Qaddafi

---

[43] North Atlantic Treaty Organization, Press Office, "NATO Defence Ministers Will Discuss Situation in Libya and Longer Term Prospects in Middle East" March 7, 2011. http://www.nato.int/cps/en/natolive/news_71277.htm.

[44] Interview with senior U.S. official, February 6, 2012.

were allowed to slaughter his people, it would encourage counterrevolutionary repression elsewhere, bringing an abrupt end to the Arab Spring. On the other hand, NATO intervention on the side of the rebels could also sap them of legitimacy and have exactly the opposite effect proponents of intervention hoped for.

The British, Canadians, and French leaned forward in favor of action. Spain and others insisted on the importance of a UN mandate. The U.S. position, while recognizing the possibility for NATO action in some areas, remained one of the more cautious – indeed close to the German position, which was the most reticent.[45] The consensus that emerged was that the alliance would improve its situational awareness by increasing its naval presence in the region, accelerating the pace of planning for humanitarian relief, and taking measures to tighten the arms embargo called for in Resolution 1970. Ministers also agreed to plan for a no-fly zone, but they emphasized that planning was not action. NATO would not undertake formal planning for military intervention, however. The British proposed three conditions for any further action, to which the ministers agreed: a demonstrable need, a sound legal basis, and strong regional support.[46] In practice, these three conditions implied a UN resolution, support from the Arab League or Gulf Cooperation Council, and a worsened situation on the ground. As of March 11, this set the bar fairly high.

The next day, the EU held a summit to discuss the Arab revolts. European leaders called for Qaddafi to step down, but there was still a

---

[45] Elisabeth Bumiller, "NATO Steps Back from Military Intervention in Libya" *New York Times*, March 11, 2011; Karen de Young and Edward Cody, "U.S. Plans to Send Aid Teams to Libya" *Washington Post*, March 11, 2011, p. A01; "West Tightens Screws as Qaddafi Forces Claim Success" AFP, March 10, 2011; interview with member of NATO International Staff, January 30, 2012.

[46] Interview with a NATO diplomat, February 7, 2012; U.S. Department of Defense, Assistant Secretary for Public Affairs, "Media Availability with Secretary Gates at the NATO Defense Ministers Meeting from Brussels, Belgium" March 10, 2011; North Atlantic Treaty Organization, Press Office, "NATO Ready to Support International Efforts on Libya" March 11, 2011. http://www.nato.int/cps/en/natolive/news_71446.htm.

glaring lack of unity in the European position. Sarkozy had just recognized the rebels and had even gone so far as to suggest that France might take action absent a UN Security Council resolution.[47] Merkel was expressing skepticism and urging a more cautious deliberation in the face of what looked like impulsiveness on Sarkozy's part. "What is our plan if we create a no-fly zone and it doesn't work?" she asked. "Do we send in ground troops? ... We have to think this through. Why should we intervene in Libya when we don't intervene elsewhere?"[48] Germany's objections to the intervention would soon become a cause of major heartburn in Washington and Brussels. At this point, however, the divide between the United States and its two forward-leaning allies, France and Britain, looked almost as wide, and French and British officials were starting to quip openly about what they felt was the sluggish pace of deliberation in Washington.[49]

---

[47] Natalie Nougayrède, "Recit: Comment la France a-t-elle décidé d'intervenir en Libye?" *Le Monde*, April 19, 2011, p. 12.
[48] "Europe's Leaders Fear Libya Could Become Next Afghanistan" *Der Spiegel*, March 14, 2011. http://www.spiegel.de/international/world/0,1518,750852,00.html.
[49] Nigel Morris and David Usborne, "Cameron Frustrated with Obama's Refusal to Act over No-Fly Zone" *Independent*, March 13, 2011, p. 8.

3 The Pivots of War

As the NATO defense ministers departed Brussels on March 11, French and British efforts to build support for military action had seen mixed results at best. Several factors worked against support for intervention in the United States. On one hand, the U.S. public was starting to pay more attention to the crisis, and the frequency with which the White House Press Office answered questions on Libya was growing: at least one senior White House official saw this as an indication that Libya had become a "water cooler issue."[1] On the whole, however, after a decade of war, and amid continuing economic troubles, the American public was sorely fatigued of military intervention. Pew Research Center polling in the second week in March found that less than a third of Americans favored helping the rebels militarily. By comparison, the Clinton administration had enjoyed 47 percent support for the 1999 Kosovo intervention at the outset. The Obama administration's focus on ending the protracted wars of the past decade meanwhile created a certain cognitive dissonance in its debates over whether or not to intervene in Libya, and a growing movement within the administration to "rebalance" U.S. commitments away from the Middle East toward Asia worked against intervention in North Africa. There was no lack of sympathy or concern for the plight of the Libyan people, but Libyans were not the only ones in the world being brutalized by their leaders, even if Qaddafi's threats to his population were the most disturbing at that particular moment. Perhaps most of all,

---

[1] Interview with senior White House official, March 29, 2012.

other than the French and British, no one else was volunteering for the job, and it was very uncertain how much even these key allies could accomplish without U.S. support. This meant that if there was to be an intervention the United States would have to play a significant role – and probably foot much of the bill. But in spite of these obstacles, in the course of a few short days, the United States pivoted from reticence about intervention to a full court press for military action that was more aggressive than anyone had so far proposed.

The Defense Department and Other Skeptics

Within Washington's halls of power, the U.S. Defense Department was the most staunchly opposed to military action. This is not extraordinary, given that the military bares the heaviest financial and human burdens of war. In this case, however, the Pentagon's initial resistance was unusually strident, in part because Secretary Gates was finishing his long, distinguished tenure as a public servant and proved willing to speak his mind with uncommon candor in public. A moderate conservative who had served both George H. W. Bush and George W. Bush administrations, Gates feared the debate over Libya was sliding rapidly down a path that seemed all too reminiscent of the debate of the Iraq war, which he once privately called "dumb."[2] He was determined not to repeat past errors in Libya and loath to further complicate U.S. relations with the Muslim world. As President George W. Bush's second secretary of defense, he had lived and breathed Iraq and Afghanistan for five years and knew the costs of cleaning up others' mistakes. Gates was, in fact, in Afghanistan the week of March 7 as the administration debate over Libya was heating up.

Gates made no fewer than six arguments against military intervention. First, he warned against taking action without clear political objectives. Did those pushing for a no-fly zone intend to topple Qaddafi, he asked, and if so, were they willing to commit the resources necessary to ensure this outcome? Alternatively, would they be satisfied if Qaddafi pulled

---

[2] David E. Sanger, *Confront and Conceal* (New York: Crown Publishers, 2012), p. 340.

back his forces but stayed in power? In this case, what was the plan for dealing with him after the conflict was over? Lack of thinking about the political objectives could prove especially detrimental to planning for the postwar period, he noted, and the last thing the United States needed was another messy postconflict situation that allowed Al-Qaeda or other nefarious groups to gain a foothold so close to Europe.

Second, Gates stressed the lack of U.S. and allied insight into the *thuwwar* themselves. (The United States eventually deployed CIA agents on the ground to gather information, as a White House leak revealed to the *New York Times*.)[3] It was unclear how unified the rebels were. The creation of the NTC had given them a voice on the world stage, but it was less clear how much loyalty the council commanded on the ground. It was one thing for the NTC to give voice the Libyan people's outrage against Qaddafi, which was nearly universal, yet quite another to command and control that outrage nationwide.

Moreover, there were reported links to Al-Qaeda and Qaddafi's claim that the *thuwwar* were actually Islamic jihadists disguised as freedom fighters, while a gross exaggeration, was not without some basis in fact. There was, for example, the case of Abdel Hakim Belhaj, who hailed from the east and had fought against the Soviets in Afghanistan in the 1980s, returning to Libya in the 1990s to help form the radical Libyan Islamic Fighting Group (LIFG), which aimed to oust Qaddafi and establish Islamic rule. When Qaddafi defeated LIFG's insurgency in the mid-1990s, Belhaj fled back to Afghanistan to fight against the United States on the side of Al Qaeda, as did many other Libyan jihadists, there or in Iraq. (The eastern town of Darnah sent more jihadis to fight in Iraq than did any other town its size, according to the U.S. Army.[4]) Belhaj claims to have been caught there by CIA and MI6 and tortured with syringes and ice cold water before he was handed over to the Libyan authorities in 2004. The Libyan

---

[3] Mark Mazetti and Eric Schmitt, "CIA Agents in Libya Aid Airstrikes and Meet Rebels" *New York Times*, March 31, p. A1.

[4] David D. Kirkpatrick, "Libya Democracy Clashes With Fervor for Jihad" *New York Times*, June 23, 2012, p.A1.

government incarcerated him in Abu Salim prison, where he renounced violence and developed a political manifesto and platform for peaceful change. He was released in 2010 under an amnesty program, and when the fighting broke out, he and other members of LIFG were at the forefront of the revolution, ascending to leadership positions in the movement.[5]

Third, Gates warned about the political fallout from another U.S.-led attack on a Muslim country. "We also have to think about, frankly, the use of the U.S. military in another country in the Middle East," he said.[6] After Iraq and Afghanistan, the reputation of the United States in the region was severely damaged. Proponents of intervention may have hoped that strikes would bolster the U.S. image in the region, he argued, but they also risked the opposite effect. Another senior administration official put a similar argument in more general terms: "There's a great temptation to stand up and say, 'We'll help you rid the country of a dictator,' but the president has been clear that what's sweeping across the Middle East is organic to the region, and as soon as we become a military player, we're at risk of falling into the old trap that Americans are stage-managing events for their own benefit."[7] Because the United States lacked legitimacy, in other words, an intervention could end up hurting the Arab Spring as much as helping it.

Fourth, Gates stressed the potential "second- and third-order consequences" of action in Libya. One of the major lessons of the past decade's wars was that modern military interventions were complex and inevitably had unintended consequences that were difficult to manage. It was very hard to predict the impact of intervention on the security situation not

---

[5] Mary Fitzgerald, "Libya Speculates on Potent Figure with a Past" *Irish Times*, September 21, 2011, p.13; Clemens Höges and Thilo Thielke, "A Questionable Form of Freedom for North Africa" Speigel Online, September 28, 2011; "Libya's Rival Military Commanders Fight War of Words" CNN Wire, October 13, 2011; "L'opposition libyenne demande l'aide de l'Europe" *Le Monde*, March 10, 2011. http://www.lemonde.fr/afrique/article/2011/03/10/direct-bataille-diplomatique-entre-kadhafi-et-l-opposition_1490863_3212.html

[6] Department of Defense, Office of the Assistant Secretary of Defense (Public Affairs), "DOD News Briefing with Secretary Gates and Adm. Mullen from the Pentagon" March 1, 2011. http://www.defense.gov/transcripts/transcript.aspx?transcriptid=4777

[7] "David E. Sanger and Thom Shanker, "Gates Warns of Risks of a No-Flight Zone" *New York Times*, March 3, 2011, p. A12.

THE DEFENSE DEPARTMENT AND OTHER SKEPTICS 47

only in Libya but also around the region. There was a risk that Qaddafi's chemical weapons might be used against his population or fall into the hands of Al-Qaeda or its affiliates.

Fifth, Gates argued, intervention in Libya would sap U.S. resources from other higher priority operations, including Afghanistan, which was a top national priority. Was Libya important enough to put those operations at risk, he asked? Even a limited no-fly zone would be a significant operation, Gates said, requiring "more airplanes than you would find on a single aircraft carrier ... a big operation in a big country."[8]

Sixth, Gates pointed out that the main strategy under discussion, a no-fly zone, would have little to no impact on the ground in Libya. True, it would strengthen the arms embargo and stop Qaddafi from using warplanes against his people, but it would have no impact on the regime's ability to attack rebel forces with tanks, artillery, rocket launchers, small arms, and other ground and naval forces. Years of experience with the likes of Saddam Hussein and Kim Jong-il had demonstrated that dictators were not normally inclined to show signs of weakness, given the repercussions that doing so could have within their own circles, so a no-fly zone itself was unlikely to be enough to get Qaddafi to stand down. A no-fly zone risked putting the United States in the uncomfortable and no doubt untenable position of watching from above as Qaddafi murdered his own people on the ground.

As Director of National Intelligence James Clapper, who shared Gates's initial hesitation, explained in testimony to Congress on March 10, Qaddafi was "in this for the long haul ... he appears to be hunkering down for the duration." Qaddafi's forces were having no difficulty replenishing their supplies, and the *thuwwar* were sorely disadvantaged against the regime's much more advanced equipment. Even if Qaddafi failed to defeat the revolt, Clapper said, the outcome might be a divided country or even a Somalia-like mess.[9]

---

[8] Budget Hearing, Department of Defense, "Hearing of the Defense Subcommittee of the House Appropriations Committee" March 2, 2011.

[9] "Hearing to Receive Testimony on the Current and Future Worldwide Threats to the National Security of the United States" U.S. Senate Committee on Armed Services, March 10, 2011.

Figure 3.1 President Obama and Secretary Clinton confer in the Oval Office, March 18.
Source: The White House.

The Administration Debate

Gates, with the backing of the vice president, national security advisor, and several other senior administration officials, spoke for the dominant view within the administration as the weekend of March 12–13 started. The public appearance of a set administration view on the issue, however, belied what was becoming an increasingly intense internal debate over whether or not to intervene. From the outside, Sarkozy and Cameron's public stance in favor of a no-fly zone, taken in conjunction with Secretary Gates's admonitions about "loose talk," gave the appearance of stasis in Washington, but discussions of the crisis within the administration were ongoing from the outset and had intensified after UN Resolution 1970.

The president was getting as many as three briefings a day on the situation in Libya.[10] The White House was consulting outside experts, including both critics such as Bush advisor Elliott Abrams and former Clinton officials such as Tom Malinowski of Human Rights Watch.[11] According to a senior administration official, the White House began "an incredibly intensive series of discussions in the Oval Office and the Situation Room" on how to handle Libya.[12] When Qaddafi began his counteroffensive on March 7, National Security Advisor Tom Donilon set up a high-level task force to examine postconflict scenarios and provide intellectual leadership on postwar military and political strategy.[13] The key question for this "post-Q" task force was what the "day after" might look like – in short, whether it would be better or worse with Qaddafi still in power. This was obviously a key question in the debate.

As is often the case in crisis situations, the perspectives of the key players in the internal U.S. debate reflected the relationship of those individuals with the post–Cold War history of U.S. military interventions and the lessons each had drawn from their own experiences with that history. If Secretary Gates and others who were raising red flags about intervention had Iraq and Afghanistan on their minds, those advocating for intervention tended to be Clinton administration veterans whose perspectives were shaped by Clinton's costly and changing policies on Bosnia-Herzegovina in the early 1990s, the world's abject failure to stop genocide in Rwanda in 1994, and the success of the NATO air campaign that drove Serbia out of Kosovo in 1999. President Clinton's regrets about not having done more to help the situation in Rwanda echoed in the heads of at least some White House staff and must have figured in President Obama's own outlook.[14]

---

[10] Karen DeYoung and Joby Warrick, "U.S., Allies Step Up Pressure on Libya" *Washington Post*, March 1, 2011, p. A01.
[11] Michael Hastings, "Inside Obama's War Room" *Rolling Stone*, October 27, 2011.
[12] Ibid.
[13] Interview with White House officials, February 13, 2012.
[14] Interview with senior White House official, March 29, 2012.

Perhaps the most prominent Clinton-era veteran on the side of the interventionists was U.S. ambassador to the United Nations Susan E. Rice. Rice, who had worked closely with the president on his election campaign, was an outspoken proponent of the Responsibility to Protect (R2P) doctrine, according to which the UN was justified in intervening in the internal affairs of a state when the national government failed in its fundamental responsibility to protect its citizens. Rice had served in 1995–97 as President Clinton's senior director for African affairs on the White House National Security Council (NSC) and as director for international organizations and peacekeeping on the NSC in 1993–95 during the Rwanda crisis. Rice later regretted the Clinton administration's failure to intervene in Rwanda and said, "I swore to myself that if I ever faced such a crisis again, I would come down on the side of dramatic action, going down in flames if that was required."[15]

In a paper on the Darfur crisis written in the run-up to the 2008 presidential campaign, Rice sharply criticized the Bush administration for leaving military action off the table, called for an immediate no-fly zone, and wrote that doing so would not only protect civilians but also "demonstrate to the Sudanese government that the international community is resolved to take tough action." In the same paper, Rice implicitly attacked the argument Gates and others would later make on Libya, namely that intervention would further harm the U.S. reputation in the region. She rejected the claim that "U.S. military action in Darfur is unthinkable in the current context because Iraq and torture scandals have left people in many nations doubting U.S. motives and legitimacy, even in humanitarian contexts ... [or] against an Islamic regime." To the contrary, she argued, deploying U.S. power to halt genocide against Muslim civilians would improve the sorry state of U.S. relations with the Muslim world.[16]

[15] Massimo Calabresi, "Susan Rice: A Voice for Intervention" *Time Magazine*, March 24, 2011.

[16] Susan E. Rice, "The Genocide in Darfur: America Must Do More to Fulfill the Responsibility to Protect" *Opportunity08*, Brookings Institution, 2007. http://www.brookings.edu/research/papers/2007/10/~/media/Research/Files/Papers/2007/10/24darfur%20rice%20Opp08/PB_Darfur_Rice.PDF.

Rice was clearly in favor of further measures to stem the violence in Libya, including the use of military force, especially as the tide began to turn against the rebellion in the second week of March. At the U.S. mission to the United Nations, she had her staff draw up a draft Security Council resolution that was tougher even than the French draft that called for a no-fly zone.[17] She had noted in a 2009 interview with National Public Radio that in situations like these, policy makers needed to make a conscious effort to put all the possible options, "conceivable and inconceivable ... before senior leadership." She would "rather be alone and a loud voice for action than be silent," she had said.[18]

Another proponent of using force was Samantha Power. Power had not been a Clinton official, but her book on genocide, *A Problem from Hell*, had won a Pulitzer Prize in 2003 for its harrowing description of a number of twentieth-century genocides and the U.S. failure to adequately respond – including in Rwanda and Bosnia. She had a history as a forceful proponent of humanitarian intervention as well as an established insider relationship with the president, who had brought her into his Senate office in 2005 and in 2009 made her his NSC senior director for multilateral affairs. Power brought with her not only a willingness to advocate for the use of military force when necessary but also a far-reaching knowledge of the tools of intervention and other options short of and including military force that the United States might employ in Libya. Speaking at Columbia University after the decision to intervene was made, Power said that to have held back would have been "extremely chilling, deadly and indeed a stain on our collective conscience."[19]

---

[17] Hastings, "Inside Obama's War Room"; Helene Cooper and Steven Lee Myers, "Shift by Clinton Helped Persuade President to Take a Harder Line" March 19, 2011, p. A1.

[18] "Rice to Take Lessons from Rwanda Genocide" *All Things Considered*, NPR, February 23, 2009.

[19] Sheryl Gay Stolberg, "Still Crusading, but Now on the Inside" *New York Times*, March 30, 2011, p. A10. See also Jacob Heilbrunn, "Samantha and Her Subjects" *National Interest* (May/June, 2011).

Contrary to some later portrayals, however, as White House officials explained, Power was no knee-jerk hawk – she acted more as an expert providing alternatives to the president than a forthright champion of military force. She wanted to ensure that the president understood and had access to the full "tool kit" of measures to stop atrocities that she described in her book, of which military force was one, though undeniably the last and most grave. She had, after all, been against the Iraq War and was fully cognizant of the many downsides of using what she called the "military tool" for humanitarian purposes.[20] Nevertheless, she clearly favored intervention, especially as the situation on the ground began to deteriorate.

In general, there were two main and one lesser arguments in favor of a military course of action. The first and most obvious was the humanitarian argument: that failing to stop Qaddafi from slaughtering Libyan civilians would amount to an abrogation of the international community's moral responsibility to protect the innocent. The second argument was a strategic one enmeshed in a wider calculus about the Arab Spring: that decisive support for the revolution would vividly demonstrate that the United States supported the uprisings across the region and could thereby deter other regional leaders from crushing legitimate civilian protests by force. If Qaddafi were allowed to cudgel his population into submission, authoritarian leaders in Yemen, Bahrain, and elsewhere could be emboldened to do the same. Not acting in Libya, in other words, would put the United States on the wrong side of history, encourage other Arab leaders to choose violent repression over peaceful reform, and could reverse a democratic surge expected to be in the U.S. interest in the long haul. A protracted civil war in Libya could moreover be expected to spill over the borders, with dire consequences for transitions underway in neighboring Egypt and Tunisia, the two epicenters of the Arab Spring.

By March 11, a third, albeit lesser concern was also that if the United States stood back, France and Britain might act on their own and at

---

[20] Interview with senior White House official, March 29, 2012.

considerable risk. Some officials were concerned that a unilateral French strike in Libya, even if backed by the British and diplomatically by a broader group, could end up making the situation worse if French strategy and capabilities proved inadequate. In that event, the United States might find itself getting pulled in to a war, but in tougher conditions.

The Decision to Intervene

As the week of March 14 opened, President Obama had called for Qaddafi to step down, but avoided intervention. In the next few days, however, discussions within the administration reached a critical turning point and pivoted abruptly toward military action. The first and most important change was Qaddafi's rout of the rebel forces. Over the weekend, Qaddafi's army began to make rapid progress, pushing rebels out of the oil port of Ras Lanuf on March 11 and crushing the uprising in Zawiyah. The *New York Times* described a macabre scene there on March 12, with apartment buildings and businesses around the central square "in ruins: broken windows, collapsed walls ... artillery holes everywhere. Mangled street lamps ... The speaker for the call to prayer ... dangling by a wire; behind it ... a tangled heap of burned-out vehicles."[21] Nearby Brega also fell back into Qaddafi's hands, and there was fierce fighting in Ajdabiya, the last town between Qaddafi's forces and Benghazi.[22] By Sunday the 13th, Ajdabiya itself fell, and Qaddafi's forces began steamrolling toward Benghazi.

Alarmed, the Arab League's foreign ministers met and, under pressure from Qatar in particular, issued a statement calling for a no-fly zone

---

[21] Anthony Shadid and David D. Kirkpatrick, "Libyan Rebels Defiant but in Disarray, as Qaddafi's Forces Gain Momentum" *New York Times*, March 11, 2011, p. A6.

[22] "Battle for Libya: Key Moments" Al Jazeera, August 23, 2011. http://www.aljazeera.com/indepth/spotlight/libya/2011/08/20118219127303432.html.

as a "preventive measure ... to protect civilians."[23] Arab League support for military action against one of its own members was unprecedented, not to mention somewhat at odds with Arab League policies elsewhere, notably in Bahrain – Just days after the Gulf Cooperation Council (GCC) and Arab League voted in favor of a no-fly zone for Libya, a GCC force composed of troops from Saudi Arabia and the United Arab Emirates (UAE) would deploy to Manama, Bahrain to help secure the capital against protests. Hence, while Saudi Arabia was willing to countenance intervention against Qaddafi in the Maghreb, it would not allow its key Sunni ally Bahrain to be threatened in the Persian Gulf.

Because Secretary Gates did not raise the Bahrain crackdown in a meeting a few weeks later with Saudi King Abdullah, some in the region speculated that Arab League support for action in Libya was a quid-pro-quo for Western silence on Bahrain.[24] There is no evidence that any such agreement was made, but it is not inconceivable that a tacit understanding to this effect emerged naturally as events unfolded over the course of the week of March 14.[25]

Qaddafi was reviled by other Arab leaders and the Saudis in particular, and this was surely a key factor in the Arab League vote. Whatever the motivations, the vote was a critical step on the road toward intervention. One senior White House official called the vote important because it was more than just "a piece of paper" in that it represented genuine Arab disapproval of Qaddafi's actions and regime.[26] To this official, at least, the vote indicated that military action against Qaddafi would have the

---

[23] Richard Leiby and Muhammad Mansour, "Arab League Asks U.N. for No-Fly Zone over Libya" *Washington Post*, March 12, 2011.

[24] Martin S. Indyk, Kenneth G. Lieberthal, and Michael E. O'Hanlon, *Bending History: Barack Obama's Foreign Policy* (Washington, DC: Brookings Institution Press, 2012), p. 157.

[25] Shashank Joshi, "The Complexity of Arab Support" in Adrian Johnson and Saqeb Mueen, eds., *Short War, Long Shadow*, RUSI Whitehall Report, 1–12.

[26] Interview with senior U.S. official, March 29, 2012.

support of the Arab street and that the United States would come out of the action with an improved reputation in the region, rather than a damaged one, as Gates and other opponents were arguing.

The momentum generated by the Arab League vote was bolstered further by meetings on Monday, March 14, in Paris between Secretary Clinton and leaders from the UAE, who said they were ready to contribute militarily to any possible anti-Qaddafi operations. Early in the administration debate, Secretary Clinton had favored keeping all options on the table, while sometimes leaning toward the more cautious position of the Defense Department, largely in hope that Qaddafi might simply yield to the rebels without an intervention. In the first two weeks of the revolt, when the rebels had seized Benghazi and so many of the regime's officials had defected, this was quite plausible. Although Clinton was one of the first senior officials to go on record that the administration was considering the possibility of a no-fly zone, she was also telling European counterparts in the first two weeks of March that the United States was not prepared to intervene. She shared Gates's skepticism of others about the wisdom of a no-fly zone, given the limited impact that it would have on the ground.[27]

The horizons for diplomacy, however, were limited – at least as long as Qaddafi continued steamrolling rebel positions. At a minimum, the secretary of state had a responsibility to insist on multilateralism, which she did before the House Foreign Affairs Committee on March 10, saying that "absent international authorization, the U.S. acting alone would be stepping into a situation whose consequences are unforeseeable." A no-fly zone was an option, she recognized, but not necessarily the best one. Echoing the concerns in the Defense Department about the mounting pressure from France and Britain, Clinton added that it was "easy for people to say 'Do this, do that,' and then they turn and say

---

[27] Joby Warrick, "Clinton's Efforts in Libyan War Called Vital" *Washington Post*, October 30, 2011, p. A1; Interview with senior U.S. official, November 24, 2011.

'Okay, U.S. go do it,'" leaving the United States to foot the bill and take all the risk.[28]

Clinton's initial hesitations, however, were alleviated and then reversed by the Arab League vote and her subsequent meetings in Paris with representatives from Arab states, which gave her further confidence in the depth of Arab support for military action. The Arabs, she was told, not only supported the operation but were ready to contribute militarily. On March 15, Clinton called the president from Paris to give him the readout and argue in favor of intervention.[29]

The same day, the French and British, with Lebanon, introduced their resolution for a no-fly zone. Combined with the Arab League vote and the rebel rout, this prompted a full meeting of the president's National Security Council in the White House. The meeting began with a dire report on the military situation on the ground by Deputy Director of National Intelligence Robert Cardillo, replete with satellite reconnaissance photos of Qaddafi's tanks headed toward Benghazi and indicating a strong possibility – based in part on Qaddafi's own statements – that Qaddafi would slaughter large numbers of people in Benghazi.[30] What, if anything, could be done about the imminent threat, however, was still very uncertain. The recent demonstrations of Arab support removed a significant obstacle to military action and put an end to one of the main concerns of Secretary Gates and others – that the United States should not be seen as attacking another Muslim country – but they did not change the basic reality that imposing a no-fly zone would not be enough to stop Qaddafi's tanks from attacking Benghazi. A no-fly zone could in fact put the United States in the awful

---

[28] U.S. House of Representatives, Committee on Appropriations, Budget Hearing, Department of State, Secretary of State, March 10, 2011. http://appropriations.house.gov/Calendar/EventSingle.aspx?EventID=236091.

[29] Interview with senior administration official, January 24, 2012. See also Cooper and Myers, "Shift by Clinton Helped Persuade President."

[30] Hastings, "Inside Obama's War Room"; Sanger, *Confront and Conceal*, p. 343.

position of flying around futilely overhead while Qaddafi massacred civilians below. As Gates told one of his top advisors just prior to the meeting, the Arab League vote had removed the diplomatic argument against intervention but not the strategic argument.[31] Gates, Donilon, and Chairman of the Joint Chiefs of Staff Admiral Mike Mullen remained skeptical. Were we really serious about this? Was the country ready to buy this problem? If the goal was to stop Qaddafi's columns from advancing on Benghazi, was the United States prepared to take more aggressive measures?

It was up to the president to make the final decision. The importance of Obama's own views and role in these deliberations was often overlooked in contemporaneous accounts of the decision. After all, his concern with the crisis had ensured it stayed on the agenda and opened the space for the White House deliberations in the first place. During his discussions with his team, he probed all sides for arguments, seeking to determine what was actually known about the situation on the ground, what the possible outcomes were, and what the costs and benefits of the response options on the table were. "It was almost a Socratic method," said one senior official involved.[32] Nor does the president appear to have been disinclined toward the use of military force for humanitarian purposes. After all, it was Senator Obama who had sought out and hired genocide expert Power and appointed her to a senior administration position (and later to a cabinet-level position). Regarding intervention, he said in 2009 that "on the one hand we think that respecting the sovereignties of nation states is important. . . . On the other hand, where you have nations that are oppressing their people, isn't there an international responsibility to intervene?" Noting that this was "one of the most difficult questions in international affairs," the president had continued, "there are going to be exceptional circumstances in which I think the need for international intervention becomes a moral imperative, the most

---

[31] Interview with senior Defense Department official, December 30, 2011.
[32] Interview with senior White House official, March 29, 2012.

obvious example being in a situation like Rwanda where genocide has occurred."[33]

In the White House Situation Room on March 15, with the sack of Benghazi imminent and the French–British draft Security Council resolution about to come up for a vote, the president expressed his dissatisfaction with the options he was being presented by his national security team. "What are we even discussing here?" he asked. "If you're telling me that this guy is tearing through his country, about to overrun this city of seven hundred thousand people, and potentially kill thousands of people – why is the option I'm looking at one that will do nothing to stop that scenario?"[34] The president agreed with Gates that there was no point in a no-fly zone if it failed to improve the situation on the ground. But weren't there alternatives? (His experience with the Afghan strategic review in 2009, in which he felt the options presented to him had been pre-cooked by the Pentagon, very likely made him suspect that he was not being shown a full range of choices now.) Irritated, the president demanded more options and then left the room for a dinner with his combatant commanders.[35]

The national security team set about the task of developing better alternatives. A cyberattack was one possibility, but it required time to prepare, and even then it was unpredictable exactly how effective it could be or how long it would take to have an effect.[36] A virus launched on the Internet will never have the precision timing of a Tomahawk cruise missile. The only other real alternatives were more aggressive military measures involving attacks on Qaddafi's forces on the ground. This, in turn, would require a much stronger UN resolution than the Franco-British resolution currently on offer.

---

[33] White House, Office of the Press Secretary, "Press Conference by the President" L'Aquila, Italy, July 10, 2009.
[34] Sanger, *Confront and Conceal*, p. 343.
[35] Ibid., pp. 343–345.
[36] Eric Schmitt and Thom Shanker, "U.S. Weighed Use of Cyberattacks to Weaken Libya" *New York Times*, October 17, 2011, p.A1; Sanger, *Confront and Conceal*, p. 343.

When the president returned from his dinner and reconvened the meeting, he was presented with new options, including ground strikes. Ambassador Rice argued that a resolution that would permit this was within reach. The president decided to pursue it. For the United States to step back at a moment when so many in the world were calling for action was unacceptable, he argued. "We can't play the role of Russia or China," Obama said. Not taking action to prevent a massacre would cost the United States credibility and legitimacy worldwide, he argued. It would signal that the United States was paralyzed by its experience in Iraq and Afghanistan, and this was unacceptable.[37] The president thus directed Rice to push for the more far-reaching Security Council Resolution. If successful, the United States would intervene.[38]

United Nations Security Council Resolution 1973

In a matter of almost twenty-four hours, the United States had swung from a diplomatic strategy to support for more aggressive military action than any other country had so far openly countenanced. But it remained to be seen whether the more aggressive resolution (whose language Rice had already started to consider the week before) would get through. Some European officials actually thought the U.S. push for a stronger resolution disingenuous and suspected the White House actually wanted a resolution so strong that it would draw Russian and Chinese vetoes, and absolve everyone from action ... or at least delay it.[39]

Negotiations in New York the following day were thus critical. The U.S. resolution called for an immediate ceasefire and an end to the violence against civilians. It included a broad mandate for military action, specifically "all necessary measures ... to protect civilians and civilian populated areas under threat of attack" in Libya. Subsequent

---

[37] Sanger, *Confront and Conceal*, p. 345.
[38] Calabresi, "Susan Rice: A Voice for Intervention."
[39] Mark Lander and Dan Bilefsky, "Specter of Rebel Rout Helps Shift U.S. Policy on Libya" *New York Times*, March 17, 2011; Ryan Lizza, "The Consequentialist" *New Yorker*, May 2, 2011.

paragraphs called for Arab League support, a no-fly zone, an extended arms embargo, and further actions against Qaddafi regime assets overseas. At the same time, however, it ruled out an "occupying force" – a phrase that left some room for interpretation but would eventually be used as one rationale for eschewing a postwar stabilization operation.[40] Russia circulated a much weaker alternative draft that called for a cease-fire but included no provisions for the use of force.[41]

France and Britain strongly backed the new U.S. draft. Speaking for France, French Foreign Minister Alain Juppé said the Security Council could not stand by and "let the warmongers flout international legitimacy."[42] Nigeria, India, Russia, China, and Brazil, however, were all refusing to support the text. This made South Africa's support critical. President Obama had called South African President Jacob Zuma (in addition to Cameron and Sarkozy) shortly after his decision to go for a stronger Security Council resolution, but when the final vote came up and the South African Ambassador to the United Nations failed to show up on the Security Council floor, Ambassador Rice personally had to go find him and summon him to the floor.[43] In the end, the resolution passed with ten of the Council's fifteen votes, with Brazil, China, Germany, India, and Russia abstaining (Nigeria ultimately voted in favor).

Russia's ambassador Vitaly Churkin said that Russia had abstained because so many questions remained unanswered, especially as regarded enforcement and what the limits of any military action would be – a line of argument that Russia would expand on as the intervention played out.[44] These reservations notwithstanding, Russia's decision not to block the resolution was a departure from traditional Russian policy. Why it did so is thus a key question, especially given Russian leaders' later

---

[40] United Nations, Security Council Resolution 1973 (2011).
[41] Interview with senior U.S. official, December 17, 2011.
[42] United Nations, "Libya: Full Text, Record of the Debate on Security Council Resolution" March 17, 2011.
[43] Cooper and Myers, "Shift by Clinton Helped Persuade President" p. A1.
[44] United Nations, "Libya: Full Text".

complaints that NATO was violating the resolution and adamant resistance to UN Security Council resolutions on Syria.

One senior Russia expert within the administration thought this may have been a case when Russian Prime Minister Vladimir Putin gave the supposedly more liberal president Dmitri Medvedev more of a say, but that it was more likely the Russians were just eager not to run athwart of European public opinion, despite their own reservations about the Arab revolts. The improved atmosphere in U.S.-Russian relations that had developed since the 2009 "reset" likely also played a role. The reset had put other issues of greater importance to Russia on the Moscow-Washington agenda, including missile defense cooperation and Russian accession to the World Trade Organization (WTO). A Russian veto on Libya might have set these efforts back. Most of all, however, the Russians had no major strategic interests in Libya, in contrast with Syria, where they had a much closer military and economic relationship and were thus willing to put up much more of a fight to thwart an intervention. The position the Russians adopted on Libya would allow them to support Qaddafi's ouster in principle and thus avoid alienating the European public, but it would also leave them free to criticize NATO, thereby garnering support elsewhere, especially in the postcolonial world.

Germany's abstention was much more of a surprise and much harder to explain. The German ambassador to the United Nations expressed concerns about risks including the possibility that many lives would be lost. Countries that intervened, he said, could be drawn into a protracted military conflict that could expand across the whole region. Germany might have gone further and voted against the resolution rather than abstaining, but the abstention was taken in Washington as tantamount to a vote against. The Russians and Chinese could effectively demonstrate tacit support by abstaining, but Germany was expected to vote with its allies, as it traditionally had. That Germany should fail to support a measure that its two most critical allies – the United States and France – both supported was indeed startling and it is not surprising that it was taken as a major affront, feeding U.S. worries that German foreign policy was more and more unmoored from its long-standing transatlantic orientation and ever more under Russian influence. Germany's vote led to one of the most acrimonious periods in Berlin's relations with Washington since the clash over Iraq in 2003. The following week, Germany would refuse to allow its pilots to man NATO AWACs aircraft assigned to the mission – thus reneging on a preexisting commitment to NATO – and there was no small amount of consternation and name-calling in Washington about Berlin's alleged perfidy. The rift across the Atlantic and within the European Union (the real loser in this decision) would take months to heal.

To a certain degree, the German vote was the result of domestic politics, and much of the blame fell on German Foreign Minister Guido Westerwelle, who had insisted on the abstention over the recommendations of his own foreign ministry staff. The desire to cater to a German electorate's pacifism and weariness with Afghanistan surely played a role.[45] But while the vote made waves at the time, it was not in retrospect as dramatic a departure as it felt. Part of the problem was likely just that Germany's political leadership had failed to appreciate the gap that had suddenly opened up between the German and U.S. positions on intervention. For the first two weeks of March, after all, the dominant position in the U.S. government was one of caution, with Germany and the United States more or less in the same camp against military action. The U.S. position then changed rapidly in the course of only a few days. Given the fact that France and Britain were the U.S. allies most likely to make significant military contributions, most of the discussion the week of the resolution had involved France, the UK, and the United States, possibly at the expense of effective communication with Germany, although the United States did make an effort to communicate the shift of course to the German Chancellery at a high level.[46]

As the operation went on, Germany would seek to repair the damage. A deal was worked out whereby Germany provided additional support

---

[45] Ralf Neukirch, "Westerwelles widersinnige Doktrin" Speigel Online, March 29, 2011.

[46] Interview with senior U.S. official, November 23, 2011; interview with senior U.S. official, January 24, 2012.

for AWACs operations in Afghanistan to compensate for pulling its crews from the Libya flights. It also refrained from pulling its entire staff from NATO headquarters, and some German officers would thus make contributions to the operation. Increasingly Germany offered financial and other assistance, but despite these efforts, it would offer no military assets.

The success of the United States and its NATO allies in getting some nonpermanent members of the UN Security Council to vote in favor of the resolution was in part due to the prior establishment of the doctrine of R2P, which had been endorsed by the Security Council in 2005. R2P developed in response to debates in the 1990s about the circumstances under which intervention could be justified. Many former colonial powers had strong reservations about intervention and insisted that national sovereignty had to be sacrosanct. Eventually, however, these postcolonial powers were persuaded to accept the proposition that sovereignty entails the responsibility to protect the citizens of the state and that when this responsibility is not upheld, a state should no longer be considered sovereign. In such cases, according to R2P, foreign intervention is justified and by definition no longer an infringement on sovereignty. R2P stipulated, however, that the United Nations would have to agree that a state had lost its sovereignty before an intervention could take place. It also stipulated that the need for military action would have to be immediate, the chances of success good, and the prospects for effective nonmilitary action poor.

With the mounting chaos across the country and Qaddafi's tanks bearing down on Benghazi, Libya seemed to fit the R2P mold, and it became the first test of whether or not the UN was willing to take action to uphold the doctrine. This was very likely a factor in the decision of some states on the Security Council – South Africa in particular, which had close ties to Qaddafi – to support the resolution. As the intervention wore on, however, some countries would begin to have second thoughts about their decision to support the resolution and charge that NATO was stretching the Security Council mandate far beyond its justification in the principles of R2P.

Figure 3.2 United Nations Security Council votes on Resolution, March 17, 1973. *Source*: United Nations, Photo # 467079.

Enabling the International Community "To Act in Concert"

Speaking from the White House the day after the passage of UN Security Council Resolution 1973, the president laid out his strategy and rationale for intervention. "Left unchecked," he said, "we have every reason to believe that Qaddafi would commit atrocities against his people. Many thousands would die. A humanitarian crisis would ensue." The region, he said, would be destabilized by mass refugee flows, democratic movements would weaken, and the demands of the international community would appear hollow. He emphasized that the United States was acting as part of a broad international coalition seeking to oust a leader who had lost his legitimacy and was engaged in a campaign of slaughter against his own people.[47]

---

[47] White House, Office of the Press Secretary, "Remarks by the President on the Situation in Libya" March 18, 2011.

In a decision that would soon become a source of controversy, the president also announced that while the United States would intervene, it would limit its own role in military operations. Not only did he rule out the deployment of U.S. ground forces, but he explicitly restricted the U.S. role to providing only "the unique capabilities that we can bring to bear to stop the violence against civilians, including enabling our European allies and Arab partners to effectively enforce a no-fly zone." As it was explained over the weekend at senior interagency meetings and would become clear in subsequent weeks in public, what this meant was that the United States would go in heavy at the start to destroy Qaddafi's air-defense systems but would then step back into an over-watch role, providing only those capabilities that other allies lacked. This was a key decision that shaped the whole intervention strategy and one of the main reasons why the Libyan case was a departure from the past.

The president met the same day with congressional leaders and explained that the U.S. lead would last only days or a few weeks at most. Allied strike aircraft would soon take the lead in strikes against the regime. As the president explained it in his speech, a central aim of the United States was to create "the conditions that would permit the international community to act in concert." This policy was reiterated several times later, when the administration started to come under fire for not doing more. As Tony Blinken, the vice president's national security advisor, explained it, "We did lead – we cleared the way for the allies. . . . But real leadership is successfully encouraging others to step up to their responsibilities. We've talked for years about burden-sharing, and either we would not let other countries act or they wouldn't or couldn't do it."[48]

The decision to restrict the U.S. role was rooted primarily in concerns about the potential political and financial costs of the operation. Gallup polls showed that only 47 percent of Americans approved of the military action as it got underway. Although more Americans approved than disapproved, the operation was still less popular than Iraq, Afghanistan,

---

[48] Sanger, *Confront and Conceal*, pp. 352–353.

Kosovo, Haiti, and even Somalia had been at the outset.[49] There was no small amount of sentiment in the Pentagon that if this was something the French felt strongly about, they could foot the bill, and Secretary Clinton had expressed a similar view in her March 10 congressional testimony. When the president called Cameron and Sarkozy to inform them of his decision to support a stronger UN resolution, he also explained that the United States was not going to do this with only token contributions from allies.[50] Any subsequent complaints on their part were therefore rather unjustified.

If there was a pragmatic side to the policy, there was also a deeper rationale behind it, which deserves note because of the criticism to which the approach would later be subject. According to one senior official, the roots of the policy could be traced in part to views expressed in a paper titled "Strategic Leadership" published in 2008 and to which several members of the future Obama administration had contributed. "Despite the prevalent assumption that America must always be in charge," the authors of this paper wrote, "effective leadership is not always centered in Washington. ... A doctrine of strategic leadership seeks effective action rather than American leadership for its own sake." This position was intended as a rebuke to what the authors considered the often swaggering leadership style of the Bush administration, a style they clearly felt unwise and not in the U.S. interest. "In a world in which power has defused," they wrote, "our interests are best protected and advanced when others step up and at times lead alongside or even ahead of us." The U.S. policy outlined by the president for Libya would later be termed "leading from behind" by an administration official – to the chagrin of the administration and delight of its critics. In the schema outlined by the authors of the aforementioned

---

[49] Jeffry M. Jones, "Americans Approve of Military Action in Libya 47% to 37%: Support is Lower than for Other Recent U.S. Military Actions" *Gallup Politics*, March 22, 2011. http://www.gallup.com/poll/146738/Americans-Approve-Military-Action-Against-Libya.aspx. Comparable Bosnia figures are not available.

[50] Sanger, *Confront and Conceal*, p. 346; interviews with White House officials, February 24, 2012.

report, however, what emerged was much closer to leading alongside, or "shared leadership," as one member of the administration put it.[51]

Why the United States Changed Course

Qaddafi had only a few hours to respond to the UN request that he cease fire and pull back his forces. As it happened, he failed to do so decisively, agreeing to the ceasefire but not withdrawing. Had he, the history of Libya might look quite different than it does today. His failure to comply immediately and comprehensively with the demands of the UN – though perhaps not surprising – was the final step that brought the weight of the U.S. and European military down upon him, setting in motion an intervention that would end in his capture and death seven months later.

At the time, some accounts of the decision to go to war emphasized the role the so-called female hawks – especially NSS senior director Power and UN ambassador Rice, but also Secretary of State Hillary Clinton – played in the rapid U.S. policy shift from relative passivity to intervention. This trio was seen as struggling against the staunch resistance of the Defense Department, led by Secretary Gates and the Chairman of the Joint Chiefs of Staff Admiral Mike Mullen. These accounts, however, were "a bit of a caricature," as one senior official said and several others confirmed. (Another called them "wildly inaccurate.")[52] Rice and Power were clearly more favorable to using force than the Defense Department, but this does not mean they were trigger-happy or eager to bomb Libya. Secretary Clinton was skeptical about intervention at first, even if she eventually came around strongly in favor of it. Moreover, while there were clearly differences of opinion, the process within the administration was not so much a debate between opposing fixed positions as it was a struggle to grapple with the unfolding crisis and understand the true range of options the United States had to address it.

---

[51] Interview with senior U.S. official, December 30, 2011.
[52] Ibid.

As one senior Defense Department official said, there was significant skepticism within the United States government about the intervention at first, but as events evolved and discussions continued, "people started to realize there was a case for it."[53] Multiple factors played a role, including French and British pressure, the Arab League vote, the imminent siege of Benghazi, and the availability of a military option that promised some amount of success. The United States obviously did not go to war because the Arab League called for it, although the Arab League vote did change the dynamics in the Security Council. Nor does the decision appear to have been overly influenced by pressure from France and Britain, contrary to some reporting at the time.[54] French and British agitation for action kept the public and national leaders focused on the crisis, and while it may have been a necessary factor, it was in itself not a sufficient one to change the debate within the administration. Ultimately it was the imminent threat Qaddafi's forces posed to the civilian population of Benghazi combined with the emergence of a military option that could save thousands of imperiled lives that led to intervention.

---

[53] Ibid.
[54] E.g., Roger Boyes, "Hesitant Obama Made Up His Mind Thanks to European Resolve" *Times*, March 18, p. 7.

4 Crippling Qaddafi and Infighting over NATO

Leaders from countries supporting the intervention gathered in Paris on March 19, two days after the UN resolution. Over the course of a few short days, the United States and its key allies had committed themselves to war with Qaddafi. Even when the president had told Ambassador Rice to push for a stronger Security Council mandate earlier in the week, it had still been uncertain what the outcome would be. But with the resolution behind them and Qaddafi's forces at the outskirts of Benghazi, leaders faced immediate pressure for swift military action. The Paris meeting emphasized the leading role France was playing. President Obama had sent Secretary Clinton in stead of himself, to underscore the lesser role of the United States. Meanwhile, in Washington, Secretary Gates delayed a previously scheduled trip to Russia to oversee the initial strikes.

At the request of the State Department, initial military operations were held back until the Paris meeting concluded, to avoid the appearance that military operations had trumped political aims. The delay was not long, however. Sarkozy walked out of the meeting and announced that French Rafale fighter jets (Figure 4.1) had just struck Qaddafi's forces in Benghazi. Few other leaders were abreast of the French operation, and it looked like a thinly veiled attempt by Sarkozy to boost his domestic approval ratings at the expense of transparency and allied coordination. In response, the Italian Prime Minister Silvio Berlusconi warned that Italy might deny the use of critical Italian bases. According to at least one European

Figure 4.1 French Air Force Rafale flies in Operation Harmattan.
Source: French MOD.

diplomat, the move "nearly broke up the coalition."[1] This was only the beginning of the problem, however. Over the course of the next two weeks, allied tensions peaked as leaders struggled to define the mission and figure out how it was going to work.

Strikes over the course of the next week took place in a coalition of the willing format, under a U.S. lead. In keeping with the president's circumscription of the U.S. military contribution, however, this was a temporary arrangement. After the United States pulled back, a new arrangement would be necessary. As a result, even as the coalition B-2s, F-16s, Rafales, Tornados, and Eurofighter Typhoons began their crippling attacks against Qaddafi, diplomats in Brussels, Paris, London, and Ankara were in a heated and lengthy debate over how the operation should be organized. The rancor got the intervention off to a rough start and exposed how thin political support really was in many countries.

[1] Joby Warrick, "Clinton's Efforts in Libyan War Called Vital" *Washington Post*, October 30, 2011, p. A1.

The Debate over NATO

The big issue was whether or not the operation would be carried out under NATO, the EU, or in a coalition of the willing format. Over the weekend, Ivo Daalder, the U.S. ambassador to NATO, who was originally skeptical about the intervention, began a full-court press to transfer operations to NATO. The U.S. Ambassador to NATO is a unique position that derives from the ambassador's role as a representative of both the Secretary of Defense and Secretary of State. Daalder was able, in part because of his own connections to the White House and force of character, to make the argument for NATO at multiple levels within the U.S. government.[2]

From his perspective, NATO offered several benefits. For one, it had well-established working relationships with non-NATO European powers and Arab states that had offered to participate. Over the course of the past decade, the alliance had established two partnership programs with Middle Eastern states: the Istanbul Cooperation Initiative and the Mediterranean Dialogue. These partnerships, which had heretofore been far from top allied priorities, suddenly took on paramount importance, because the military participation of the Arab partners would reinforce the political message that Qaddafi's actions were universally deplorable.

NATO also had command and control systems that could bring the broad coalition that would participate in the operation together into a single, coordinated chain of command. Allies and partners were familiar with how NATO command and control worked and could quickly plug into it. Using only French or British national command and control assets to run an operation with such a broad array of participants might or might not have been possible, but it would surely have been more difficult and increased the need for improvisation. Only the United States had comparable capabilities, but these were ruled out on the grounds that they

---

[2] Multiple interviews.

were not "unique" U.S. capabilities and using them would therefore have been against Presidential guidelines.[3]

Theoretically, one alternative might have been to conduct operations under the aegis of the EU, with the United States and NATO providing the enabling capabilities the EU lacked. This is an arrangement known as "Berlin Plus" that had worked recently in Bosnia, though not easily on account of ongoing tensions between Cyprus, an EU member, and Turkey, a NATO member. Germany's outspoken opposition to the intervention, however, meant there was little reason to pursue this option seriously. As for the UN, while it had peacekeeping forces to offer for a potential postwar stabilization operation, it had none of the firepower necessary for the intervention itself.

Arguing via secure teleconference from Brussels to Washington, Ambassador Daalder was making the case for NATO. Others agreed, and by Monday, March 21, a consensus was forming in Washington around the view that NATO was the best organization for the operation. As Assistant Secretary of State for European Affairs Philip H. Gordon would later explain, "We believed strongly that with such European support and such an important European role to play we wanted to see [NATO] formally take on this mission."[4]

The U.S. view was shared by some allies, but not all. The day after Resolution 1973 passed, NATO ambassadors had convened in Brussels to discuss NATO's options. Three basic camps had already begun to emerge. The first camp, led by the United States and Britain, with varying degrees of support from Italy, NATO Secretary General Rasmussen, and several smaller states, pushed to bring operations under NATO command. Daalder and Rasmussen led the charge. An energetic former Danish prime minister, Rasmussen had the political instinct to grasp early on the potential benefits a successful intervention in Libya might bring an

---

[3] Interview with senior U.S. official, December 7, 2011; interview with senior U.S. official, February 7, 2012.

[4] "The Democratic Wave in the Arab World: Transatlantic Perspectives" Remarks at the EU Washington Forum, Sofitel Lafayette Square Hotel, October 27, 2011.

alliance that had been strained politically and militarily from nearly a decade of war in Afghanistan. (Several NATO observers also noted that his enthusiasm for a NATO operation was not unconnected to his own craving to be back in the limelight.)[5] NATO had been planning for the possibility of an intervention for several weeks, but the EU had also undertaken its own plans for the humanitarian aspects of the operation, creating something of a competition between the two organizations. Rasmussen was determined to see NATO get the whole mission set out in the UN resolution, not just parts of it.[6]

Turkey was initially against the intervention altogether, but soon changed its position. Turkish public opinion was against intervention, and Turkey had more than $10 billion in investments in Libya, with thousands of Turkish citizens on the ground in the construction and other industries. Since the outbreak of the crisis, Turkey had represented British interests in Tripoli and maintained relatively close contact with the Qaddafi regime. The Turks also feared they were especially vulnerable to any regional blowback an intervention might cause. To complicate matters, Turkish leaders felt snubbed by the French, who had failed to invite them to the March 19 Paris meeting – Turkish Foreign Minister Ahmet Davutoglu had complained that it was "inappropriate that an operation [sanctioned by the United Nations] ... is launched at a meeting attended by a small group of countries."[7] French officials noted that given Turkey's opposition to any intervention, it would have made no sense to invite them. "We only invited like-minded countries," a French diplomat explained.[8] But the impression persisted that long-standing animosity between Sarkozy – who had opposed Turkey's bid for EU membership – and Turkey's government was the real reason for the snub. On March 21,

---

[5] Interview with former member of the NATO International Staff, January 30, 2012.
[6] Interview with member of the NATO International Staff, February 6, 2012.
[7] "Turkey Criticizes France's Role in Libya Intervention" *Today's Zaman*, March 22, 2011.
[8] Fulya Ozerkan, "Alliance of the Unaligned Split on Libya Intervention" *Hurriyet Daily News*, March 21, 2011. http://www.hurriyetdailynews.com/default.aspx?pageid=438&n= turkey-draws-red-lines-on-libya-operation-2011-03-21.

Turkey thus held up a vote that would have moved NATO operational planning ahead.[9] Soon, however, recognizing that the intervention was going forward with or without their support, the Turks joined the U.S. camp and sought to bring it under NATO auspices, if only to gain some control over it.

Italy fell into the same camp, but for different reasons. The Italians wanted a more restricted interpretation of Resolution 1973 to protect their interests on the ground and supported using NATO in the hope that this would increase their influence over operations.[10] Italy would face the brunt of any refugee crisis, it imported Europe's largest share of Libyan oil (22 percent) and gas (13 percent), and had invested heavily in Libyan industry. Moreover, the Libyan state owned significant shares in Italian firms, including the bank Unicredit, the automaker Fiat, and the soccer team Juventus. Later, the imperiled Berlusconi government would waver, at one moment offering to send more aircraft, the next calling loudly for a cease-fire.

Several smaller allied states, including Norway and Belgium, joined the pro–NATO camp on the grounds that it was easier for them to participate – both technically and politically – if the intervention was a NATO mission rather than a coalition of the willing. These smaller states supported the intervention largely out of a fundamental support for the United Nations and international law. Enthusiasm from Eastern European allies was more mixed. Some expressed concern that the intervention might detract from NATO readiness for territorial defense (i.e. vs. Russia), while others recognized it as an opportunity for NATO to show resolve and thereby gain strength overall.[11] In any case, because

---

[9] Daniel Dombey and Peter Spiegel, "Rift over Command of Libya Campaign" FT.com, March 22, 2011.

[10] Franco Venturini, "Incertezze e dubbi fuori tempo" *Correiere Della Sera*, March 22, 2011. http://www.corriere.it/editoriali/11_marzo_22/incertezze-e-dubbi-fuori-tempo-franco-venturini_a895ce5e-544f-11e0-a5ef-46c31ce287ee.shtml.

[11] "Analysts Say Allies Have 'Very Different Motives' for Joining Attacks on Libya" AFP, March 22, 2011; interview with senior U.S. official, February 6, 2012.

they lacked the capabilities the operation called for, the views of most Eastern European states naturally carried less weight in alliance deliberations.

The second camp, led by Germany, was against the intervention but not prepared to block a NATO action. The Germans took the position that as long as members of the alliance who supported the action understood they had no intention of supporting it militarily, Germany would agree to "join consensus" and allow NATO to play a role. In other words, having effectively voted against the operation on the Security Council, Germany would now be content to sit on the sidelines. Poland also pitched its tent in this camp, but it withheld participation not on political grounds but on the grounds that its F-16 pilots were not sufficiently well trained to participate – a somewhat questionable excuse.

The third camp was the French camp, strongly in favor of intervention but against using NATO. France's relationship with the alliance is notoriously complicated. In 1966, French president Charles de Gaulle had withdrawn France from NATO's integrated command structure, infuriating many in the United States. France would remain a member of the alliance, still bound by the commitment to come to the defense of other members, but more independent operationally and in its nuclear planning. French intellectuals had often disparaged NATO as a symbol of U.S. power in Europe, while France persistently encouraged the development of the EU's security capabilities as their preferred (and French-dominated) alternative to the alliance – most recently by calling for an independent EU headquarters during the transatlantic rift over the 2003 invasion of Iraq. Since his election in 2007, however, President Sarkozy had made a concerted effort to normalize France's relationship with NATO. While continuing to support the EU's military aspirations, Sarkozy insisted there should be no competition between the two institutions and announced France's reintegration into the NATO command structure at the 2008 Bucharest Summit, thus overturning long-standing Gaullist policy.

Despite this more amicable attitude, the French still strongly objected to using NATO when it came to Libya.[12] First, they cited potential delays in getting the NATO machinery started, as well as the challenges that had arisen in the 1999 Kosovo operation, when the practice of giving NATO governments the right to scrutinize choices of military targets had led to postwar complaints of interference from the military leadership. (That such oversight had been insisted upon by then French president Jacques Chirac was rather ironic.) The French were keen to minimize the influence of Italy and especially Turkey, two countries they feared would use their seat on the North Atlantic Council (NAC) to tightly restrict and possibly undermine NATO operations.[13] Turkish leaders riposted by accusing the French of coveting Libya's oil.[14] The French also claimed the alliance's poor reputation in the Arab world would undermine the legitimacy of the operation, creating divisions among the rebel factions and limiting the participation of Arab partners.[15] French leaders expected a short war, and the three key powers were already involved in the attacks, they argued, so why, bother with NATO? Better to continue the existing ad hoc arrangement – the "pick-up game" formula, as one senior U.S. official put it – adding only an overarching political body for strategic direction to military operations.[16] Perhaps it also seemed inappropriate – even unfair – that the responsibility for an intervention that France had done so much to orchestrate should abruptly be handed over to NATO, an organization widely viewed as dominated by the United States. As Juppé explained, it was not NATO that had taken "the initiative" on Libya.[17]

---

[12] Jean-Pierre Stroobants, "Libye : batailles diplomatiques en coulisses" *Le Monde*, March 24, 2011, p.1.

[13] Nathalie Nougayrede, "Libye: La menace d'une guerre longue fragilise la coalition" *Le Monde*, March 31, 2011, p. 1.

[14] Ian Traynor, "Turkey and France Clash over Libya Air Campaign" *Guardian*, March 24, 2011.

[15] Stroobants, "L'Alliance atlantique."

[16] Interview with senior U.S. official, January 24, 2012.

[17] Jean-Pierre Stroobants, "L'Alliance atlantique étale ses divisions à Bruxelles sur la gestion de la crise libyenne" *Le Monde*, March 23, 2011.

As airstrikes continued, however, French arguments against NATO started losing steam. The French were isolated and began to recognize their campaign against NATO was alienating their European counterparts, especially the British. Another factor was probably that the real challenge of conducting such a complex coalition operation from French and British military headquarters alone dampened the French push against the NATO option. This issue is not so much about capacity but about the ease of integration of key partners such as Sweden, Qatar, and the UAE into operations outside NATO. The French proposed that NATO might loan its command and control structures to the coalition, thereby enabling a smaller coalition to conduct the operation outside the alliance, but this was a nonstarter.[18] Meanwhile, Turkey's change of heart and subsequent support for the NATO option helped pull the Arab states closer to the alliance, thus weakening the French claim that NATO was unacceptable in the Middle East.

Intra-alliance tensions came to a head on March 21, when the French and German ambassadors stormed off the floor of the NAC in response to sharp barbs from Rasmussen. (To complicate matters, the Germans had just pulled their crews from the existing NATO AWACs.) The Turks, meanwhile, continued their rhetorical campaign against the French position, with Prime Minister Reçep Tayyip Erdogan saying, "I advise our western friends, when they look at this region, to see the hungry children, the suffering mothers, the poverty.... I wish they would not only see oil, gold mines or underground wealth."[19]

By midweek, however, the lack of good alternatives to NATO was becoming more and more clear. Obama called Qatari Emir Sheik Hamad Bin Khalifa Al-Thani, Prime Minister Cameron, and President Sarkozy, after which the French dropped their objections to using NATO for the naval and no-fly zone missions but continued to push to keep the more demanding and riskier civilian protection mission outside the alliance – in

---

[18] Interview with senior U.S. official, February 6, 2012.
[19] Delphine Strauss, "Turkey Attacks France on Libya 'Crusade'" *Financial Times*, March 24, 2011.

other words, a dual mission where NATO handled the no-fly zone and a smaller coalition went after Qaddafi's forces.[20] (A somewhat similar model had, for a time, been used in Afghanistan, with NATO doing counterinsurgency operations while the United States led a coalition for the counterterrorism mission.)

The breakthrough came on Thursday, March 24, in a phone call brokered by Secretary Clinton among the French, British, and Turks. The French agreed that all the military missions outlined in Resolution 1973 would fall to NATO, and the Turks agreed not to use their position on the NAC to meddle or otherwise hold them up. To mollify the French and the Turks alike, a political "chapeau" for the intervention would be created in the form of a contact group for Libya on the basis of the March 19 meeting in Paris. The contact group would set broad political guidelines and handle diplomacy but have no direct authority over NATO. As a senior French official later explained, the contact group was needed to show there was a political dimension to the intervention "beyond the strikes."[21] The NAC would remain in charge – "sacrosanct," as one senior U.S. official put it.[22] At the end of the four-way call, the State Department reported, Juppé and his Turkish counterpart Ahmet Davutoglu both congratulated Secretary Clinton.[23] This put NATO in charge of all the UN-mandated missions of the operation. Operational transition would begin soon.

Unfortunately, just as the intra-alliance spat appeared to have been quelled, another problem had emerged. As the footage of strikes against Qaddafi's systems were broadcast around the world, NATO's Arab partners, who a week before had pledged their support to the operation, now

---

[20] Scott Wilson and Karen DeYoung, "Coalition Nears Agreement on Transition for Operations in Libya" *Washington Post*, March 23, 2011, p. A09; Interview with senior U.S. official, February 6, 2011.

[21] Interview with senior French official, November 15, 2011.

[22] Interview with senior U.S. official, February 6, 2011.

[23] Ibid.; U.S. Department of State, Undersecretary for Public Diplomacy and Public Affairs, "Teleconference Background Briefing on North Atlantic Council (NAC) Discussions on Libya" March 24, 2011.

got cold feet. Jordan and the UAE withdrew their initial offer of combat aircraft, saying they would provide only humanitarian assistance. The four Qatari aircraft that had been promised were also still to arrive in the theater as of March 24. Again, it took a long conversation between Secretary Clinton and the Qatari foreign minister Sheik Hamad Bin Jasim al-Thani and multiple calls to the UAE's Sheik Abdullah bin Zayed al-Nahyan and Jordan's King Abdullah II to bring the Arab partners back into the tent.[24]

Coalition Operations under Odyssey Dawn

Throughout the debate over whether to use NATO, British, French and U.S. strikes were leveling Qaddafi's air-defense system and forcing his troops to take cover. Several factors made operations in Libya easier than recent operations elsewhere, for example, in Afghanistan. For one, Libyan targets were near European bases in the southern Mediterranean, making complicated overflight arrangements from third-party states unnecessary. The desert topography is also relatively conducive to air strikes, and although Libya's territory is vast, most of the population is near the coast, and all of the significant fighting so far had taken place there. This was the land across which Erwin Rommel and Field Marshall Montgomery had struggled back and forth in their epic World War II battle for mastery of North Africa. Rommel described it in his memoirs as the "arid and monotonous wastes of the great Sirte."[25]

The French strikes on March 19 had been launched from bases in eastern France and struck at least four armored vehicles and possibly several more outside Benghazi in the first live-fire of the conflict.[26] The French strikes addressed the most immediate threat to the civilian

---

[24] Warrick, "Clinton's Efforts in Libyan War Called Vital."
[25] B.&H. Liddell Hart, *The Rommel Papers* (New York: Da Capo Press, 1982), p. 373.
[26] Radio France Internationale (Paris), "French Fighter Jets Fly over Country" March 19, 2011.

population, whose protection the UN had mandated. The mission was regarded by some in the United States as somewhat risky, because the strikes on Qaddafi's integrated air-defense system had not yet begun, but it demonstrated French resolve – and showcased the Rafale's defensive capabilities to potential foreign buyers, such as India, which subsequently decided to purchase $20 billion worth of the aircraft. Some French analysts would later argue that the success of these strikes also showed that Qaddafi's air defenses were not so big a threat as some U.S. officials would later claim and that subsequent heavy U.S. strikes against those defenses were overkill driven by a particularly expensive U.S. concept of operations.[27]

Nevertheless, very few NATO allies had the evasive capabilities of the French Rafale, so before a full-blown no-fly zone could be established and patrolled by all the participating nations, Qaddafi's air-defense systems had to be destroyed. Qaddafi had Soviet long-range surface-to-air batteries and radars that, while old, were still lethal. These defenses were deployed primarily along the coast, including Tripoli, Benghazi, and the major oil ports.[28] There were five regions with up to six air-defense brigades per region. Six of those brigades had SA-2 Guideline systems; three had SA-3 Goa systems; four had SA-5 Gammon systems. The total number of surface-to-air missiles (SAMs) was estimated at a little more than 200, far less, for example, than Syria's. It is also likely that some or all of the Benghazi air-defense system was already in the hands of local rebel brigades (*kata'ib*), further weakening the defense in the area where the initial French strikes occurred. These systems also lacked the capability to track multiple incoming aircraft and were much less effective against targets with low radar profiles, such as cruise missiles or the Rafale.[29] Qaddafi also had an air force of roughly 180 planes, including MiG-21s,

---

[27] Interviews with French analysts, Washington, D.C., July 2013.

[28] Jeremiah Gertler, "Operation Odyssey Dawn (Libya): Background and Issues for Congress" CRS Report for Congress, March 30, 2011.

[29] See Sean O'Conner, *Imint and Analysis*, April 2012; relevant articles on SAM capabilities in *Jane's Defense and Security Intelligence;* "Libya" *The Military Balance 2012*, International Institute of Strategic Studies.

MiG-23s, and MiG-25s, Mirage F-1s, and Sukhoi Su-17s, Su-20s, and Su-24s, but these were poorly maintained and manned by pilots who had relatively little flying time. Many of the jets were old and just sitting on runways, unable to take off.[30]

But even if Qaddafi's defenses were no match for NATO, they still could have destroyed allied military and humanitarian aircraft and killed NATO troops. As U.S. chief of naval operations Admiral Gary Roughead put it, "If someone is going to put a missile in the air, you don't say 'OK, it's an old one, I'll worry about it later.'"[31] Even after the fixed systems were destroyed, there were the regime's mobile SAMs, which included SA-6s and SA-8s, as well as SA-24 man-portable air-defense systems (MANPADs), to contend with.[32]

Consequently, shortly after the Rafales struck their targets in Benghazi, the coalition hit Qaddafi's air-defense systems with a combination of air- and sea-launched weapons, of which the United States fired the vast majority. U.S. and British navies together fired 110 Tomahawk missiles, striking some twenty radar, missile, and command and control sites of the Libyan air-defense system – a ratio that some observers later thought excessive, given that each missile costs approximately $1 million, depending on the configuration. The U.S. missiles were fired from two U.S. Arleigh Burke-Class destroyers (Figure 4.2) and three submarines in the region, while Britain fired from the submarine HMS *Triumph*. The United States then flew B-2 stealth bombers all the way from Whiteman Air Force Base in Missouri to drop forty-five precision-guided bombs on Qaddafi's airfields.[33] Like the Tomahawk

---

[30] Department of Defense, Public Affairs Office, "Transcript: DoD News Briefing with Adm. Locklear via Teleconference from USS Mount Whitney" March 22, 2011; Jeremiah Gertler, "Operation Odyssey Dawn (Libya): Background and Issues for Congress" CRS Report for Congress, March 30, 2011.

[31] "Navy EW Plane" *Defense Daily*, March 25, 2011.

[32] David A. Fulghum, "Libya's Secret SAMs" *Aviation Week and Space Technology*, vol. 173, no. 11 (March 28, 2011), p. 25.

[33] Defense Department, Office of the Assistant Secretary of Defense for Public Affairs, "DOD News Briefing with Vice Adm. Gortney from the Pentagon on Libya Operation Odyssey Dawn" March 19, 2011.

Figure 4.2 Arleigh Burke-class guided-missile destroyer USS *Barry* (DDG 52) launches a Tomahawk missile in support of Operation Odyssey Dawn.
Source: U.S. Navy, photo 110319-N-7231E-001.

volley, this was a demonstration of power that may have gone beyond the immediate needs of the operation, but it was no doubt intended to demonstrate U.S. capabilities to other regional powers – such as Iran and Syria. Additional cruise missile strikes destroyed Qaddafi's command and control facility in Tripoli, and a Scud missile ground-ground facility. (The F-22 Raptor could have also have participated in these strikes, but none were in the theater at the time.)[34]

The British flew Tornado GR4s for strikes against air defenses directly from RAF Marham in the UK. Libya's Bussetta naval base six miles east of the capital was also bombed, and there were strikes against radar installations at airbases near Benghazi. Meanwhile, the French continued to target regime armored forces headed toward Benghazi.[35] Operation Odyssey Dawn – so named by a group of U.S. majors and lieutenant colonels confined to a codename whose first word had to start with "O" and second word with a letter between "A" and "S" – had begun.[36]

Qaddafi's air force and long-range surface-to-air systems were flattened in a matter of a few short days. The regime was incapable of getting even a small number of its planes aloft to strike back. Coalition aircraft could now patrol Libyan airspace to collect intelligence, enforce the no-fly zone, and carry out the civilian protection mission. U.S. Air Force F-15Es flying from Lakenheath, UK, F-16CJs from Spangdahlem, Germany, and AV-8B Harrier attack jets from the USS *Kearsarge* conducted additional strikes against Qaddafi forces. B-2 stealth bombers destroyed aircraft shelters at an airfield outside

---

[34] "Raptors Missed the Window" *Aviation Week*, March 28, 2011.
[35] Tom Coughlan and Catherine Philp, "Third Night of Coalition Airstrikes to Extend No-Fly Zone" *Times*, March 22, 2011, pp. 4–5; Ben Potter, "Allies Split over Libya Endgame" *Australian Financial Review*, March 23, 2011, p. 1; "Gaddafi Compound Rocked by Blasts" *New Zealand Herald*, March 22, 2011.
[36] Ed O'Keefe, "An Odd Mix Produced This Operation's Name" *Washington Post*, March 23, 2011, p. A17.

Misrata, while French pilots attacked sites along the coast and near Benghazi.[37]

Meanwhile, other countries were joining the operation. By the time Resolution 1973 had passed, Danish leaders were already in the process of working on parliamentary support for a Danish contribution. Their proposal passed unanimously on March 19, a first for Danish military action in the post–World War II era. The relatively low risk for Danish personnel, combined with the legitimacy of a UN Security Council Resolution, helped secure Danish participation. Six Danish F-16AM fighters joined operations on March 20, under the command of U.S. Africa Command's (AFRICOM's) air operations command (AOC) at Ramstein Air Force Base in Germany.[38]

Support for the UN Security Council was also important to Norway's decision to join early on. On the Norwegian left, the operation was popular on humanitarian grounds, while in conservative circles it was seen as a way to demonstrate continued military relevance after Afghanistan. Norway's leaders were originally somewhat taken by surprise when the resolution passed, but, after receiving an invitation to the March 19 Paris meeting, they quickly offered up aircraft for strike operations as a show of political support.[39] Initially, as the tussle over Libya played out in Brussels, Norway held back its fighters pending clarification of command and control arrangements, but they joined operations on March 23 after a royal decree authorizing their participation for three months.[40]

---

[37] Peter Goodspeed, "Disputed Target" *National Post*, March 22, 2011, p. A8; Christian F. Anrig, "Allied Air Power over Libya" *Air and Space Power Journal* (Winter 2011), pp. 89–109; Defense Department, Office of the Assistant Secretary of Defense for Public Affairs, "DOD News Briefing with Rear Adm. Hueber via Telephone from USS Mount Whitney" March 23, 2011.

[38] Christian F. Anrig, "The Belgian, Danish, Norwegian, and Dutch Experiences" in Karl P. Mueller, ed., *Precision and Purpose: Airpower in the Libyan Civil War*. Santa Monica, CA: RAND, forthcoming.

[39] Interviews with Norwegian officials, Oslo, September 28, 2012.

[40] Anrig, "The Belgian, Danish, Norwegian, and Dutch Experiences."

Belgium also passed a parliamentary vote in favor of military support to Resolution 1973 on March 18. This was particularly notable given that the country had been in the throes of a political crisis that threatened to rend the country apart. On March 21, Belgian F-16s joined operations with air patrols and, six days later, with air-to-ground strike missions flying from Araxos, Greece.[41] By March 21, Belgian F-16s, Canadian CF-18s and CC-150 tankers, Danish F-16s, Italian F-16s, Spanish F-16s, and a Spanish tanker were also participating in the operation. Norwegian F-16s were en route.

Late that Monday night, the coalition suffered its first – and only – significant loss when a U.S. F-15E Strike Eagle malfunctioned near Benghazi, forcing its two crew members to eject. The plane crashed and the pilots were separated from each other during their ejection, posing the possibility that a U.S. airman might be captured and killed or held for ransom by regime forces – or someone else. One of the crew managed to contact another airborne F-15, which radioed in his location. Within three hours, he was rescued in an operation that involved an F-16, two Harriers, two Chinook helicopters, and two V-22 Osprey tilt-rotors.[42] Luckily for him, the other member of the crew was picked up by pro-rebel forces and returned to safety.[43]

A few days into the operation, with Qaddafi's advance on Benghazi stopped and his forces in retreat, the coalition shifted its attention westward to Ajdabiyah and Misrata, where it attacked regime mechanized forces, artillery, mobile SAMs, command and control capabilities, and supply lines. On the night of March 21, there were also further strikes against the port of Tripoli, destroying more regime military supplies, including Soviet multiple rocket launchers. Libyan officials reported millions of dollars in damage, but no civilian casualties. Coalition efforts to neutralize regime forces outside Misrata and

---

[41] Ibid.
[42] "Timeline of F-15 crew rescue in Libya" AFP, March 22, 2011.
[43] Department of Defense, Public Affairs Office, "Transcript: DoD News Briefing with Adm. Locklear via Teleconference from USS Mount Whitney" March 22, 2011.

Benghazi continued, for example, with British Tornados destroying Libyan armored vehicles outside Ajdabiyah and French jets destroying a Libyan air force plane.[44]

F-16s from Qatar meanwhile joined the operation. By Thursday, the United States had flown in five EA-18G Growler jamming aircraft from Iraq in response to concerns about the persistence of SAMs on the ground.[45] The United States also added A-10 and AC-130 ground-attack aircraft and fired Tomahawks against the headquarters of Qaddafi's 32nd Brigade, his elite unit responsible for most of the attacks against the rebels. The coalition also struck regime ammunition storage facilities and bunkers, tanks, armored personnel carriers, and other mobile military vehicles, weakening its ability to fight back.[46] On March 28, a U.S. Navy P-3C maritime patrol aircraft fired on Libyan coast guard vessels, forcing them to beach. Two smaller Libyan vessels were then attacked by an A-10, destroying one and forcing the crew of the other to abandon ship.[47]

By the end of the first week of strikes, rebel *kata'ib* had retaken Ajdabiyah, the next town outside Benghazi on the road to Tripoli, and were headed toward the town of Brega. This put them in a much stronger position, but they were still 530 miles from Tripoli, with several pro-regime strongholds along the way.[48] The F-15 malfunction aside, these initial coalition operations were free of significant error, although the lack of time to organize and negotiate command and control made it difficult to know exactly who was leading, who was following, and

---

[44] Tom Coughlan and Catherine Philp, "Allied Strikes Rain Down as Gaddafi Forces Attack Civilians in Rebel Town" *Times*, March 23, 2011, pp. 10–11; Brad Norington, "Libyan Command Handed to NATO" *Weekend Australian*, March 26, 2011, p. 17.

[45] "Navy EW Plane Makes Combat Debut over Libya" *Defense Daily International*, vol. 13, no. 12 (March 25, 2011); Craig Hoyle, "How 'Odyssey Dawn' Tamed Libya's Air Defences" *Flight International*, March 29, 2011.

[46] Defense Department, Office of the Assistant Secretary of Defense for Public Affairs, "DOD News Briefing with Vice Adm. Gortney from the Pentagon on Libya Operation Odyssey Dawn" March 28, 2011.

[47] Joint and Coalition Operational Analysis, "Libya: Operation Odyssey Dawn (OOD)" September 21, 2011, p. 3.

[48] Liz Sly and Scott Wilson, "Airstrikes in Libya Help Rebels Advance" *Washington Post*, March 27, 2011, p. A01.

what the overall strategy was going to be. According to the French, national military staffs commanded their assets and coordinated with each other. According to the United States, however, Africa Command (AFRICOM) was in command of the whole coalition.[49] The French had actually thought the operation was going to be jointly run from French and British headquarters, and French officers actually showed up in the UK to start planning the operation only to find that their British counterparts had deployed to Ramstein Air Force Base in Germany, where the United States was running its operations. Disagreements like these led Norway to hold its six F-16s at Crete pending clarification of command and control.[50]

The reality was that command and control of a fifteen-member coalition where each member came with their own rules of engagement and caveats was inherently quite difficult, even for an operation of moderate size. Joint task force Odyssey Dawn had originally been set up to support the earlier Security Council Resolution (1970), and most of the command and control arrangements had been established as the crisis was building.

The challenge of establishing effective command and control with multiple partners was compounded by the fact that within the U.S. military itself, there was considerable debate about who should be in charge. Libya was in AFRICOM's area of responsibility, which clearly suggested that it should lead operations on the U.S. side. Before the intervention, AFRICOM had been given the task of evacuating U.S. nationals from Libya by the secretary of defense. Soon, they were also asked to assist the U.S. State Department in humanitarian operations to move Egyptian refugees from Tunisia to Egypt. But AFRICOM had been designed largely to help African militaries train – building partnership capacity – rather than for kinetic operations of the kind now called for in Libya. It lacked the requisite staff of planners and analysts. To complicate matters, the cross-theater nature of the crisis automatically involved two

---

[49] "Norway Insists on Acting under US Command in Libya" AFP, March 22, 2011.
[50] Christian F. Anrig, "Allied Air Power over Libya" *Air and Space Power Journal* (Winter 2011), pp. 89–109.

other commands – U.S. European Command (EUCOM) and U.S. Central Command (CENTCOM) – that were better equipped for kinetic operations. This created further tensions. As one senior U.S. military official put it, you had "a geographic command set up to do one thing but you are asking it to do another."[51] There was, moreover, an argument that EUCOM ought to be in the lead, given that the Mediterranean was in EUCOM's area of responsibility (AOR), many of the assets that would be necessary for the operation were in Europe, and most operations would be based from there.

In the end, however, AFRICOM was given the lead, although it would rely heavily on EUCOM, CENTCOM, Strategic Command (STRATCOM), and Transport Command (TRANSCOM) for support. To some extent, the challenges inherent in crossing AORs were ameliorated by the fact that some of the commanders were dual hatted to both EUCOM and AFRICOM. While the commander of U.S. forces in Africa, General Carter Ham, was responsible for operations in the theater, Admiral Samuel Locklear, who commanded the U.S. Navy forces for both Europe and Africa, headed the NATO Joint Force Command in Naples, Italy and had tactical command of operations from aboard the USS *Mount Whitney* in the Mediterranean.[52] French and British admirals, as well as liaison officers from other countries participating, were aboard the *Mount Whitney* with Admiral Locklear to coordinate operations.[53]

One novel development in Odyssey Dawn was the use of social media as a means of amplifying the strategic communications of the coalition. Social media had played an important role in sparking the Arab uprisings, but here the U.S. military took advantage of the new technologies for situational awareness and strategic communications, using Twitter, Facebook, and YouTube, for example, to warn civilians of impending attacks and deliver demands to the regime forces. In addition to the

---

[51] Joint and Coalition Operational Analysis, "Libya."
[52] Defense Department, Office of the Assistant Secretary of Defense for Public Affairs, "DOD Press Briefing by Admiral Samuel J. Locklear III, Commander, Joint Task Force Odyssey Dawn" March 22, 2011.
[53] Ibid.

usual leaflets dropped in this kind of operation, NATO relied on these technologies to tell civilians NATO sought to protect them and warn them to stay indoors. Regime forces were told to lay down their arms and stop moving on the cities.[54]

France provided a significant portion of the air assets for Odyssey Dawn, as it would for the eventual NATO operation. These included several Rafale and Mirage multirole fighter jets flying from France, Italy, or the aircraft carrier *Charles de Gaulle* in the Mediterranean. British support would soon include Typhoon and Tornado fighter jets as well as support aircraft flying from the UK and bases in the Mediterranean. Britain also fired sea-launched Tomahawk missiles. Italy made contributions on several fronts, most importantly as a base for operations but also with Tornado and F-16 fighter jets. Canada sent CF-18 fighters in the first days of coalition operations. Belgium, Denmark, the Netherlands, Norway, Qatar, Spain, and the UAE also contributed.[55]

Odyssey Dawn was nevertheless dominated by the United States. Nine days into the operation, the United States had fired 192 Tomahawks, with Britain firing only 7. The United States dropped 455 precision-guided munitions, with 147 from the coalition.[56] The United States also played an essential role in other key areas, flying 80 percent of all air refueling, almost 75 percent of aerial surveillance, and 100 percent of the electronic warfare missions with its EC-130s and EA-18Gs. Totals varied from day to day, but the United States conducted more overall flights than the combined totals of other coalition members, and it completed nearly as many strike missions.[57]

If one accepts the French argument that the initial U.S. strikes on Qaddafi's air-defense systems were unnecessarily heavy, the discrepancy

[54] Joint and Coalition Operational Analysis, "Libya."
[55] Gertler, "Operation Odyssey Dawn (Libya)."
[56] Defense Department, Office of the Assistant Secretary of Defense for Public Affairs, "DOD News Briefing with Vice Adm. Gortney from the Pentagon on Libya Operation Odyssey Dawn March 28, 2011.
[57] Ibid.

between U.S. and European contributions might look less stark. But even then there would be no question that the United States was dominant and indispensable to these initial operations that crippled the Qaddafi regime.

Rearticulating the Strategy and Objectives

Despite its success in averting what would surely have been a slaughter in Benghazi, the attacks on Libya had been roundly criticized throughout the week. Beyond the difficulties within the alliance and with the Arab partners, tensions were already emerging among the allies over the interpretation of the Security Council mandate. Simultaneously, international support was flagging as images of the bombing circulated around the world. Arab League Secretary General Amr Moussa complained: "What is happening in Libya differs from the aim of imposing a no-fly zone, and what we want is the protection of civilians and not the bombardment of more civilians."[58] Secretary General of the GCC Abdul Rahman Bin Hamad Al-Attiyah made similar comments. Russian Prime Minister Vladimir Putin meanwhile likened the operation to a "medieval crusade" in remarks that even President Medvedev criticized as excessive. Although Moussa later adjusted his position, insisting on his support for the operation, the impression that the coalition had immediately gone beyond its mandate of civilian protection was fairly widespread.[59] The shift from complaining about U.S. inaction to criticisms of overkill may have been predictable, but it stuck in the craw of at least one senior defense department official, who later lamented that "at one moment it seemed we were under fire for doing too little. A few days later, we were under the microscope for doing too much."[60]

There was also criticism back in Washington. The international wrangling over the interpretation of Resolution 1973 and the intensity of the

---

[58] Peter Finn and Greg Jaffe, "U.S. Jets Strike Gaddafi's Ground Forces" *Washington Post*, March 21, 2011, p. A01.
[59] Simon Tisdall, "Front: Libya: Reaction" *Guardian*, March 22, 2011, p. 6.
[60] Interview with senior U.S. official, December 16, 2011.

strikes had left some frustrated. On March 23, after a number of members of Congress from both sides of the aisle had expressed reservations about the intervention, Speaker of the House John A. Boehner sent the president a letter that called for closer consultation and a more clearly defined strategy. "I and many other members of the House of Representatives," he wrote, "are troubled that U.S. military resources were committed to war without clearly defining for the American people, the Congress, and our troops what the mission in Libya is and what America's role is in achieving that mission."[61]

The White House rebuffed these criticisms, citing multiple congressional testimonies of senior officials, but the administration was also under fire for allegedly lacking a strategy from less partisan quarters.[62] Gideon Rose, for example, the editor of *Foreign Affairs*, criticized the administration in the *Washington Post* for lacking a clear view of its desired end-state in Libya. The "administration has launched the United States into battle with no clear vision of what successful and stable outcome looks like," he wrote, adding that the administration's strategy of limited engagement did not preclude the need for clear objectives. "In insisting that it is only a little bit pregnant – or that it will not be, or be held to be responsible for supporting its offspring – the administration is kidding itself (or us)."[63] Statements by allied leaders were not helping much to clarify matters. "Mission accomplished would mean the Libyan people free to control their own destiny," said British defense secretary Liam Fox, adding, however, that "regime change is not an objective" of the operation.[64] These kinds of statements made easy fodder for those who wanted to take aim at the U.S. administration or the intervention as a whole.

---

[61] Letter from John A. Boehner to the president, March 23, 2011. http://www.speaker.gov/UploadedFiles/POTUSLetter_032311.pdf.

[62] Mark Landler, "Even While Taking a Chance with Libya, Obama is Playing it Low Key" *New York Times*, March 25, 2011, p. A10.

[63] Gideon Rose, "Tell Me How This One Ends" *Washington Post*, March 27, 2011, p. B01.

[64] Robert Marquand, "Splits Widen among Western Leaders over Way Forward in Libya" *Christian Science Monitor*, March 22, 2011.

Figure 4.3 President Barack Obama delivers his address on Libya at the National Defense University, March 28.
Source: National Defense University.

The transition from the coalition to NATO a week later provided the chance for the president to address his critics and lay out in greater detail the U.S. objectives and strategy. In a speech at the National Defense University (NDU) (Figure 4.3), Obama stressed that the United States was enabling an international coalition to take collective action against a common threat. This was a humanitarian intervention, the president said: "To brush aside America's responsibility as a leader and – more profoundly – our responsibilities to our fellow human beings under such circumstances would have been a betrayal of who we are . . . . As president, I refused to wait for the images of slaughter and mass graves before taking action." (This is a statement the administration would later come to have mixed feelings about a year later when tens of thousands had died in civil strife in Syria.)

Obama also stressed the strategic rationale for the operation, however, and especially the importance of taking a stand in favor of the uprisings in the Arab world: "America has an important strategic interest in preventing Qaddafi from overrunning those who oppose him," he said. "A massacre would have driven thousands of additional refugees across Libya's borders, putting enormous strains on the peaceful – yet fragile – transitions in Egypt and Tunisia. The democratic impulses that are dawning across the region would be eclipsed by the darkest form of dictatorship, as repressive leaders concluded that violence is the best strategy to cling to power." Qaddafi was a tyrant, a threat not only to his own people but also a man whose agents had taken American lives, the president added.

At the same time he made the argument for the operation, however, Obama also reiterated the limits on the scope of the U.S. role. Unique U.S. capabilities had played a major role in the initial phase of the operation, but the United States would now transfer responsibility for operations to the alliance, he said. The United States would not send ground forces, he repeated, and regime change was not an objective of the military operation. "Broadening the military operation to include regime change would be a mistake," he said, because the international political and diplomatic will for regime change did not exist. Qaddafi needed to leave, to be sure, but his departure was not the objective of the military operation.[65] The latter distinction between the goals of the military operation and overall U.S. goals was one that worked in theory, but would be increasingly difficult to keep in practice as the operation stretched out over the summer and Qaddafi refused to back down.

A Country Divided

Several months later, U.S. major general Margaret H. Woodward, who served as joint forces air commander for the operation, admitted that "at the very beginning ... I thought we may have been given the mission too

---

[65] White House, Office of the Press Secretary, "Remarks by the President in Address to the Nation on Libya" March 28, 2011. http://www.whitehouse.gov/the-press-office/2011/03/28/remarks-president-address-nation-libya.

late" to keep Qaddafi's forces out of Benghazi.[66] In ten days, however, Operation Odyssey Dawn had accomplished a great deal. Qaddafi's air force was grounded and his air-defense systems and command and control systems were seriously degraded. More important, the assault on Benghazi had been stopped and possibly thousands of lives had been saved. The cost to the United States was approximately $400 million, a large part of which came from the expense of the Tomahawk missiles.[67] Of the more than 3,200 Tomahawks in the U.S. inventory, however, the portion consumed was relatively small.[68] The United States had also lost an F-15, but there were no military casualties, and civilian casualties and damage to civilian infrastructure were minimal, an accomplishment that would be sustained throughout the intervention.[69]

In addition to the humanitarian benefit, Benghazi's rescue would prove strategically important as the war progressed. Had Benghazi fallen, it would not only have been a devastating blow to the morale of the uprising. As a free city, it gave the rebels a political and military operating base from which they could continue to fight. In subsequent months, rebel leaders in Benghazi would gain broad international recognition. They were able to begin the arduous task of building political institutions, an independent media, and civil society. Meanwhile, Benghazi was a safe haven to train and equip the growing anti-Qaddafi army.

Even if Qaddafi's forces were reversed at Benghazi, however, the regime was far from defeated. As April started, the country was divided: the east was free, but the west was still largely under Qaddafi's heel. A long and frustrating struggle to force Qaddafi to relinquish his grip on the cities and towns of the west now ensued. Benghazi became the face of the revolt, but it was also cut off from the real fighting and sometimes heroic feats being performed elsewhere in Salutin, in the western Nafusah Mountains on the border with Tunisia, and the Tripolitanian cities of

[66] John Tirpak, "Lessons from Libya" *Air Force Magazine* (December 2011), pp. 34–38.
[67] Gertler, "Operation Odyssey Dawn (Libya)."
[68] Jim Garamone, "Roughead: Ships Were Ready for Odyssey Dawn" American Forces Press Service, March 23, 2011. http://www.defense.gov/news/newsarticle.aspx?id=63272.
[69] See Chapter 7.

Zintan, Zawiya, and especially in the streets of Misrata, a key city that rose up against Qaddafi early on and was now beginning to suffer a long and bloody siege at the hands of regime forces. This was a problem. The distance between Benghazi and these other areas – both geographical and in terms of the intensity of the fighting – made it hard for the rebel leadership to assert its authority. This was especially true after the war, when it faced a country policed by a proliferating number of *kata'ib*, most of whom had not been connected meaningfully with the Benghazi leadership and many of whom had sacrificed even more to liberate the country.

5   Stalemate

NATO's Operation Unified Protector (OUP) thus began with Security Council backing, strong regional support, and a battlefield well prepared by the U.S.-led coalition that preceded it. As many of those interviewed for this study acknowledged, some senior officials in both U.S. and allied governments expected Qaddafi would collapse or capitulate quickly. It was seven months, however, before he was killed and NATO's mission was brought to a close. In retrospect, a lengthier operation might have been expected given the political and military constraints allied militaries operated under and the tenacity with which dictators have historically held onto power. Nevertheless, it came as a surprise to some key participants, as is too often the case with this kind of war.

Two underlying dynamics would determine success or failure. On one side there was the pace of the rebel advance on the ground; on the other, the strain on allied resources and cohesion, neither of which was great to begin with. The rebel *kata'ib* needed to take Tripoli before NATO consensus fell apart. The longer Qaddafi held out, the more the fragile consensus within the alliance risked an all-out breakdown and the more the pressure grew to hit Qaddafi harder. But herein lay a central dilemma of the whole operation: if more strikes on Qaddafi might accelerate his demise, they would also increase the risk of civilian deaths and collateral damage, which also could split the coalition apart. NATO thus continued operations at a pace sufficient to give the *thuwwar* a fighting chance but insufficient to ensure their victory. The result was an apparent stalemate on the ground and a war that dragged out much longer than some officials had expected – or at least hoped would be the case.

Handoff and Operational Structure

After the war, NATO leaders were quick to point to the speed with which the NATO operation got going as a sign of the resolve and overall unity of the alliance. "Within 10 days of the U.N. Security Council voting a resolution mandating the protection of Libya's civilians, policing of a no-flight zone, and prevention of illicit arms transfers by air and sea, NATO took command of a significant force of dozens of ships and hundreds of airplanes and commenced military operations," wrote Ambassador Daalder and NATO's supreme allied commander, Europe (SACEUR) James G. Stavridis in the *International Herald Tribune* after Qaddafi's death. It is indisputable that the whole process between initial discussions at the North Atlantic Council (NAC) and the start of NATO operations, which lasted a little over a month, was much faster than in Kosovo, where discussions lasted over a year, and in Bosnia, where deliberation lasted several months. But this speed was hardly a sign of underlying allied unity. The fact was, the Germans and others continued to object to the operation, even as they let it move ahead.

NATO's response to the crisis was fairly rapid, however, given the circumstances. Operational plans were needed for each of the four tasks outlined in the UN resolution: the arms embargo, humanitarian relief, the no-fly zone, and civilian protection. Operational planning for each of these missions passed through the alliance crisis response system, a process that requires the allied military leadership to generate and allied political leadership to agree on a concept of operations, contributions to the mission (i.e., force generation), and then decide to execute the plan. The full agreement of the NAC is needed at each stage of this process. In this case, all the operational plans were developed and passed within ten days of the UN resolution. This is impressive, although in most cases formal NATO planning drew heavily on preexisting plans developed by

U.S. European and Africa commands as well as the prudent planning that SACEUR had begun several weeks earlier. Existing U.S. tasking orders for air operations were simply handed over to NATO. Had NATO been starting from scratch, the process of initiating operations would surely have been lengthier and less smooth.

The handoff to NATO was then facilitated by the fact that some of the key officers running Odyssey Dawn also stayed close to the action. Admiral Locklear ceded operational command to his deputy at Joint Forces Command Naples, Lt. Gen. Charles Bouchard of Canada, who would now lead the NATO combined joint task force. This was clearly and widely recognized as an effort to get the U.S. military off the stage and a non-U.S. officer in front of the television cameras. A separate command center was set up in a building across from Joint Forces Command on the Naples base for Libya operations. Locklear was technically still in the overall chain of command, however, between Bouchard and Admiral Stavridis, and from the background he would play an important role in calming frayed nerves in Washington when the going got iffy later in the war.[1] Lt. General Ralph J. Jodice, who was commander of the U.S. 16th Air Expeditionary Task Force, was also the commander of NATO air operations. He initially commanded the air operations from the NATO base at Izmir but eventually transferred operations to the tactical headquarters at the NATO Combined Air Operations Center (CAOC) in Poggio-Renatico, Italy, because he lacked the information necessary to make certain decisions in Turkey. After a somewhat hectic time getting up and running, Poggio-Renatico would become the critical node for the air campaign.[2] The ultimate political authority for military operations remained the North Atlantic Council.

The key non-NATO partners in the operation – Sweden, Qatar, the UAE, and Jordan – linked into NATO structures through direct liaison officers at the CAOC in Poggio-Renatico and at Bouchard's headquarters in Naples. In areas where the partners played key roles, such as

[1] Interview with senior U.S. official, January 30, 2011.
[2] Interview with NATO official, February 10, 2012.

intelligence, the number of liaison officers could be significant.[3] Given the effort to show broad regional support for the mission, there was a significant effort to get the Arab partners to take a lead in the public diplomacy as well as an effort to put an Arab face on the operation itself – for example, by putting an Arab officer in the deputy commander's role.[4] The latter never panned out, but as one senior U.S. official explained, "the red, green and black of Arab nations' flags were expected to be prominent in military operations."[5]

The willingness of the Arab partners to join NATO in operations against the regime arose in large part from long-standing animosity between Qaddafi and the Gulf state leaders. This was especially true in the case of Saudi Arabia, as already noted, but it was also true in the case of Qatar. Qaddafi had singled Qatar out in his February 22 rant against the uprising, attacking Qatari-owned news agency Al Jazeera for its reporting on the violence. France's relations with Qatar were also strong, and Qatar had been particularly important in Sarkozy's efforts to develop closer ties with the Gulf. Both Qatar and the UAE played an important role in getting the Arab League to support the no-fly zone.[6]

Qatar flew Mirage 2000s from Souda Bay in Crete in joint patrols of the no-fly zone with the French. They also played a key part in liaising with the *thuwwar*, providing transport for humanitarian supplies and eventually providing them with direct financial and military support, as did the Emirates. The UAE deployed six F-16s and six Mirage 2000s for more than 100 strikes, some with their Black Shaheen cruise missiles.[7] Jordan's role has not been officially acknowledged, but multiple

[3] U.S. Mission to NATO, "Remarks to the Press on Libya and Operation Unified Protector, Ambassador Ivo Daalder" September 8, 2011. http://nato.usmission.gov/libya-oup-90811.html.

[4] Interview with senior U.S. official, December 16, 2011.

[5] Steven Erlanger, Elisabeth Bulmiller, and David D. Kirkpatrick, "Europeans Press Libya Showdown" *International Herald Tribune*, March 19, 2011, p. 1.

[6] John Irish and Regan E. Doherty, "Libyan Conflict Brings French-Qatari Ties to the Fore" Reuters, April 13, 2011; Tim Ripley, "Power Brokers, Qatar and the U.A.E. Take Center Stage" *Jane's Intelligence Review*, December 21, 2011.

[7] Ripley, "Power Brokers."

open-source documents and statements by U.S. officials indicate that Jordan flew F-16s in no-fly zone operations alongside the Royal Air Force (RAF).[8]

At the start of NATO operations, fourteen NATO nations were participating with four non–NATO partners.[9] Only five, however, were conducting air-ground strikes, and of this group only France and Britain were flying without restrictions.[10] Within NATO, the nations engaged in offensive operations had established an informal group, known variously as the "striker group," "le petit groupe," and the "OP-4 group" – a reference to paragraph four of Security Council Resolution 1973, which mandated the civilian protection mission. The striker group would soon grow from its initial six – Belgium, Britain, Canada, Denmark, France, and Norway – to eight when Italy and the United States rejoined strike operations.

The role of the striker group was key. It discussed most decisions informally prior to deliberation with the full complement of allies and in the process decided many of the important issues and organized a good deal of the necessary logistical and other support.[11] This was an important innovation from the Kosovo air campaign, when NATO capitals scrutinized and rejected targets – much to the frustration of U.S. military officials. Most targeting decisions in Unified Protector

---

[8] Richard Norton and Taylor Simon Rogers, "Special Report: Libya War Audit: Arab States Hold Fire in Battle against Gaddafi Regime: Qatar, Jordan and United Arab Emirates Play Defensive Role" *Guardian* (London), May 23, 2011; "Andrew J. Shapiro, Assistant Secretary, Bureau of Political-Military Affairs Speaks on Ensuring Israel's Qualitative Military Edge" *Targeted News Service*, November 4, 2011; "NATO General Rules Out Any Threat from Pro-Gaddafi Remnants in Libya" *Kuwait News Agency*, October 24, 2011; "Speech by Admiral Giampaolo Di Paola, Chairman of the NATO Military Committee at the 57th Annual Session of the NATO Parliamentary Assembly, Bucharest, Romania" *State News Service*, October 8, 2011; "A Timeline of the Conflict in Libya" CNN.com, August 18, 2011; Ivo Daalder, "Libya – A NATO Success Story" remarks at the Atlantic Council of the United States, November 7, 2011.

[9] Ivo H. Daalder and James G. Stavridis, "NATO's Victory in Libya" *Foreign Affairs*, March/April, 2012.

[10] Edward Cody, "France, Britain Want NATO to Fight Harder against Qaddafi's Forces" *Washington Post*, April 12, 2011.

[11] Interview with French official, February 7, 2012; Interview with U.K. official, February 7, 2012.

were made at the operational level, with very few pushed up for discussion by NATO ambassadors. Even when there were discussions at that level, preliminary consensus was reached within the striker group before the issue was brought to the floor of the NAC for decision, thereby accelerating the process. As one allied official put it, unlike in Kosovo, where political oversight had hindered operations, in Libya the striker group mostly worked "to facilitate" them.[12]

"NATO Is Disappointing Us"

Despite the relatively smooth handover to NATO, the next few weeks were near fatal, as the limits of allied capabilities became clear, overarching strategic objectives remained murky, and Qaddafi's forces repulsed the initial rebel breakout. On April 16, rebel military chief Abdel Fattah Younes complained publicly that "NATO is disappointing us."[13] At the start of Odyssey Dawn, *thuwwar* from Benghazi had pushed over 500 kilometers west, all the way to Qaddafi's hometown of Sirte. But their breakout had been short lived, and in the first weeks of NATO operations the rebels were forced back to Ajdabiya, 160 kilometers from Benghazi. This was an obvious embarrassment for the alliance. On April 10, sandstorms made it impossible for NATO jets to strike regime forces on the ground, allowing Qaddafi's troops to outflank the rebels and nearly dislodge them from Ajdabiya. People fled the town and the regime troops were suddenly back within striking distance of Benghazi. The next day, heavy fire from NATO aircraft forced them back to Brega, 75 kilometers to the southwest. The rebels were then able to deploy outside Ajdabiya in a position they would hold for the remainder of the war. A static line of confrontation emerged on the eastern front as a result. On March 26, Juppé had said he expected a short war: "The elimination of Libya's military potential could take

---

[12] Interview with allied official, February 7, 2012.
[13] Graeme Smith, "Rebel Military Chief Rebukes NATO" *Globe and Mail*, April 16, 2011, p. A14.

several days or several weeks, but by no means several months."[14] Such hopes, however, which were clearly not Juppé's alone, proved misplaced.

Meanwhile, attention shifted to the increasingly dire situation in Misrata, which had been under siege since rebels seized control in February. Situated between Ajdabiyah and Tripoli, Misrata is Libya's third largest city, with a population of 300,000. Misrata is the site of the battle of Qasr Bu Hadi in 1915, where imperial Italian forces suffered a heavy defeat at the hands of one of their supposed allies, Ramadan Al-Suwayhli, and the city's citizens now displayed their fighting fortitude against Qaddafi. Their control was nevertheless extremely tenuous. Regime forces shelled the city indiscriminately from positions to the south, east, and west of Misrata's Mediterranean port.[15] Qaddafi sent armored personnel carriers, multiple rocket launchers, and other weapons to the suburb of Tuwerga and bombarded the city relentlessly, including with cluster munitions.[16] Small *kata'ib*, sometimes no stronger than a dozen men at the start, fought a house-to-house, block-to-block street war to keep the regime forces at bay. They had the advantage of in-depth knowledge of the city landscape, but their weapons and ammunition, limited to begin with, were dwindling rapidly.[17] The civilian population lacked food, water, and electricity. Hospitals overflowed with casualties, dysentery was rife, and corpses lay strewn in the streets. Regime snipers targeted civilians and *thuwwar* indiscriminately and were reported to be killing children. There was evidence of systematic rape by regime militias, sometimes proudly reported by regime troops themselves. By April 15, Human Rights Watch reported that 267 bodies had been brought to the

---

[14] "Coalition Members Differ on Duration of Libya Operation" *Russia Daily*.

[15] Diederik Wandewalle, *A History of Modern Libya* (New York: Cambridge University Press, 2012), p. 27.

[16] "Press Briefing on Libya" April 19, 2011. http://www.nato.int/nato_static/assets/audio/audio_2011_04/20110419_110419a.mp3.

[17] Harriet Sherwood, "It Will Be a Massacre in Misrata if NATO Doesn't Send Ground Troops, Say Rebels" *Observer*, April 17, 2011, p. 19; C.J. Chivers, "Taking Airport, Rebels in Libya Loosen Noose" New York Times, May 12, p. A1.

city morgue, with the total number of dead likely far higher. A week later, that number was estimated to be nearly 1,000.[18]

The sea was the city's only lifeline. Ships from Benghazi, as well as Turkey, Malta, and other foreign ports, brought in food and medical supplies. Ships also eventually brought arms and ammunition that the *thuwwar* desperately needed, although not in the amounts they sought – an issue that would create tensions between Misratans and the NTC when the war was over. Qaddafi had agreed not to attack the humanitarian vessels, but the promise could hardly be taken as ironclad, and much-needed shipments were risky.[19] Misrata's civilian population meanwhile took flight by boat abroad or to the relative safety of Benghazi. By mid-April, thousands of civilians had been evacuated with the help of the United Nations International Office of Migration, but thousands more were still crowded in the port.[20] If Qaddafi's forces were to recapture the city, Western leaders feared, the consequences for the people would be dire, rebel morale could be crushed, and the country could end up being permanently split along its historical east-west divide.[21] By mid April, *thuwwar* were protesting that what had been prevented in Benghazi was now happening in Misrata, and calling for more help from NATO.

In an effort to alleviate the pressure on Misrata's stricken population and help the rebels hold the line against Qaddafi's forces farther east, NATO divided its air strikes between tactical strikes against regime forces on the Ajdabiya-Brega front and in Misrata on the one hand, and strategic

---

[18] Marie Colvin, "'We Had Our Orders: Rape All the Sisters'" *Sunday Times*, May 22, 2011, p. 30; Xan Rice, "Front: The Graveyards Are Filling Up in Misrata's Unexpected War" *Guardian*, p. 1, April 22, 2011.

[19] "For Beseiged Libyan City, the Sea Is a Sole Lifeline" AP, April 21, 2011.

[20] UN Integrated Regional Information Networks, "Libya: Traumatized Evacuees Describe Misrata Horror" *Africa News*, April 18, 2011; UN Office for the Coordination of Humanitarian Affairs, "Libya: Misrata Is Difficult to Access: Humanitarian Assessment Finds People in Need of Medical Supplies" *OCHA Situation Report no. 49*, July 16, 2011.

[21] Barack Obama, David Cameron, Nicolas Sarkozy, "Libya's Pathway to Peace" *International Herald Tribune*, April 15, 2011.

strikes against the regime command and control and resupply capabilities on the other. To put pressure on regime forces to back off from Brega, air strikes hit regime ammunition storage facilities, tanks, armored personnel carriers, rocket launchers, surface-to-air missiles, and other weapons. To put pressure on the regime to withdraw from Misrata and stop shelling the city, NATO bombed its ammunition stores, tanks, radars, rocket launchers, and other military equipment. Meanwhile, NATO hit the command and control center of Qaddafi's 32nd "Khamis" Brigade, which was directing attacks on Misrata and Ajdabiya from south of Tripoli. Allies also worked to coordinate national efforts to evacuate civilians from Misrata and facilitated the shipment of humanitarian aid into Libya's other major cities.[22]

In the first three weeks of operations, NATO flew more than 1,300 strike sorties. This was an average of sixty-two per day, although not all of these flights dropped bombs, and the rate was somewhat lower at the start. To the consternation of France, Obama lived up to his promise and withdrew U.S. fighter aircraft on April 4.[23] The French concentrated their efforts on the Brega-Ajdabija front, while other countries focused on Misrata and Tripoli. Nevertheless, the situation on the ground did not budge. Misrata was still under siege and fighting continued back and forth between Ajdabiya and Brega. Qaddafi still had a firm grip on Tripoli and the rest of the west and showed no sign of relenting. Figure 5.1 shows targeting in the first phase of the NATO operation.

Relative Weakness of the *Thuwwar*

"I've not had any training," said one *tha'ir*, "but I've seen plenty of action films."[24] The fact was, *thuwwar* sorely lacked experience and equipment.

---

[22] NATO Press Office, "Secretary General's Annual Report 2011" January 26, 2012. http://www.nato.int/cps/en/natolive/opinions_82646.htm.

[23] Natalie Nougayrède, "La guerre de Libya met à l'épreuve le lien transatlantique" *Le Monde*, May 24, 2011.

[24] Adrian Blomfield and Nick Meo, "For Ragtag Rebels, Little Training, Less Choice" *National Post*, March 8, 2011, p. A1.

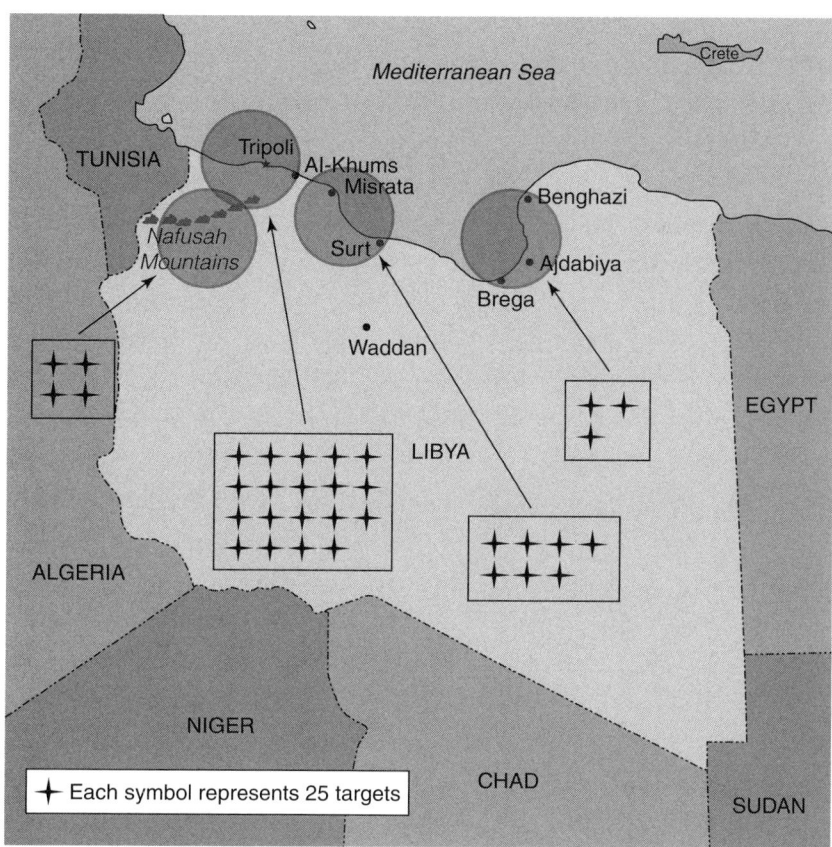

Figure 5.1 The early phase of the operation focused heavily on Tripoli and Misrata (Targets April 11–May 15).
Source: NATO, Operational Media Updates, April 11–May 15, 2011.

They fought bravely, but few were professional soldiers. By early April, the number of training camps in Benghazi had increased and there were reportedly more than 1,000 young men training in some of them.[25] Depictions of the state of affairs inside the camps, however, were discouraging. One report depicted a "teen remake of the Dirty Dozen: a

[25] Chris McGreal, "Libya: Rebel Training Camp" *Guardian*, April 8, 2011, p. 27.

shambolic line of soldiers, many under 18 and at least 3 only 15, mixed with a scattering of older educated professionals of varying fitness."[26]

At the outset, the *thuwwar* had very few weapons. Those they did have had been captured from an arms depot in Benghazi and were rusting and in a state of disrepair, Soviet vintage or older. Some of the guns were even Italian Carcano rifles that dated from the interwar period.[27] There were other small arms: heavy machine guns, rocket-propelled grenades (RPGs), and mortars. They had Katyusha rockets, as well as a few Russian Grad multiple rocket launch systems, but they initially lacked the know-how to use them. They also had a few old Soviet-era T-55 tanks, but these were outgunned by Qaddafi's more modern T-72s. For the most part, *kata'ib* deployed in so-called technicals – pickups with 12.7-mm anti-aircraft or other machine guns mounted on the back (Figure 5.2). The rebels' attempts to repair the more broken-down pieces of equipment with makeshift welding jobs imparted a "Mad Max" quality to the whole scene.[28]

Moreover, even if the ranks of the *thuwwar* had grown to the thousands by early April, a much smaller fraction of these actually fought on the main fronts, and nearly all the recruits lacked basic fighting skills. It is one thing to learn to aim and fire a Kalashnikov and another to learn to operate successfully as a fighting unit, employ effective ground tactics, and maintain discipline against a superior force. At the front, *thuwwar* often fought in an uncoordinated and chaotic manner, retreating quickly and then charging regime positions when morale recovered, often with disastrous and bloody results.[29] One military observer likened many of

[26] Doug Saunders, "Rebels Rely on Teens to Fill Ranks" *Globe and Mail*, July 11, 2011, p. A1.
[27] "Accidental Heros" RUSI, (n.a.), September 2011; "Libyan Rebels and Their Arab Spring Armament" Al Jazeera, July 18, 2011. http://www.aljazeera.com/programmes/faultlines/2011/07/2011718132823320628.html.
[28] Jerome Starkey, "It's a Mad Max Conflict" *Times*, May 14, 2001, p. 44; Peter Godspeed, "Disputed Target: The Attack on Qaddafi's Base Has Sparked Debate about the West's Mission" *National Post*, March 22, 2011, p. A8.
[29] C.J. Chivers, "Libyan Rebels Don't Really Add Up to an Army" *New York Times*, April 7, 2011, p. A1.

the rebel attacks in the early weeks of the war to "coastal tourism. They would get in their 4x4s and charge up the coast encountering little opposition," he explained. Then, they would "break for a cup of tea and decide they had taken the land. Then Qaddafi's forces would come charging back and they would scurry back. These were phoney advances."[30] Defectors from Qaddafi's army did provide some experienced leadership, but those who had recently served Qaddafi were not always viewed as legitimate by *thuwwar* rank and file. The other group of fighters with experience were the hardened jihadists, returned from Iraq and Afghanistan – a fact that Qaddafi relentlessly sought to draw attention to.

Underlying many of these weaknesses were the financial problems the rebels faced. Despite implicit international support for their efforts, the NTC struggled to fund its war effort. Sanctions from two UN Security Council resolutions restricted the flow of funds, as did the fact that most countries, including the United States, had not at this point recognized the NTC as the legitimate government in Libya. In early April, the United States dispatched veteran diplomat and regional expert Chris Stevens as its representative to Benghazi, thus getting the process started, but it would be months before the official U.S. recognition, and the UN vote to unblock Libyan monies for the NTC came only toward the end of the war, after Tripoli had fallen..

Finally, if the *thuwwar* were poorly trained and equipped, they were also highly disorganized. A look at rebel organization in Misrata is a case in point. According to a postwar study of rebel organization there, the initial rebel units were small, neighborhood fighting cells that only over time coalesced into larger *kata'ib*. Even then, however, there were some two hundred *kata'ib* in Misrata alone at the end of the war. Although the sizes varied, they were on average roughly fifty members, composed largely of the student population and men who had been employed in

---

[30] Patrick Wintour and Nicholas Watt, "Cameron's War: Why PM Felt Gaddafi Had to Be Stopped" *Guardian*, October 3, 2011, p. 13.

the private sector. Professionals such as doctors and servants of the state, not surprisingly, made up a smaller proportion.[31]

Early in the war, these rebels were simply fighting to keep Qaddafi's forces away from their own homes. Only later, as the regime began to weaken, would some begin to focus on overthrowing it. This, in turn, would increase the pressure for consolidation into larger groups and then coordination between these groups. As rebel leader Fawzi Bukaatf, who established the Revolutionary Brigades Commission in the east, put it, "In the early days, Misratans were fighting for Misrata and Zintanis for Zintan. By the end of May 2011, it was clear that we had to gather coalitions of brigades. We couldn't fight well if we did not coordinate ourselves."[32] As a result, larger organizations eventually emerged (with some guidance from external actors) in Benghazi, Ajdabiyah, Misrata, and Zintan. But this process did not occur until late May and did not begin to have an impact on the battleground for at least another month.

The "shambolic" state of the rebel fighting forces would improve gradually, beginning with shipments of weapons from Qatar, which Emir Sheik Hamad Bin Khalifa al-Thani announced in mid-April. These rebel acquisitions were combined with growing ingenuity on the part of the rebels – for example, in the deployment of sand-filled trucks to block the advance of regime tanks.

Qaddafi's own military was also not very strong. Since the early years of his rule, he had largely neglected the formal Libyan military institutions, favoring security organizations such as the Revolutionary Committees, which existed outside the state and were controlled entirely by him. Although he sought to maintain rough parity with Algeria and had an army some 50,000 strong, only a fraction of this number remained loyal to him – likely closer to 10,000–12,000. The only truly loyal brigade

[31] Small Arms Survey, Research Note #19, June 12; Adam Forbes, "Small Arms/Light Weapons and Physical Security in Misrata" *Journal of ERW and Mine Action*, vol. 16, no 2. (June 2012). Forbes puts the number of brigades at 168, while SAS research note puts them at 236.

[32] International Crisis Group, "Divided We Stand: Libya's Enduring Conflicts" *Crisis Group Middle East North Africa Report no. 130*, September 14, 2012, p. 18.

RELATIVE WEAKNESS OF THE THUWWAR 109

Figure 5.2 A Rebel technical.
Source: Al Jazeera English.

within that army was the 32nd, commanded by his son Khamis. With roughly 3,000 troops chosen for their loyalty to the regime, the Khamis brigade was also the best equipped, in part because Qaddafi trusted it not to defect and turn the weapons against him.

Still, for many weeks, even if weak relative to NATO and hollowed out by Qaddafi, regime forces had a significant military advantage over the rebels on the ground.[33] The regime forces were larger and more experienced than the rebels. They also had more modern weaponry, and Qaddafi had reinforced it with mercenaries from Africa and Eastern Europe.[34] Although the regime's weapons stocks had deteriorated in the years when Libya was under international sanctions, it still had large numbers of artillery, multiple rocket launchers, tanks, armored personnel carriers, and small arms.[35]

[33] Rod Nordland, "Arms Said to Reach Libyan Rebels" *International Herald* Tribune, April 18, 2011, p. 4; IISS, "NATO Steps Up the Pace in Libya" *Strategic Comments*, August 24, 2011; Gary Li, "Libyan Rebels' Weapons Deficit" IISS Experts Report, March 8, 2011.
[34] "Libya Jails Russia, Ukraine, Belarus 'Mercenaries'" *Agence France Press*, June 4, 2012.
[35] IISS, "Libya" *The Military Balance*, 2011, p. 320; *Janes World Armies*, "Libya" January 2012.

Qaddafi's forces had also begun to adapt to the NATO air strikes, thereby blunting the advantage the rebels initially gained from the intervention. Regime forces had quickly recognized they were exposed and vulnerable in the Libyan desert if they presented a conventional profile for NATO jets. They also figured out that NATO was highly preoccupied with civilian casualties and collateral damage. Accordingly, they dispersed, camouflaged themselves as *thuwwar*, and sought to blend in with the civilian population to increase the chances NATO strikes would accidentally cause civilian deaths. It thus became much harder for NATO to target them, and the importance of getting good targeting intelligence from the ground – intelligence that was at this point in the operation unreliable at best – greatly increased.

Allied Capability Shortfalls

Meanwhile, NATO had faced its own shortages and difficulties getting started. Bad weather in the desert held up initial operations for a few days, and there were some legal obstacles to overcome before NATO could fully take over from the coalition. The result was a struggle even to maintain an operational tempo that was significantly lower than for the Kosovo air campaign in 1999.[36] To make matters worse, NATO bombers accidentally hit a rebel convoy, killing thirteen *thuwwar* outside Brega – a deadly error later attributed to the absence of communication with the rebels.

One reason for the relatively low operational tempo was that at the start of the operation, fewer than 70 of more than 7,000 combat-capable allied aircraft – less than 1 percent – were flying the civilian protection missions.[37] Even without counting the United States, which owns more than 4,000 of NATO's fighter jets, the portion of jets flying was still very small. In some cases, the obstacles were technical or owing to a lack of maintenance of aircraft. In other cases, the obstacles were political, as

[36] See Chapter 8.
[37] Calculated from multiple sources.

with Germany, which had some 300 jets but offered none. In still others, the obstacles appear to have been a mix of political and technical, as with Poland, which has over 120 jets but also offered none. Deployments in Afghanistan meanwhile restricted somewhat the ability of those countries that were participating to offer what they could, although this was largely because of the additional cost rather than a lack of equipment – the requirements in the two theaters being quite different.

To complicate matters, as the NATO operation began, there was a need to shift from "static" to "dynamic" targeting. Initial strikes hit known fixed or static sites, but as these were destroyed, fighter jets increasingly had to take off without a specific target set and search for targets while in the air, a task that required more specialized equipment that some allied aircraft lacked.[38]

Other bottlenecks were more serious, however. The jets were essential, but there were other aircraft that were relatively scarcer, especially those designed for close-in ground attack missions, such as the A-10 Warthog and AC-130 gunship. The United States had briefly introduced these weapons in the first week of Odyssey Dawn but withdrew them after NATO took over. Additionally, munitions were a problem. After three weeks, NATO had to reduce its number of sorties because munitions were in short supply.[39] Large countries such as France could fill their gaps by accelerating production, but the shortages were more problematic for smaller states that had to buy them from other countries. Efforts to get precision guided munitions from nonstriker members of the alliance were difficult, and the United States filled the gap.[40]

Even more important were the shortages in refueling tankers and intelligence, surveillance, and reconnaissance (ISR). As in so many

---

[38] Telephone interview with senior U.S. official, July 9, 2012; Paul Koring, "Air War on Qaddafi Struggling for Lack of Planes" *Globe and Mail*, April 16, 2011, p. A3.

[39] Karen DeYoung and Greg Jaffe, "NATO Runs Short on Some Munitions in Libya" *Washington Post*, April 15, 2011.

[40] Michale Codner, "Military Doctrine and Intervention" in Adrian Johnson and Saqeb Mueen, eds., *Short War, Long* Shadow, RUSI Whitehall Report 1–12; Koring, "Air-War on Qaddafi Struggling."

other areas, the United States possessed the vast majority of the tanker capacity in the alliance – some five times the number of tankers of other allies combined. Nevertheless, together, non-U.S. tankers totaled more than sixty, which should have been a suitable number for the operational tempo of this campaign, but the nonparticipation of countries such as Germany and the caveats placed on the use of tankers by some participating allies meant that air-to-air refueling was perpetually in short supply, especially in the early weeks of the operation.[41] The tanker shortfall – together with another shortfall in search and rescue capability – increased the challenge involved in striking deep into Libya and therefore made air assets closer to Libya all the more valuable.[42] In this respect, the French aircraft carrier *Charles de Gaulle* was particularly beneficial – at least until it had to return to base in Toulon for scheduled maintenance in August.

Most U.S. officials, however, argued that the critical shortfall was in ISR. Good ISR was in high demand because allies were determined to ensure that their air strikes caused the absolute minimum possible collateral damage and civilian casualties. This was essential for humanitarian reasons (a principal rationale for the war), but good optics were also critical to holding the coalition together. Minimizing damage to Libyan infrastructure was also important, both because excessive damage would saddle postconflict Libya with a much more difficult reconstruction challenge and because major energy concerns in some allied countries – Turkey and Italy in particular – owned much of that infrastructure. There were also broader implications for the legitimacy of the whole operation, as UK Defence Secretary Liam Fox later explained: "We would need to exorcise the ghost of Iraq post-Gaddafi, and we could do that if we showed we had a higher regard for the lives of civilians, and had a different perception of the value of life, than the regime that was being replaced."[43]

---

[41] Interview with U.S. official, February 6, 2012.
[42] Interviews with U.S. and NATO officials, February 10, 2012.
[43] Wintour and Watt, "Cameron's War."

A number of unusually strict requirements for situational awareness and precision bombing were therefore written into the rules of engagement for the strikes. For every strike on a fixed target, for example, a minimum of thirty minutes of observation was required to ensure the site was free of civilians. Smaller precision munitions were often used in the place of larger bombs to minimize collateral damage, and the importance of having sufficient stocks of these smaller precision weapons – Hellfire and Brimstone missiles, for example – would become one of the main military lessons of the operation.

Beyond aircraft, there were also insufficient staff for the analysis of the intelligence that was available. Precision strikes require staff that are trained and available to assess, analyze, and prosecute potential targets (called targeteers). Libya is a large country, with at least three areas of operation, thus creating a significant demand for ISR. At the start of the operation, the alliance found itself woefully short of such staff, especially targeteers. Initially, non–U.S. allies managed only a fraction of the hundreds needed, and many of those who were made available to the CAOC in Poggio-Renatico were trained only for national air defense and thus lacked the skills for offensive air operations.[44] In part, the shortfall was due to the speed with which the operation got underway, which left limited time to identify and deploy staff with the requisite skills. In part, however, it was also due to a basic shortage of qualified targeteers. The United States had to scramble to fill in the gap. Despite the fact that U.S. assets were already stretched from other operations, hundreds of U.S. staff were transferred from the regional U.S. commands and other theaters to fill in the lacuna and keep the operation going.[45]

To further complicate matters, there was difficulty sharing information within the coalition. Different computer networks and multiple intelligence-sharing arrangements meant that the information processing element of the targeting process was sometimes opaque to key striker

---

[44] Interview with senior U.S. official, February 7, 2012.
[45] Ibid.; interview with U.S. official, February 6, 2012.

nations such as France – causing much exasperation.⁴⁶ Because France lacked intelligence-sharing arrangements with other key NATO allies, French officers lacked visibility into the full targeting process and were forced to wait outside the facility where the intelligence was being processed while decisions were made inside by other states.⁴⁷ This led to no small amount of agitation on the part of the French – and even some American – officers.

Lacking adequate targeting and key capabilities, the pace of operations slowed, and pressure on Qaddafi's forces slackened, just at the moment when political leaders started coming under the gun to up the tempo. As Secretary Gates would put it later, it was "the spectacle of an air operations center designed to handle more than 300 sorties a day struggling to launch about 150."⁴⁸ Figure 5.3 shows sortie rates over the course of the operation. In the end, the United States would provide over three-quarters of the ISR, furnishing not only targeteers but eventually deploying other assets, including U-2s, E-8 JSTARS, navy EP-3s and EA-18G Growlers, air force EC-130Hs, Reapers, and Predators to the theater.⁴⁹

It should be noted, however, that some French officials have downplayed in private the significance of these ISR shortfalls. As some analysts have pointed out, a "vast proportion" of the air strikes conducted during the campaign were at the dynamic targets, where strike aircraft seek out their own targets, and thus rely less on NATO ISR than on capabilities they carry with them. Figure 5.4 shows the evolution of targeting patterns over the course of the mission and the larger proportion of fixed buildings vs. mobile vehicles in the early stages of the operation. The French are

---

[46] Robert Densmore, "French Pilots over Libya Decline US Intel; Clearance Just Too Slow" aolnews.com, September 21, 2011; Eric Schmitt, "NATO Sees Flaws in Air Campaign against Qaddafi" *New York Times*, April 14, 2012.
[47] French military source.
[48] Office of the Assistant Secretary of Defense (Public Affairs), "Speech: The Security and Defense Agenda (Future of NATO), as Delivered by Secretary of Defense Robert M. Gates, Brussels, Belgium, Friday, June 10, 2011." http://www.defense.gov/speeches/speech.aspx?speechid=1581.
[49] Densmore, "French Pilots over Libya Decline US Intel."

ALLIED CAPABILITY SHORTFALLS

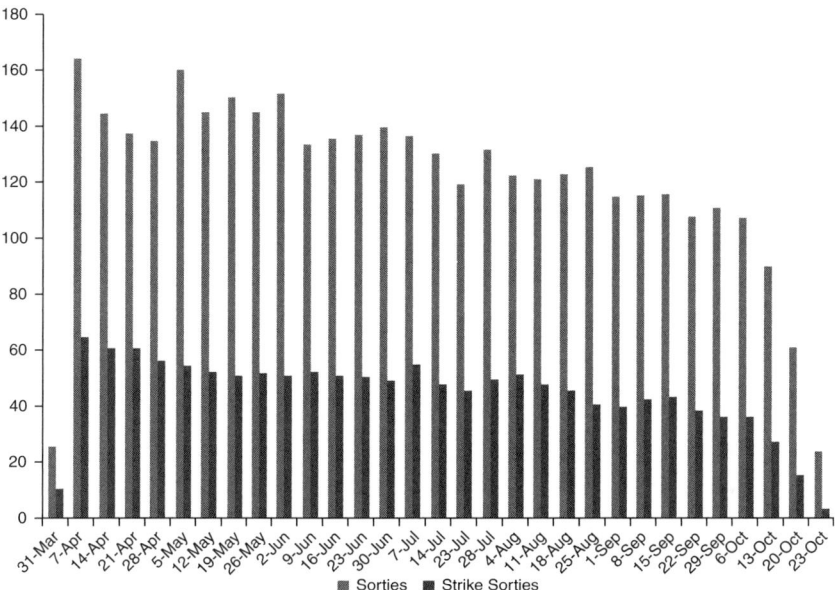

Figure 5.3 Operation Unified Protector average daily sorties per week.
Source: NATO, Operational Media Updates, April 16–October 23, 2011.

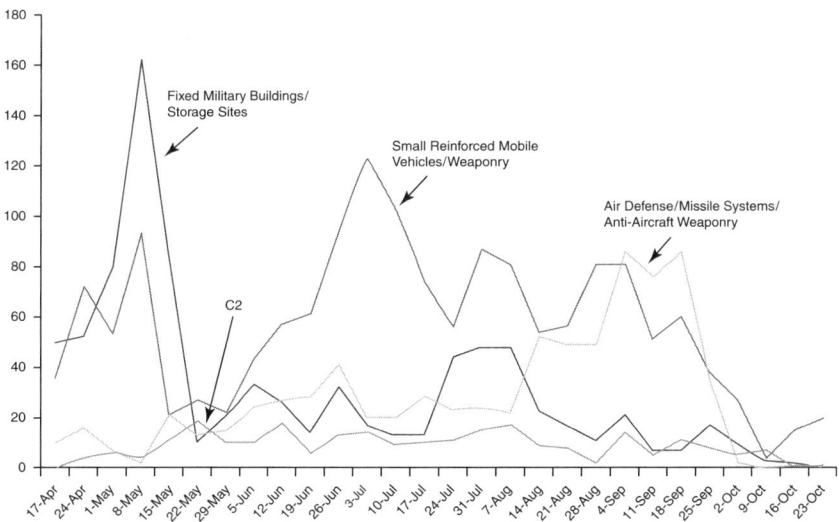

Figure 5.4 Evolution from static to dynamic targets (weekly totals: April 17–October 23).
Source: NATO figures.

adept at this dynamic hunt-and-kill type of targeting, and for this reason they may have been more nonplussed about the ISR shortfalls that so dismayed the far better resourced U.S. military. It is also possible, however, that French efforts to downplay the significance of the ISR shortfalls were at least in part an effort to counter the U.S.-led drive to establish a native NATO ISR capability through the Aerial Ground Surveillance system. If so, they failed, because that system was agreed upon in early 2012.

As General Ham later explained, ISR was a shortfall, but this was in part because given the pressure for extremely low civilian casualties, it would have been difficult to ever have enough ISR. Whereas there was never any shortage of tankers – because the United States was supplying them in large numbers – ISR was a somewhat different story. "ISR is tougher.... And I'm sure Admiral Locklear and the JTF commander would say, yeah, I would like more.... But you have to prioritize what you do have and say, OK, these are the most important areas for me to collect."[50]

A final factor in the emerging stalemate, frequently cited by military officials, was the absence of clear strategic guidance. The speed with which the decision to intervene had been made coupled with the need to sustain a broad coalition behind the mission resulted in somewhat vague picture of the specific goals of the intervention beyond stopping the immediate assault on Benghazi. The U.S. president had called for Qaddafi to step down long before the decision was made to use military force, but, as discussed earlier, his March 28 speech clearly said that regime change was not an objective of the military operations themselves. Resolution 1973, moreover, called only for the protection of civilians rather than regime change (although UNSCR 1970 did refer the situation to the International Criminal Court, implying that, even in Russian and Chinese eyes, Qaddafi had stepped beyond normal bonds of legitimacy).

---

[50] Remarks at Defense Writers Group Breakfast, Washington, DC, September 14, 2011. http://www.airforce-magazine.com/DWG/Documents/2011/September%202011/091411ham.pdf.

Military planners were uncomfortable with the apparent discrepancy and argued that without clarity on end-states, strategy and targeting were inherently difficult. What was the specific objective, they wondered, of their operations?

Protecting civilians could mean several things, after all. The immediate goal of stopping the imminent attack on Benghazi had been accomplished, but what where they supposed to be doing now, and how far were they authorized to go to achieve it?[51] A limited view of the mandate might imply focusing only on specific units that were attacking civilians – for example, destroying Qaddafi's tanks as they attacked Libya's cities – and generally aiming to separate the regime forces from the rebel-held areas. This limited view, however, would not have made much sense militarily even against a relatively unsophisticated modern army such as Qaddafi's, so allied political leaders eventually took the position that all of Qaddafi's military forces were viable targets as long as some of them were threatening civilians somewhere in the country. This allowed for strategic attacks against facilities in Tripoli and elsewhere that would wear the regime down and eventually undermine its ability to defend itself against the rebels.

This position was accepted at the April 14 NATO foreign ministerial meeting. Qaddafi had "lost all legitimacy" and had to step down, the ministers agreed, adding that NATO would continue its operations until the following three conditions were met:

1. All attacks and threats of attack against civilians and civilian-populated areas have ended.
2. The regime has verifiably withdrawn to bases all military forces, including snipers, mercenaries and other para-military forces, including from all populated areas they have forcibly entered, occupied or besieged throughout all of Libya, including Ajdabiyah, Brega, Jadu, al Jebal al Gharbiyah, Kikla, Misrata, Nalut, Raslanuf, Yefrin, Zawiyah, Zintan and Zuara.

---

[51] Interview with NATO official, February 6, 2012.

3. The regime must permit immediate, full, safe and unhindered humanitarian access to all the people in Libya in need of assistance.[52]

These goals stopped short of regime change but helped military strategists and planners develop a more precise set of targets.

On April 15, President Obama, President Sarkozy, and Prime Minister Cameron published a joint op-ed that specifically called for Qaddafi's ouster, although not specifically by military means.[53] This drew fire from Russia. Speaking immediately after a meeting of the NATO–Russia Council held on the sidelines of the Berlin ministerial meeting, Russian foreign minister Sergey Lavrov stated flatly that "the UN Resolution did not authorize regime change." For good measure, Lavrov added that "Al-Qaeda and other terrorists" were benefiting from the rebellion, a claim that Qaddafi had already put forward a number of times.[54] That Al-Qaeda might benefit from the operation was an exaggeration. It was true, however, that while clearly authorizing the use of force in broad terms, the UN resolution did not specifically call for regime change, so NATO was operating in a gray zone.

Russia would continue its criticisms of NATO, while maintaining that it also wanted Qaddafi out. That this would ever have happened without NATO military strikes is dubious. In any event, Russian criticisms cost Russia little and allowed the Russian leadership to maintain enough distance from the operation to not upset Russian clients elsewhere in the world, without being so callous as to undermine Russia's relationship with European publics that favored the operation.

---

[52] NATO Press Office, "Statement on Libya Following the Working Lunch of NATO Ministers of Foreign Affairs with Non-NATO Contributors to Operation Unified Protector" April 14, 2011.
[53] Obama et al., "Libya's Pathway to Peace."
[54] Russian Ministry of Foreign Affairs, "Transcript of Replies by Russian Minister of Foreign Affairs Sergey Lavrov to Media Questions at Press Conference Following Russia-NATO Council Meeting" Berlin, April 15, 2011. http://www.mid.ru/.

The Naval Dimension

As attention focused on the slowness of the progress on the ground, naval operations were making a somewhat underappreciated contribution to the mission. NATO warships were involved not only in policing the arms embargo but also in the no-fly zone and the civilian protection missions. The composition of the coalition differed from that of the striker group in that Bulgaria, Greece, the Netherlands, Romania, Spain, and Turkey also participated, while Denmark and Norway did not.[55]

The evacuation of U.S. and other foreign citizens from Libya in the early days of the revolt, prior to NATO's engagement, had largely been a naval operation. The initial volley of Tomahawk missiles against Qaddafi's air defenses was launched from sea. Later, naval guns were fired at Qaddafi's forces onshore; for example, on May 7 when the French navy frigate *Courbet* engaged rocket launchers onshore that were firing into Misrata. On other occasions, Royal Navy vessels fired illumination rounds to allow aircraft to strike targets with greater accuracy onshore.[56] Throughout the operation, seabasing of helicopters and jets brought allied airpower much closer to Qaddafi's shores, despite the fact that the French aircraft carrier *Charles de Gaulle* had to be removed from operations for routine maintenance in August.

Without the arms embargo and NATO blockade, Qaddafi would surely have been able to mount a more lethal campaign against the rebels. It was especially important because the strategy of patience required grinding down his capabilities and the morale of his forces. Given the relatively low rate of NATO air strikes, if Qaddafi had been able to access outside suppliers he may have been able to reequip his forces more quickly, thereby frustrating the air campaign.

---

[55] Interview with NATO military official, February 10, 2012.
[56] Christian F. Anrig, "Allied Air Power over Libya" *Air and Space Power Journal* (Winter 2011), pp. 89–109.

Enforcement of the arms embargo was inherently complicated, however. A strict interpretation of the UN mandate would have implied that all shipments of arms into Libya be stopped. In practice this would have meant blocking rebel access to weapons and other materiel they needed, which in turn would have undermined efforts to break the stalemate on the ground. On one occasion at least, when a rebel vessel carrying arms from Benghazi to Misrata was stopped, a request for guidance was sent to the NAC, which directed General Bouchard to allow the vessel to pass on the grounds that the arms embargo was intended to deny supply of arms from outside the country, not the movement of arms within it. By contrast, later in the operation, naval forces blocked a shipment of fuel they suspected was headed for Qaddafi's forces, this time on the grounds that it would support regime operations against civilians.[57]

Naval operations were not without some problems, the most notable of which was that no arrangements had been made for holding vessels in violation of the arms embargo. The eleven vessels that were eventually turned back had nowhere to go. Problems were also created by refugees fleeing the fighting for Italy. Operating guidelines tasked NATO vessels to intervene only if the boats carrying the refugees were in imminent danger; otherwise, they became a problem for the Italian authorities. In at least one case, where several hundred people died during the voyage to Italy, the Italian government came to loggerheads with the alliance leaders over who was responsible.[58]

In the end, of some 3,100 ships hailed during the mission, only 11 were diverted, most of these early in the operation.[59] The small numbers, however, may belie the success of the naval arms embargo, as it is likely

---

[57] Multiple interviews.

[58] Nick Squires, "Libya: Italy Demands Investigation into whether NATO Warship Ignored Refugees" *Telegraph*, August 5, 2011.

[59] NATO Press Office, "Operation Unified Protector Final Mission Stats" November 2, 2011. http://www.nato.int/nato_static/assets/pdf/pdf_2011_11/20111108_111107-factsheet_up_factsfigures_en.pdf.

that once word was out that NATO was stopping any shipments of arms to Qaddafi, many arms dealers stopped trying.

Return of the Predators

Under pressure from allies and the emerging stalemate, Italy reintroduced its fighter aircraft into strike operations, from which they had been absent since the handover to NATO. The United States also reengaged in strikes, adding two Predator drones on April 21. Because the Predators offered high precision and the ability to operate closer in for strikes and surveillance, they could be very useful in circumstances where Qaddafi's forces were moving out of the open areas, hiding under awnings and other structures in the urban shadows.[60] Unlike F-16s, moreover, they were unique U.S. capabilities and thus fell within the guidelines Obama had set out.[61]

The United States could, in theory, have done much more: sending in fighter jets, for example, or reinserting the A-10s and AC-130 gunships that it had used in initial strikes against Qaddafi, but large-scale U.S. involvement of this kind would have gone against the president's directive – in spirit, at least. Moreover, it would have been humiliating for the European allies leading the strike operations and hence something of a defeat for NATO.

Given the controversy their use in Pakistan and elsewhere had occasioned, the decision to reintroduce Predators into strike missions met with some criticism. Predator operations in Pakistan had generated significant public outcry, and the concern was that the use of Predators would be bad public relations and erode support for the operation in Arab countries and potentially on the street in Libya itself.[62] In Libya, however, this

---

[60] Interview with senior Defense Department official, December 30, 2011.
[61] "Comments by Secretary Robert Gates, Secretary of Defense and General James Cartwright, vice chairman of the Joint Chiefs of Staff, Washington, DC, Thursday, April 21, 2011." http://www.jcs.mil/speech.aspx?ID=1589.
[62] David Ignatius, "Drone Attacks in Libya a Mistake" *Washington Post*, April 21, 2011.

skepticism proved misplaced. The Predators may not have conducted a large number of strikes, but their impact on the morale of the regime's forces was almost certainly real and helped tip the momentum of the operation in favor of the *thuwwar*. With the Predators circling in the air, regime forces were at much greater risk when they exposed themselves, for example, on the streets of Misrata, where the situation had now become dire.

6 Grinding Away

As NATO operations entered their second month, the standoff between the regime and rebels west of Benghazi had not budged, and the suffering of the population of Misrata had become the focal point of the war. Qaddafi's forces were still shelling the city with heavy weapons, including self-propelled artillery, Grad rockets, and cluster bombs fired from 120-millimeter mortars. These cluster bombs killed indiscriminately, and often left behind unexploded yet still lethal "bomblets" that threatened the civilian population even after the shelling had stopped. The civilian death toll mounted.[1]

Continued pressure from NATO bombing and the heroic efforts of the cities' urban revolutionaries finally yielded some progress by mid-May, pushing regime forces to retreat away from the port back to the town center. On May 14, rebel *kata'ib* pushed even further, taking the airport and some of the suburbs from which the regime had been shelling the city. From then on, rebels would hold their positions despite continued bombardment. Humanitarian aid flows would increase, and life would slowly start returning to the city.

The relief of Misrata was an important breakthrough after more than two months of siege. It forced Qaddafi to reinforce his troops outside the town and sent a much-needed signal that the tide of war might be turning in favor of the rebels. Given that many Libyans were fence-sitting out of

---

[1] C.J. Chivers, "Taking Airport, Rebels in Libya Loosen Noose" *New York Times*, May 11, 2011.

fear of ending up on the losing side, this kind of signal was important. Unfortunately, however, momentum in Misrata was not followed up with advances elsewhere, and for three more frustrating months little changed on the ground. Qaddafi remained defiant. "I tell the coward crusaders," he said, "I live in a place where you can't get me. I live in the hearts of millions."[2] "We're grinding down the regime," said the American officer who commanded the NATO and British AWACs engaged in the operation at the end of May.[3] It was true, but the war was still less than halfway over, and there were now serious concerns that the price of toppling the regime could end up being higher than the alliance and its partners were prepared to pay.

Allied leaders were increasingly exasperated as public and private pressure for more aggressive action against the regime intensified. In the United States, approval of the intervention was starting to drop off, according to Gallup polls, which showed 47 percent approval on March 21 and 39 percent three months later.[4] "We are eager to hear from the president about what additional nonmilitary pressures he is rallying to finally end Col. Muammar el-Qaddafi's murderous reign," the *New York Times* editorialized in June.[5] Roughly half the public in France and Britain supported the operation, but in France support had also declined, with disapproval overtaking approval in June polling.[6] Cameron and Sarkozy were worried that pressure from some allies to end the war might force them to accept a negotiated settlement on

[2] John F. Burns, "Qaddafi Boasts of Survival as Libya Protests Airstrike That It Says Killed 11 Clerics" *New York Times*, May 14, 2011, p. A8.
[3] Eric Schmitt, "NATO Air War in Libya Faces Daunting Task" *New York Times*, May 25, 2011, p. A1.
[4] Jeffrey M. Jones, "Americans Shift to More Negative View of Libya Military Action" *Gallup Politics*, June 24, 2011.
[5] "Libya and the War Powers Act" *New York Times*, June 16, 2011. See also, Ruth Walker, "Libya's Chess Game" *Christian Science Monitor*, May 9, 2011; Jonathan Marcus, "Libya Stalemate Leaves NATO without 'Plan B'" BBC, May 11, 2011; Anne Applebaum, "What to Do about Libya's Stalemate?" *Washington Post*, June 6, 2011.
[6] "Approval of the Military Intervention in Libya" IFOP, June 2011. http://www.ifop.com/media/poll/1558-2-study_file.pdf.

unfavorable terms. As a result, they pressed for further and more direct measures to aid the rebels and bring the operation to a successful conclusion. "We will not be in Libya forever," said Juppé after an EU meeting in Brussels on May 23. "Without changing strategy," he said, it was time to up the tempo.[7]

In addition to being bad political optics, the longer the operation dragged on the more the chances were that the coalition might fall apart. By early May, the expiration of NATO's initial ninety-day authorization was fast approaching and reauthorization was looking like less than a sure thing.[8] Within the alliance, there was disagreement about what to do. Between the need to stay within the UN civilian protection mandate, the relatively low participation rate of allied militaries, broad political opposition to ground forces, and the continued need to avoid civilian casualties, the options for bringing the operation to a rapid close were few. Concerned that going too far beyond the UN mandate or causing more civilian deaths would break the coalition apart, the United States wanted a steady but cautious approach. Daalder thought the rate of progress, though slow, was sufficient. Defections were continuing, and Qaddafi was no longer able to mount a major offensive against the rebels, who were slowly gaining experience and weaponry and thus fighting more effectively.[9] British and French leaders, however, felt more pressure to demonstrate forward progress and thus were more willing to accept risks and take steps to stretch the UN mandate. They pushed for options to broaden the campaign against Qaddafi, including with ground forces if necessary.

Ultimately, NATO compromised, taking political and military measures to increase the pressure but not going as far as France and Britain wanted. On the political side, the coalition bolstered the rebels through meetings of the Contact Group, while simultaneously continuing efforts

---

[7] Jean-Jacques Mevel, "La France pousse les alliés à accélérer le tempo en Libye" *Le Figaro*, May 24, 2011, p. 8.
[8] Interview with senior U.S. official, February 6, 2012.
[9] See Appendix C for a list of defections. Interview with senior U.S. official, February 6, 2012.

for a negotiated settlement. On the military side, France and Britain added helicopters, intensified the bombing somewhat, sought to deflate the morale of Qaddafi's forces, and eventually strengthened the rebel *kata'ib* with direct military assistance on the ground in the form of arms and training, advice, and combat contributions from small numbers of allied and partner special forces. The latter efforts, although officially undertaken outside NATO's remit in a bilateral capacity, were the most controversial because they clearly amounted to siding with the *thuwwar* and hence went beyond what the UN had authorized. Arms shipments in particular appeared to be a violation of the arms embargo, although according to the official U.S. interpretation of Security Council Resolution 1973, the "all means necessary" clause took precedence over the clauses imposing an arms embargo: arms shipments that helped protect civilians were thus legal.

Controversy aside, these gradual increases in pressure had their desired effect in tipping the balance against the regime. They could not have had this effect absent the space created by the air and sea campaigns, but they were a necessary catalyst generating the ground-force momentum that would ultimately bring Tripoli down.

Attacking with Helicopters

The steps to increase the pressure on Qaddafi were incremental. After the United States agreed to add the Predators in late April, the French and British decided to deploy attack helicopters to the theater in May. The initial proposal came at a meeting of allied military chiefs in Brussels early in the month at which French and British argued that the slower, lower-altitude strike capability the helicopters offered would be useful for targeting regime forces that were going to lengths to conceal themselves. The addition could also have a beneficial psychological impact by demonstrating a new level of NATO commitment. Despite concerns that using helicopters could significantly increase the risk not only of civilian casualties but also of NATO losses, because of the presence of man-portable

Figure 6.1 A French Tigre flying from the amphibious assault ship *Tonnerre*.
Source: NATO.

air-defense systems on the ground, the United States eventually agreed to the British and French proposal.[10]

The decision was announced a few weeks later and on June 4, British Apaches flying from the HMS *Ocean* and French Tigre (Figure 6.1) and Gazelles flying from the *Tonnere* hit twenty targets along the coast, including a radar installation, a regime checkpoint, and military vehicles near Brega, thus helping to loosen the deadlock between there and Ajdabiya.[11] These helicopters operated in close coordination with fixed-wing aircraft, which supplied reconnaissance.[12] The British deployed a

---

[10] Interview with NATO official, February 7, 2012.
[11] "Libya: UK Apache Attack Helicopters Launch First Strikes" *Telegraph*, June 4, 2011. http://www.telegraph.co.uk/; "Libya: UK Apache Helicopters Used in NATO Attacks" BBC News, June 4, 2011. http://www.bbc.co.uk/news/uk-13651736; "Des helicopters français participent aux frappes" *France2.fr*, June 4, 2011. http://info.france2.fr/monde/des-helicopteres-francais-participent-aux-frappes-69065831.html.
[12] Christian F. Anrig, "Allied Air Power over Libya" *Air and Space Power Journal*, (Winter 2011), pp. 89–109.

total of four helicopters, while the French sent twenty.[13] A *thuwwar* commander in Brega, where initial helicopter strikes focused, claimed to be in "constant contact" with the Apaches, although it is a little unclear exactly what that meant and NATO would never confirm such reports.[14]

Compared with the fixed-wing aircraft, attack helicopters would carry out only a small proportion of the total strikes, but their psychological impact – like that of the Predators – was likely significant. The helicopters could fly slower and closer to the ground than the fighter jets, allowing them to identify targets more easily. Moreover, with fewer fixed regime targets remaining, the smaller munitions carried by the helicopters were valuable because they could be used more easily for smaller targets such as military vehicles.[15] In addition, because their sorties were inherently riskier than fighter-bomber missions that dropped their loads from 20,000 feet, the helicopters also demonstrated a renewed NATO commitment to winning the war. Anecdotal reporting suggests that they had a positive impact on *thuwwar* morale. "With the Apaches, we are ready," one *kata'ib* commander said. "Before, when we were attacked, we were not experienced. But now we have leaders. We are stronger than they are."[16]

French helicopters contributed much more than the British, who incorporated their helicopters into NATO air tasking orders and thus flew at much higher altitudes than the French. The French struck some 85 percent of the total helicopter targets, at least by French estimates. The large number of French strikes was an indication of the willingness to take risks – a performance that impressed more than one U.S. military

---

[13] "Libye: Le point sur les moyens militaires engagès par la France" AFP, June 12, 2011; "British Apaches Hit Targets Near Libya's Brega: Ministry" AFP, June 4, 2011. Eventually Britain deployed five: "Britain Pulls Apache Helicopters from Libya Mission" AFP, September 24, 2011.

[14] "Libyan Rebels Cannot Break Brega Deadlock" AFP, June 12, 2011.

[15] See "Accidental Heros" RUSI, September 2011.

[16] Richard Norton-Taylor and Chris Stephen, "Ex-SAS Men on Ground in Libya to Spot Targets as Fighters Dig in for NATO Attacks" *Guardian*, June 1, 2011, p. 15.

official.[17] French helicopters flew within 50 meters of the ground, striking targets of the crew's choosing within a predesignated "kill box."[18] It is difficult to judge the overall impact of adding the helicopters, because complete data is lacking. At a tactical level they do appear to have had an impact and given that there were so few other options for upping the pressure on the regime, even if the impact was small, it was worth it.

NATO also continued its operations with fighter jets and at sea. In the immediate aftermath of the relief of Misrata, naval operations came to the fore, as Qaddafi's forces attempted to mine the harbor and set a booby trap to threaten allied patrols and interrupt the flow of humanitarian aid into the city. The regime had been mining the harbor using small inflatable boats since April, and NATO had started countermining operations to establish a safe corridor from the Mediterranean through the harbor. Other regime tactics included booby trapping a small boat of human mannequins with a ton of explosives in hope of killing a would-be NATO rescue operation. The threat from Qaddafi's naval forces was eventually deemed serious enough to warrant a direct attack on Qaddafi's navy, and NATO destroyed eight Libyan warships in the western ports of Tripoli, Khums, and Sirte.

In later May and June, with Misrata more secure, the main line of fighting shifted westward to the nearby towns of Zlitan and Dafniyah. NATO continued pounding regime forces there with fixed-wing and helicopter strikes, while also continuing to hit regime forces dug in at Brega in the east. It also struck Qaddafi's weapons storage sites in the middle of the country – for example, at Waddan – and continued to hit command and control facilities in Tripoli. It also destroyed an important antenna at the Tripoli airport that Qaddafi was using to track NATO air operations.

---

[17] Interview with French official, February 7, 2012; interview with senior U.S. military official, February 10, 2012.
[18] Nathalie Guibert, "Près de deux mois de frappes intensives pour les hélicoptère" *Le Monde*, July 27, 2011, p. 4.

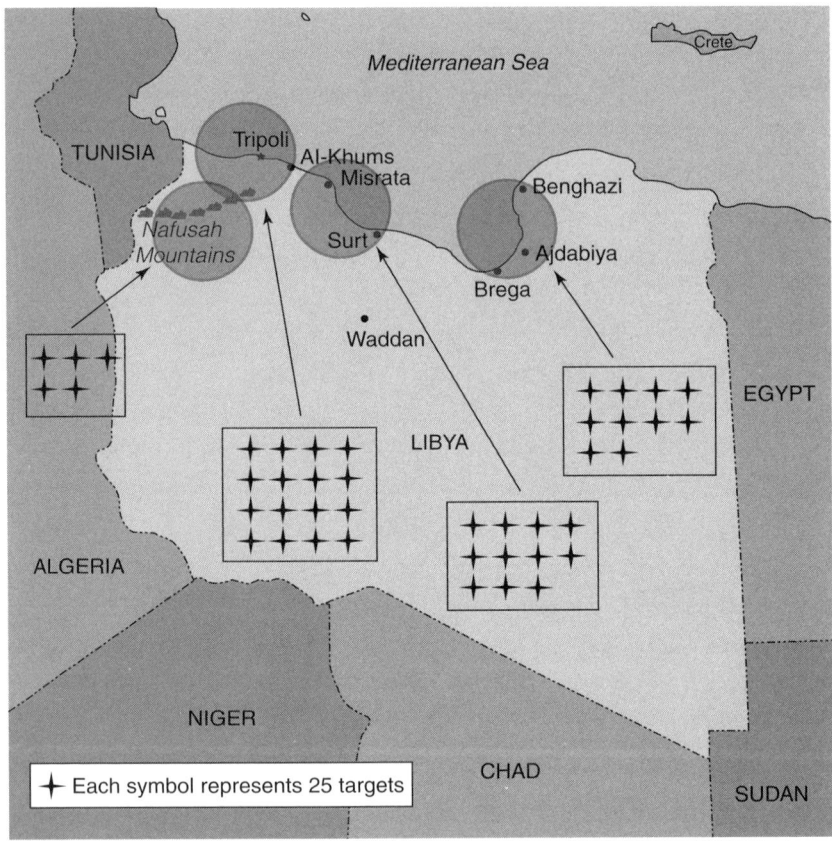

Figure 6.2 Northwestern Libya was the most targeted region, followed by the northeast, May 16–July 17.
Source: NATO, Operational Media Updates, May 16–July 17, 2011.

By July, Qaddafi's forces had dwindled to the point where they no longer could mount a major offensive against the rebels. But they maintained the capacity to fight and continued to shell civilians. The progress of the rebel *kata'ib* was still slow, but civilian life in Benghazi, Misrata, and Ajdabiyah was improving and some of those who had fled were returning to their homes. Very gradually, therefore, the tide was shifting against the regime. But the light at the end of the tunnel still seemed a long way off for NATO. Figure 6.2 shows the progression of NATO strikes in this intermediate phase of the war.

Upping the Political Pressure: The Contact Group

The political push to oust Qaddafi was meanwhile gaining steam through the diplomatic efforts of the Contact Group. With membership on the basis of the March 19 Paris meeting, the Contact Group had been officially established in London on March 29, just before NATO took over the reins. On the most basic level, the Contact Group provided a political conduit for the rebels to communicate with NATO and its partners. This was important because, while there was communication between the rebels on the ground and liaison officers from NATO nations, there was no direct military link between NATO and the *thuwwar*. Meetings also helped bolster the prestige and legitimacy of the NTC while simultaneously serving as a forcing mechanism to get the NTC to articulate a postwar vision and broaden its membership to include representatives from western Libya, where the critical fighting was increasingly focused. On a more practical level, the Contact Group was a means of generating and channeling funds to the rebels as well as working on getting them officially recognized.

Diplomats also sought to use each meeting to ratchet up the political pressure on the regime and emphasize that its time was running out. Meetings alternated between Europe and the Middle East in order to remind the world that it was a broad coalition, not just NATO, attacking Qaddafi. Five meetings were held over the course of the conflict – London, Doha, Rome, Abu Dhabi, and Istanbul – and even when the group was not meeting officially, discussions among its members continued; for example, on the margins of the G8 meeting in Deauville in May or at the UN General Assembly in September. Plenary meetings were preceded by small group meetings that set the agenda and helped maintain focus as the plenary sessions grew larger and larger.[19]

At meetings in April in Doha and May in Rome, rebel leaders began to lay out their plans for postwar Libya. This helped demonstrate their commitment to constitutional democracy and increased confidence about

[19] Interview with senior U.S. official, January 24, 2012.

their postwar intentions within the alliance, countering Qaddafi's repeated claims that they were just a bunch of terrorists. It was important that the rebels had postwar plans if they were going to govern effectively and for obvious reasons these plans had to be congruent with the broader principles for which the intervention was being conducted. Discussions of the postwar situation were also intended to telegraph the message that Qaddafi was not going to win.

At the Rome meeting, the focus of the Contact Group's work began to shift to finding ways to aid the rebels financially. The *thuwwar* were sorely in need of resources both to fight the regime and to keep the lights on in the eastern areas they controlled. The two rounds of UN sanctions on Libya also hit the NTC, whose uncertain legal status further restricted their access to funds from many foreign governments. Some funds were flowing to them in the form of cash from Qatar and the UAE, but these were not enough for the challenges they faced as the war dragged on. A financial mechanism to allow countries to channel funds to the rebel leaders was finalized at the June 9 meeting in Abu Dhabi. The mechanism allowed $300 million in support from Kuwait and Qatar to go forward and paved the way for additional support from other countries. The $300 million was still much less than NTC officials had asked for, however, and disbursement would be slow. The council's foreign minister, Ali Tarhouni, complained that it was "beyond frustration."[20] Moreover, it was one thing to send the rebels financial aid. It was another to unlock the billions of dollars in Libyan state assets that had been frozen by Resolution 1970 back in February. Doing this would take even more time.

Meanwhile, the question of "recognition" of the NTC had been confounding officials and confusing publics alike ever since Sarkozy first decided to "recognize" the rebels in early March. The fact was, recognizing a group such as the NTC was not a simple and straightforward political decision that could be made independent of certain legal criteria. While

---

[20] Steven Lee Myers, "$1 Billion Is Pledged to Support Libya Rebels" *New York Times*, June 10, 2011, p. A4.

UPPING THE POLITICAL PRESSURE: THE CONTACT GROUP 133

the group itself could be recognized as a legitimate entity, recognizing it as the official government of Libya was another thing altogether. The problem was complex – far more so than most of those involved realized it would be.[21] For a government to be legally recognized, it must meet certain minimal requirements, and it was not altogether clear what these requirements were. According to some experts, they included being broadly based, having reasonable fighting strength, and having effective control over the state's territory.[22] Lacking the requisite qualities, recognition of the rebels as the legitimate state of Libya might be challenged after the fact as contrary to international law, creating major headaches down the road.

A significant amount of time was thus spent working through the legal issues recognition raised in Washington.[23] As it turned out, the United States eventually recognized the NTC in stages. At the onset of the intervention, the U.S. position was that it was "a" legitimate representative of the Libyan people. This gave the council a certain status and legitimacy and opened the door to financial assistance and even representation of some kinds. It did not, however, amount to a legal renunciation of the Qaddafi regime's claim to represent the Libyan state. In Abu Dhabi in June, the United States then recognized the council as "the" legitimate representative of the Libyan people, thus inching a step further but without going so far as to establish legally that the council was synonymous with the Libyan state. Other states followed their own course, depending upon their own internal laws, interpretation of international law, and existing relationship with the Qaddafi regime. By July, however, there was a broader consensus that recognition was possible, and at the Istanbul Contact Group meeting the United States and several allies formally recognized the NTC as the state of Libya. This opened the door to formal diplomatic relations, severed any remaining diplomatic

---

[21] Interviews with U.S. officials, February 13 and February 17, 2012.
[22] Stefan Talmon, "Recognition of the Libyan National Transitional Council" *American Society of International Law: Insights*, vol. 15, no.16 (June 16, 2011).
[23] Interview with senior U.S. official, February 27, 2012.

links countries might have to the Qaddafi regime, and was a key step in unlocking access to the $30 billion in Libyan state funds frozen overseas.

Unfortunately however, it was only the first step. Sanctions themselves also had to be lifted, and this required a consensus on the UN sanctions committee. Given their ongoing criticism of the operation, the South African members of the committee blocked moves to lift the sanctions – especially because doing so now effectively meant aiding the rebels in their fight against Qaddafi. Despite high-level attention in the White House, it would take several more weeks to break the logjam.

The Coalition Starts to Creak

When allied defense ministers met in Brussels on June 9–10, the anti-Qaddafi coalition had strengthened politically. Germany was now offering its diplomatic backing with less equivocation and also promising financial support for postconflict reconstruction. Militarily, however, the strain the operations had placed on the alliance was starting to show through and nerves were wearing thin. Allies agreed to extend the mission for another ninety days, but many officials were privately concerned about whether operations could be kept going beyond that. If NATO had to back out, operations could have reverted back to the coalition of the willing format originally preferred by the French, but not without a major blow to legitimacy and to morale – not to mention a defeat for those who had fought to go with NATO in the first place.

Allied armies continued to strain under the demands of the operation. By late May, British air chief marshal Sir Simon Bryant sent a paper to the UK Parliament citing the strains the operation in Libya was placing on the Royal Air Force (RAF), especially given the need to sustain simultaneous operations in Afghanistan. "Two concurrent operations are placing a huge demand on equipment and personnel," Sir Bryant said. Fighters and transport aircraft were being stretched;

THE COALITION STARTS TO CREAK 135

manpower was overworked.[24] Munitions stocks were also low. As one U.S. official put it, the rapidity with which some countries had run out of bombs was "stunning."[25] Britain was reported to be running low on Brimstone missiles, the low-yield precision-guided munition that was being heavily used (although there was later debate over how serious the problem was).[26] The UK's relatively small supply of Tomahawk missiles had already limited its participation in the initial strikes against Qaddafi's air-defense system, and Britain had turned to the United States for purchases to top up its stocks.[27]

By early June, Norway had dropped 370 bombs on targets over Libya but was now at risk of running out. They signaled they would curtail their role in May and announced just after the NATO ministerial that all six of their F-16s would be withdrawn by early August.[28] Norwegian pilots had been some of the more effective in the striker group and were increasingly called upon for riskier and more difficult missions – for example, on Tripoli itself. The grounds for political agreement on the operation in Norway had always been somewhat thin, with the left supporting the intervention for humanitarian reasons and the right eager to flex its muscle to prove the relevance of Norwegian military power. Eventually the strains within Norway's governing coalition and a sense that Norway had done its share and shown its support led Norway to reduce and finally terminate its participation. The official reason given was the need for

---

[24] Thomas Harding, "Future RAF Missions under Threat if Libyan Intervention Continues" *Daily Telegraph*, June 20, 2011. http://www.telegraph.co.uk/news/uknews/defence/8588125/Future-RAF-missions-under-threat-if-Libyan-intervention-continues.html.

[25] Interview with senior U.S. official, February 7, 2012.

[26] See Parliament of the United Kingdom, "Defence Committee – Ninth Report," January 25, 2012, Chapter 4.

[27] Thomas Harding, "Libya: Navy Running Short of Tomahawk Missiles" *Telegraph*, March 23, 2011. http://www.telegraph.co.uk.; James Kirkup, "Navy Chief: Britain Cannot Keep Up Its Role in Libya Air War Due to Cuts" *Telegraph*, June 13, 2011. http://www.telegraph.co.uk.

[28] Alison Kennedy, "Norway to End Libyan Fighter Contributions" *Foreigner* (Oslo), June 12, 2011.

fighters and crews to patrol its long border, and this likely played a factor, but political calculations were also important.[29]

Meanwhile, Denmark was also feeling the strain. Danish fighters had carried out 274 sorties and dropped 494 precision bombs, but on June 9 it was reported that they were also at risk of running out of munitions and needed to buy more.[30] Soon thereafter, Sweden announced that it would also reduce its operations in support of the no-fly zone.[31]

At the NATO ministerial, Secretary Gates pressed the Dutch, Spanish, and Turks to bolster their participation by moving beyond no-fly zone enforcement and striking ground targets. He also pressed Germany and Poland to contribute militarily.[32] These overtures, however, had no effect on allied participation, and the day after the meeting, in his last major address as U.S. secretary of defense, Gates lambasted the allies for falling short and warned that it boded badly for the future of the alliance. "It has become painfully clear," he said, that "shortcomings – in capability and will – have the potential to jeopardize the alliance's ability to conduct an integrated, effective and sustained air-sea campaign" in Libya. Although all the members of the alliance had voted for the mission, Gates lamented that less than half were participating and only a third were flying strike missions. This was not just because allies didn't want to participate, he said; in some cases it was simply because they lacked the capabilities to do so.[33]

Gates did note that some countries, especially Norway and Denmark, were making contributions that were remarkable given the smaller size of

---

[29] Interviews with Norwegian officials, Oslo, September 28, 2012.
[30] "Denmark Running Out of Libya Bombs," June 9, 2011. http://politiken.dk/news inenglish.
[31] Gerard O'Dwyer, "Libya Operations Threaten Nordic Budgets" *Defense News*, June 19, 2011.
[32] Thom Shanker and John F. Burns, "Nations Bombing Libya Ask for Help Amid Strain" *New York Times*, June 9, 2011, p. A9.
[33] Office of the Assistant Secretary of Defense (Public Affairs), "Speech: The Security and Defense Agenda (Future of NATO), as Delivered by Secretary of Defense Robert M. Gates, Brussels, Belgium, Friday, June 10, 2011." http://www.defense.gov/speeches/speech.aspx?speechid=1581.

THE COALITION STARTS TO CREAK

their militaries, and he called out others – Canada and Belgium – that he thought were performing well. But he stressed that the overall situation was not good and warned that if nothing were done NATO was doomed to irrelevance.

The sharp tone of his address, much of which Gates himself had added to his prepared text, struck some as unfair – or at least undiplomatic – given that it came at precisely the moment when some European allies had stepped up to the challenge and were carrying a much larger share of the operational burden than in any of NATO's past interventions. As one French official put it, "Well, he's the secretary of defense, not the secretary of state."[34] Even if rather undiplomatic, however, Gates's comments pointed to real problems and voiced a general frustration within the U.S. defense establishment about the limits of allied defense capabilities.[35]

Lt. General Ralph Jodice, who commanded the CAOC in Poggio-Renatico, would later claim that despite the difficulty in getting the munitions, he always had what he needed. "I never once had to cancel or postpone a sortie because I didn't have the right munitions that I needed," Jodice said.[36] This, however, was in part because of the ongoing U.S. efforts to ensure that the participating allies were sold the munitions they ran out of. Through October 28, 2011, the United States would sell allies and partners approximately $261 million worth of ammunition, repair parts, fuel, technical assistance, and other support. Of this, $114 million was provided as foreign military sales (FMS). Another $148 million included fuel ($141 million), host nation support ($6 million), and airlift ($1 million) through acquisition and cross servicing agreements and similar programs.[37]

Meanwhile, French and British pressure to accelerate the pace of operations continued. Day raids on Tripoli commenced the same week as the defense ministerial. Qaddafi's compound in the capital was bombed

---

[34] Interview with French official, February 8, 2012.
[35] Multiple interviews.
[36] John Tirpak, "Lessons from Libya" *Air Force Magazine* (December 2011), pp. 34–38.
[37] Unclassified Defense Department figures provided at author's request, December 14, 2011.

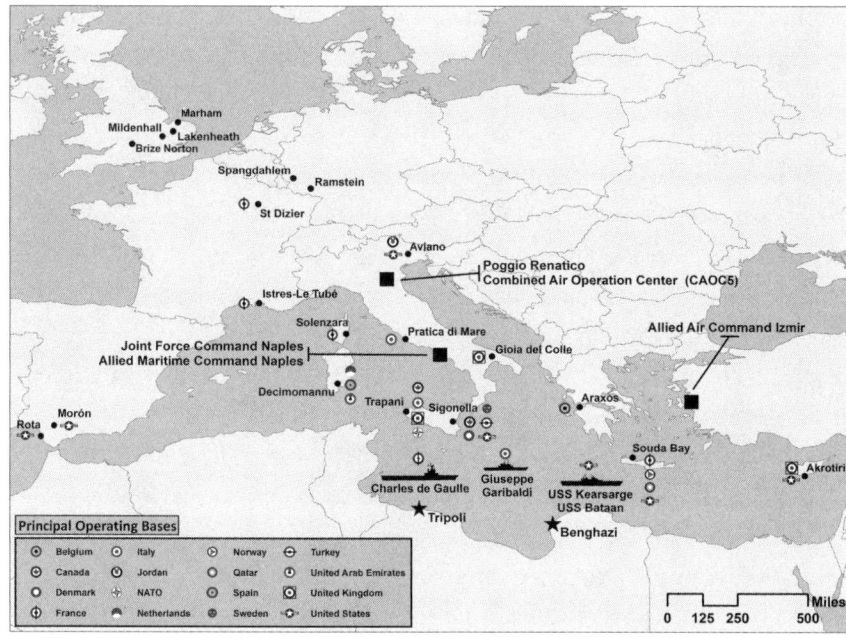

Figure 6.3 Operation Unified Protector European Basing.
Source: Mueller, ed., *Precision and Purpose*.

heavily.[38] The talking points in Washington meanwhile aimed to make victory of the *thuwwar* look inevitable and dishearten the regime. "I think it is just a matter of time before Qaddafi goes," President Obama said at a White House lunch with Chancellor Merkel. "What you're seeing across the country is an inexorable trend of the regime forces being pushed back, being incapacitated."[39]

Taken too far, however, acceleration could upset the coalition if it resulted in excessive collateral damage or overly stretched the mandate. The Canadian government, for example, was under criticism from the

---

[38] On escalation, see John F. Burns, "Qaddafi Compound Is Pounded in Day Raid" *New York Times*, June 7, 2011, P. A4.

[39] Helene Cooper, "Obama and Merkel Tell Qaddafi to Go" *New York Times*, June 7, 2012. http://www.nytimes.com/2011/06/08/world/africa/08prexy.html?_r=1&ref=libya.

opposition for mission creep.[40] On June 18, NATO accidentally hit a rebel column outside Brega. The next day it hit a home in Tripoli, killing nine civilians.[41] In the wake of these incidents, Italy's foreign minister Franco Frattini called for the "immediate suspension" of hostilities to establish aid corridors.[42]

Figure 6.3 shows the layout of NATO forces operating from Europe during the campaign.

Troubles with Congress

Back in Washington, the White House had come under increasing fire from Congress, where there was widespread discontent with the administration's failure to consult extensively or seek congressional approval prior to the commencement of hostilities. Some members of Congress claimed the administration was close to violating the War Powers Resolution, which limits U.S. participation in a conflict to sixty days without congressional approval. By mid-May, that deadline was approaching, and the White House had made no move to request authorization or invoke the allowed thirty-day extension.

At the start of the intervention, the administration's hesitancy to invoke the War Powers Resolution was probably due to concern that seeking approval would give the impression that military operations were heavier and more involved than intended and thus send the wrong signal to the world about the U.S. role.[43] The White House has not traditionally sought congressional approval for military actions – it did not in Kosovo, even though the mission went over sixty days, and in other recent cases Congress passed legislation authorizing military action without a

---

[40] Paul Koring, "It's a Knife-Fight in a Phone Booth" *Globe and Mail*, June 13, 2011, p. A1.
[41] David D. Kirkpatrick, "Errant Missile Hit Civilian Home in Libya, NATO Says" *New York Times*, June 19, 2012, p. A8.
[42] Campbell Clark, "Cracks Showing in NATO's Libya Strategy" *Globe and Mail*, June 23, 2011, p. A18.
[43] Interview with senior U.S. Official, December 16, 2011.

formal request from the Executive Branch. The fact that the U.S. role was even more minimal here, coupled with the expectation that Qaddafi was only going to last a few weeks, probably made authorization from Congress seem unnecessary in addition to being potentially bad optics.

Nevertheless, the lack of a formal request would create problems for the White House on both sides of the aisle on the Hill. When the sixty-day deadline passed on May 20, Congress and public commentators started to complain.[44] On May 23, Representative Dennis Kucinich introduced a resolution to "remove United States armed forces in Libya" within fifteen days, which generated unexpectedly strong bipartisan support. In response, Speaker of the House of Representative John Boehner introduced an alternative resolution on June 2, 2011, which, without taking any concrete action to stop the intervention, required the White House to explain why it had not sought congressional authorization and report on the costs of the operation.[45] In the context of ongoing struggle over the U.S. budget deficit, anything involving costs was potential tinder for partisan fires. Boehner's resolution passed along mostly partisan lines on June 3 and the Kucinich resolution failed.[46]

The Boehner-drafted reporting requirement came into effect at precisely the moment when a lengthy debate within the administration over the War Powers Resolution was coming to a head. The Defense Department had concluded that requesting congressional authorization was advisable. State Department legal advisor Harold Koh, however, argued that authorization was unnecessary because the type of operations the United States was engaged in and the frequency of its strikes did not amount to "hostilities." The president sided with State's interpretation, and the White House released a report to Congress on June 15 stating that no authorization was necessary because U.S. operations in Libya

---

[44] George F. Will, "Obama's Illegal War" *Washington Post*, May 29, 2011.

[45] Jennifer Steinhauer, "House Rebukes Obama for Continuing Libyan Mission without Its Consent" *New York Times*, June 4, 2011.

[46] Interview with congressional staff, August 28, 2011.

"were distinct from the kind of 'hostilities' contemplated by the War Powers Act."[47]

When it emerged in a *New York Times* report a few days later that the Defense Department Legal Office and the White House's own legal counsel had had concluded, contrary to the position adopted by the White House, that U.S. activities and Predator strikes in particular did amount to hostilities, a furor broke out on the Hill.[48] Several Republican lawmakers started pushing legislation that would deny funding for any future Predator strikes. Overall, however, chaos reigned and neither party was united. Thirty-seven conservative former officials and experts sent a letter to Congress criticizing the effort, while Republican Senator Marco Rubio coauthored an op-ed in the *Wall Street Journal* with Senator Lieberman that called for continued support.[49] Senator McCain pressed for more, not less, aggressive action. Traditional Republican foreign policy circles had after all never been very supportive of the War Powers Resolution, as Senator Lindsey Graham reminded the public on "Meet the Press" when he deemed it "unconstitutional, not worth the paper it is written on."[50] The split within the Republicans was indicative of the growing chasm within the GOP over the relative priority of fiscal rectitude and national security.

For their part, the Democrats were split along familiar lines, with the left wing of the party critical, even shocked, by the president's decision not to ask for approval, while moderates fell in behind the White House. The apparently cavalier attitude toward the War Powers Resolution was an affront to the left wing of the party, which has long viewed it as an much needed bastion against the abuse of executive privilege. But not all

---

[47] David A. Fahrenthold and Peter Finn, "Anger Ramps Up in Congress over Libya" *Washington Post*, June 19, 2011.

[48] Charlie Savage, "Two Top Lawyers Lose Argument on War Power" *New York Times*, June 18, 2011.

[49] Jennifer Steinhauer, "Letter Highlights Divisions among Republicans on Libya" New York Times Blogs, June 20, 2011; Joe Lieberman and Marco Rubio, "Victory Is the Answer in Libya" *Wall Street Journal*, June 23, 2011.

[50] Michael D. Shear, "Best Political Quotes of the Weekend" New York Times Blogs, June 20, 2011.

Democrats felt this way. Senator John Kerry, chairman of the Senate Foreign Relations Committee, likened the uprisings in the Middle East to the fall of communism and staunchly supported the White House.[51] On June 23, Secretary Clinton was dispatched to the Hill to shore up support with her former congressional colleagues, but she had little success in quelling the rising revolt.

The next day, Boehner brought two bills to the floor: a resolution by Representative Hastings on the basis of a Kerry–McCain Senate resolution that would fully authorize combat operations in Libya (H.J. Res. 68) and a bill sponsored by Representative Tom Rooney that would eliminate funds for further U.S. strikes and limit U.S. participation to ISR, refueling, search and rescue, and planning (H.R. 2278).[52] The House then proceeded, in the course of a few hours, to vote down both the authorizing and the limiting bills. Neither would it approve of the operation nor would it try to stop it. The apparent contradiction was indicative of the confusion and turmoil that had engulfed both sides of the aisle (eighty Republicans and thirty-three Democrats had voted *against* both bills).[53] When Senate majority leader Harry Reid tried to introduce the authorizing bill in the Senate the following week, he was forced to pull it when Republicans complained that they had canceled a planned recess to discuss the larger issue of the debt ceiling, not foreign policy. This was all true, but it only indicated the weakness of Congress as a whole on the issue. As so often in past interventions, Congress failed to have much impact. As freshman GOP Senator Rand Paul aptly put it, "We've sort of made ourselves irrelevant."[54]

A side effect of the White House position on the congressional authorization was that, while it allowed U.S. military operations to continue, it also capped U.S. involvement more or less at current levels, at least as long as congressional approval was outstanding. This meant that if the alliance

[51] Chris' Strohm, "Kerry, McCain Push One-Year Authorization for Libya Operations" *National Journal*, June 21, 2011.
[52] Jennifer Steinhauer, "House Deals Obama Symbolic Blow with Libya Votes" New York Times Blogs, June 24, 2011.
[53] Jonathan Allen, "How Libya Push Tripped the GOP" Politico, June 25, 2011.
[54] Scott Wong, "Kerry Stands by Resolution" Politico, June 23, 2011.

was going to ramp up the pressure on Qaddafi, the allies would need to provide the forces. The allies recognized this, so the whole affair with Congress had the unintended – yet from a U.S. perspective salutary – a consequence of increasing the pressure on them to do more.

In retrospect, it would probably have been better if the White House had consulted with Congress more closely from the start of the operation in March. Bombing commenced only hours after a hastily arranged conference call with members, many of whom were commuting back to their districts for recess. Even staunch supporters of the president felt out of the loop. Other members who had been calling for bombing and a no-fly zone immediately questioned the president once operations commenced. The lack of consultation at the outset made going to Congress more difficult later. It remains unclear whether Congress would have authorized the operations given the political costs involved, but the scant consultation unnecessarily politicized the situation.[55]

Postconflict Conundrums

As the military campaign progressed, postwar planning proceeded on a number of fronts. The May 5 Contact Group meeting in Rome set up an international stabilization and response team for Libya, led by the UK's Department for International Development (DFID). At the White House, Donilon had set up a post-Qaddafi or "post-Q" high-level task force soon after the military operations began. This group was headed by White House senior director for strategic planning, Derek Chollet, and tasked with providing intellectual leadership on questions about postconflict military and political strategy. Chollet, who had been brought into the White House at Donilon's own request, was extremely capable, but was unfortunately soon inundated with managing the intervention itself. Staff evacuated from the U.S. Embassy in Tripoli also worked the issue in Washington under U.S. ambassador to Libya, Gene Cretz.[56]

---

[55] Interview with congressional staff, August 28, 2011.
[56] Interviews with White House officials, February 13, 2012, and February 17, 2012.

The post-Q task force worked with the rebels' own postconflict team in Doha, which was some seventy strong.[57] It was unclear, however, to what extent the Libyan team was linked up with the evolving situation on the ground and its counterparts in Benghazi. They produced plans, but how coherent these plans were and whether they had any juice was unclear.[58] At a minimum, liaison with the Libyan postconflict team likely provided insight into internal rebel politics, while serving as a useful source of information about the rebel's underground preparations within Tripoli for its overthrow.

Despite these multiple efforts, there were many challenges involved in planning for postconflict Libya. The United States had built up substantial knowledge and capabilities for postwar planning over the past two decades, and it entered the conflict with a bureaucracy familiar with the challenges postwar efforts entailed and geared up to respond. Most of that knowledge and administrative capacity, however, was born of Iraq and Afghanistan wars in which large numbers of civilians had been deployed to rebuild, retrain, reequip, and generally reestablish normal life in poor, war-torn societies. In Libya, however, the operating assumption was always that the U.S. postconflict footprint would be light compared not just with these more recent wars but with prior decades of nation-building efforts in Somalia, Haiti, Bosnia, and Kosovo. A major challenge from the outset was thus how to do postconflict planning for a country where others would be in the lead and U.S. influence would be comparatively low.[59]

Another challenge was basic uncertainty about what the postconflict situation would actually look like. There were a number of conceivable outcomes. If the country ended up divided between a liberated east and Qaddafi ruled west postconflict planning would only be necessary in the east. If there was a negotiated settlement in which Qaddafi stepped down

---

[57] Shashank Joshi, "What Will Free Libya Look Like?" Telegraph.co.uk, August 22, 2011.
[58] William Maclean, "If Libyan Rebels Force Gadhafi's Fall, Can They Fill the Power Vacuum?" *Daily Star* (Lebanon), August 22, 2011.
[59] Interviews with White House officials, February 13, 2012.

but the regime stayed in power, it was unclear how reconstruction would proceed. There was also uncertainty about how much damage there would be and growing concern that Qaddafi might conduct a scorched-earth campaign that could make postwar resource requirements skyrocket. Moreover, planners wondered to what extent the constraints the president had placed on U.S. participation would also apply to the postconflict operations. The United States was not going to send in ground troops, that was clear, but what other capabilities would it make available? These questions only became clear over time, and in the interim, thinking about post-Q became inextricably intertwined with the management of the war itself.[60]

On June 24, the Pentagon held a post-Q table-top exercise dubbed "Island Breeze" that brought together several people working on Libya in the U.S. government and gave them the chance to discuss and play out a number of scenarios for the fall of Tripoli and the postconflict situation. This helped clarify some key issues, including the particular limitations likely to exist in the Libyan postconflict environment and the importance of keeping China and Russia on board, despite their criticisms, to help out once the war was over.[61] It also helped clarify the circumstances under which international "boots on the ground" might be advisable. Subsequent discussions of this subject, however, went nowhere. The United States was set against sending in ground forces, even in a minor security role. Other good candidates – Turkey, for example – were also reluctant. The *thuwwar* leadership continued to resist any such proposals, fearing that foreign boots on the ground would undermine their already tenuous legitimacy. Under these conditions and given that the relative calm that prevailed in Tripoli immediately after the war, discussions of a postconflict stabilization force eventually came to naught.[62]

On the surface, the slow and extremely tenuous progress that Libya experienced following Qaddafi's death suggests that not enough resources

---

[60] Interviews with White House officials, February 13, 2012, and February 17, 2012.
[61] Ibid.
[62] Ibid.

were given to postwar planning. In theory, the United States and its allies should have worked from the start to bolster the NTC's legitimacy across the country, including with strategic communications. They should also have done more to ensure the NTC had the capacity for decision making that would be required in the postwar period by beefing up its personnel with allied and third-party experts in a coordinated way and moving faster to establish police, financial management, and other forms of training that would be sorely needed in the immediate postwar period. Had they done so, it would have helped for a smoother transition from war to peace.

All of the officials interviewed for this book – U.S. and allied – insisted adamantly, however, that little more could have been done under the circumstances to make the NTC more inclusive or more effective after the war. Ongoing military operations were everyone's main concern, and even if the United States had a major capacity for postconflict planning it would have been unwise and violated the principle of local ownership for the United States to just plan to the whole postconflict operation for the Libyans.

7   Sudden Success

By mid-July, the front lines of the war had hardly changed at all since mid-May. There were three fronts: Rebel *kata'ib* were still fighting to break out from Ajdabiyah, strike west from Misrata toward Zlitan, and push east from the Nafusah Mountains into Zawiyah and toward Tripoli itself, where they had been furtively preparing for an uprising. The rebels now had satellite phones that allowed them to coordinate more effectively across the disparate fronts, as well as radios that enhanced their coordination at the tactical level, but progress was still painfully slow and it was beginning to look like the war might drag on indefinitely.[1] After initially overestimating how quickly Qaddafi would fall, many observers were now predicting a long battle ahead. Some reporting claimed Qaddafi had a "suicide plan for Tripoli," and officials in Washington were concerned about how far he might go to keep his grip on power.[2] An editorial in the *Financial Times* warned that "an all out assault on Tripoli ... would almost certainly result in a bloodbath among rebels, regime supporters, and civilians. The seeds of vengeance and anarchy would be sown."[3] Signs of fissures among the *thuwwar* were furthermore

---

[1] David D. Kirkpatrick, "Libyan Rebels Trumpet Coordination in Attacks" *New York Times*, June 17, 2012, p. A15.

[2] Interview with White House officials, February 17, 2012; Andrew Osborn, "Libya: Col Gaddafi Has 'Suicide Plan' to Blow Up Tripoli" *Telegraph*, July 14, 2011. http://www.telegraph.co.uk/.

[3] "Prepare for Libya's Coming Transition" *Financial Times*, August 8, 2011, p. 6.

raising concerns about possible violence in the aftermath of a rebel victory.[4]

To make matters worse, having destroyed most of the regime's command and control, bunkers, air-defense, and other fixed systems, NATO did not have much headroom to intensify the pressure on the regime. NATO spokesman Col. Roland Lavoie explained the situation as follows: "Pro-Qaddafi forces are losing their ability to conduct massive offensives. This does not preclude them, however, from operating in covert locations in agricultural, administrative, or even residential facilities or schools from where they command and conduct attacks."[5] Concerns were growing that further air strikes would just be "pounding sand" to make it look like the operation was still achieving something. There was a shift, however, to smaller and smaller targets, as Figure 5.4 indicates, just to keep the pressure up, but the air operation was coming up against the problem of diminishing marginal returns.

Negotiating a Way Out

With growing international and domestic criticism, strained allied militaries, doubts about NATO's staying power, and concerns about the lengths to which Qaddafi might go to hold on, allied leaders pushed harder and harder for a negotiated settlement that would provide some relief. Unfortunately, efforts to get a deal proceeded in an uncoordinated and haphazard fashion, with multiple freelance initiatives that tended to undermine one another.

From the start, the biggest advocate for negotiation was South Africa, which had especially close relations with Qaddafi before the conflict, thanks in no small part to his largesse within the African Union. In April, President Zuma had traveled to Tripoli to propose an African Union peace plan that called for an immediate ceasefire, international

---

[4] Doug Saunders, "Stalemate, Struggle and the Hunt for an End" *Globe and Mail*, July 16, 2011, p. A15.

[5] NATO press briefing, August 9, 2011.

supervision of the truce, and negotiations for a political settlement. Qaddafi "accepted" the plan but did not pull back his troops. The rebels rejected it outright, insisting Qaddafi go before any negotiations would take place. Zuma returned at the end of May with the same plan but with no more luck.[6]

Meanwhile, at the May 28 G8 meeting in Deauville, France, President Obama and President Medvedev discussed Libya and Qaddafi's fate. Russia's position was still that Qaddafi needed to go, but that the military strikes had exceeded the UN mandate. The presidents agreed that Russia would seek to negotiate Qaddafi's departure. "If he makes this responsible decision himself," Medvedev said, "then we can talk about how it can be done, what country will take him under what conditions... But in any case, international society does not see him as the leader of Libya now."[7]

Mikhail V. Margelov, Russia's special envoy to the Middle East and Africa, was dispatched to Benghazi to negotiate a deal with the rebels. He opined that Russia was in a particularly favorable position to mediate because Russian soldiers had "never fought against African countries and against the African people."[8] In Benghazi, he tried to persuade the rebels to bring the negotiations to the African Union for mediation, but they again refused, continuing to insist that Qaddafi had to step down and leave Libya before they would ceasefire and negotiate.[9] Instead, they suggested that Russia join the Contact Group.[10] In this, Russia demurred, but Margelov still flew to Tripoli on June 16, where he met with Qaddafi's prime minister, Al-Baghdadi Ali Al-Mahmudi, who told him that the rebels would have to lay down their arms before the regime would negotiate with them. The latter was a nonstarter for the rebels, who had

---

[6] John F. Burns, "Qaddafi and Zuma Meet but Reach No Agreement" *New York Times*, May 31, 2011, p. 10.

[7] Ellen Barry, "In Diplomatic Reversal, Russia Offers to Try to Persuade Qaddafi to Leave Power" *New York Times*, May 28, 2011, p. 10.

[8] Ibid.

[9] "Source Details Russian Envoy's Talks with Libyan Opposition" BBC Monitoring Former Soviet Union, June 8, 2011.

[10] "Russia Steps Up Libya Mediator Role" *Moscow News*, June 10, 2011.

little reason to trust that Qaddafi would negotiate in good faith once they stopped their attacks. Margelov told reporters that he was "cautiously optimistic" about resolving the crisis, but in reality he had accomplished nothing.[11]

Rebels remained steadfast, and not without reason they insisted that "Qaddafi staying in Libya is Qaddafi staying in power." A negotiated settlement was therefore off the table until he departed. The prospects that the Libyan ruler would step down further weakened, however, when the International Criminal Court (ICC), following up on Resolution 1970, issued an arrest warrant for him on June 27. The warrant increased the overall legitimacy of the intervention, which was welcome, but it also meant that any negotiated settlement now needed to involve finding Qaddafi sanctuary in a country without an extradition agreement with the ICC (or consent to stand trial himself). Meanwhile, Qaddafi's son Saif told *Corriere della Sera* that his father was open to the idea of elections – a dubious claim amid its continued shelling of the population.[12]

Still undeterred in their efforts to negotiate a settlement, the Russians then invited Zuma to Moscow and sent the head of the World Chess Federation, Chirsan Ilyumzhinov, to Tripoli to play chess with Qaddafi and discuss what might be done. Illyumzhinov succeeded in checkmating Qaddafi (at which point he wisely offered a draw), but he otherwise had no more luck than Margelov.[13] These Russian efforts were no doubt earnest, but Russia's position of calling for Qaddafi's departure on the one hand while rebuking NATO on the other was obviously calibrated to garner support in the developing world while not alienating Russia from European publics – a balance that Russia would find more difficult to maintain months later when the crisis in Syria intensified.

---

[11] "Russian Envoy Says Nothing New Heard during Tripoli visit" BBC Monitoring Former Soviet Union, June 16, 2011.

[12] Ernesto Londono, "Qaddafi's Officials Are Defiant as Russia Seeks Talks" *Washington Post*, June 17, 2011, p.A11.

[13] Andrew E. Kramer, "Russia Meets with NATO in New Push for Libyan Peace" *New York Times*, July 5, 2011, p. 9.

In early July, shuttle diplomacy between regime and rebel representatives was reportedly underway in Cairo and Tunis, coordinated by Western governments, although the rebels denied that any such discussions were taking place.[14] By the second week of the month, however, it was clear from press reports that a new effort to get a negotiated settlement was under way. With Ramadan approaching, it appeared the rebels might be more ready for a ceasefire. Meanwhile, statements by French and Italian leaders suggested that a negotiated settlement was in the making. Prime Minister François Fillon of France said that a political solution "was beginning to take shape," Juppé reported that regime emissaries had said that Qaddafi was ready to go, and Frattini called for a political settlement.[15] French defense minister Gerard Longuet also made statements implying that, unlike the rebels, France supported talks even with Qaddafi still in the country.[16] *Le Monde* then reported that Sarkozy himself had met with Qaddafi's chief of staff, Bashir Saleh, bolstering a claim by Saif that a special envoy from the regime had met with Sarkozy.[17] The French government denied these reports but confirmed that it was "passing messages" to the regime in an effort to get a negotiated settlement and said it was also pressuring the rebels to come to the negotiating table.[18] Saif then repeated the claim that the regime was ready to agree to elections under international supervision, while also endorsing the idea of a government of national unity and a new constitution.[19]

---

[14] "Libyan Sources Say Al-Qaddafi Supervising His Envoys' Negotiations with Rebels" BBC Monitoring Middle East, July 6, 2011.

[15] Howard LaFranchi, "Libya Conflict: Is Qaddafi Exit in the Offing?" *Christian Science Monitor*, July 12, 2011.

[16] Foreign Staff, "France Calls for Peace Talks with Qaddafi" *Daily Telegraph*, July 11, 2011, p. 14; Jacky Rowland, "French Contact with Libyans over Gaddafi" Al Jazeera, July 12, 2011. http://www.aljazeera.com/news/africa/2011/07/201171214412794693.html.

[17] "Paris dément négocier directement avec la Libye" *Le Monde.fr*, July 11, 2011.

[18] Ruth Sherlock and Richard Spencer, "It's Time for Talks with Qaddafi, Says France" *Daily Telegraph*, July 12, 2011, p. 15.

[19] Scott Sayare, "France Denies Libyan Claim It Is in Direct Talks with Tripoli" *International Herald Tribune*, July 12, 2011, p. 4.

The French effort, however, had raised hackles within the alliance, especially because it had sidelined the UN special envoy Abdel Al-Khatib, who was a former Jordanian foreign minister. To mend fences, the United States tried to corral other efforts behind Khatib through the Contact Group in the hope that this would reduce freelancing and end efforts by the regime to play the various parties off against one another.[20]

The July 15 Istanbul Contact Group meeting thus reaffirmed the leading role of the United Nations in the negotiations. Speaking after the meeting, Frattini underlined that Khatib would be the "sole interlocutor" between the regime and the rebels. In an apparent rebuke of France's efforts to get Qaddafi to step down, he criticized such efforts as "very counterproductive."[21]

So far, the U.S. position had been to eschew direct negotiations with the regime. Signals through other channels, however, indicated Qaddafi was misinterpreting U.S. silence and absence of its forward role in the military operation as a sign of U.S. openness to his staying in power. By July the White House decided direct contacts were necessary to set the record straight. On July 16, the U.S. assistant secretary of state for Near Eastern affairs, Jeffrey D. Feltman, flew with Cretz and Chollet to Tunisia and met with senior members of Colonel Qaddafi's government in the ambassador's residence in Tunis.

In a heated and emotional three-hour session, members of the regime expressed their shock that the United States, so recently a friend of Libya, was now bombing them in support of what they insisted was an Al-Qaeda backed rebellion that would reduce the country to rubble. For their part, the U.S. envoys repeated that there was no solution that left Qaddafi in power. They also stressed, however, that the same did not apply to other members of the regime: as long as Qaddafi was gone, all options were on the table. If Qaddafi refused to leave, NATO would continue its operations until he did.[22]

---

[20] Interview with White House official, February 27, 2011.
[21] Christophe Schmidt and Nicolas Cheviron, "Pressure on Qaddafi as West Boosts Libya's 'Leaders'" AFP, July 15, 2011.
[22] Interview with senior U.S. official, February 17, 2012.

This was a relatively straightforward appeal, but the regime officials were incredulous. As one official later recounted, they seemed unable or unwilling to accept that these were the only alternatives they had. With no progress after hours of discussion, however, the U.S. team departed for Washington, leaving their interlocutors to drive the now perilous road back to Tripoli.[23]

Subsequent efforts by Khatib yielded rebel agreement in principle on the formation of a transitional government that would include ex-regime officials, provided these officials did not "have blood on their hands," and *thuwwar* leaders noted that they had already welcomed several regime defectors into their ranks.[24] Then, in an apparent reversal of previous rebel positions, NTC President Jalil told the *Wall Street Journal* on July 26 that Qaddafi could stay in Libya, noting that "we will decide where he stays and who watches him."[25] The possibility was amenable to the United States and Italy, provided the rebels agreed. Although Jalil quickly denied having made the comment, hopes for a settlement peaked.[26]

The next day Jalil confirmed that the NTC had in fact offered Qaddafi a chance to remain in the country, provided he was willing to relinquish all responsibilities. In the very same statement, however, Jalil said that the offer no longer stood and that Qaddafi would have to leave the country before negotiations could begin. Given the ICC indictment, this was a high bar. A few countries that were not members of the court were considered (including Equatorial Guinea), but none were willing to take him.[27]

---

[23] Helene Cooper and John F. Burns, "Plan Would Keep Qaddafi in Libya, but Out of Power" *New York Times*, July 28, 2011, p. 12; "US Sends 'Time to Go' Message to Gaddafi" Al Jazeera, July 19, 2011. http://www.aljazeera.com/news/africa/2011/07/2011718233615749270.html.

[24] James Hider, "'We All Want Qaddafi Dead and Buried'" *Times*, July 26, 2011, p. 13.

[25] Charles Levinson, "World News: Rebel Chief Says Qaddafi, Family Can Stay in Libya" *Wall Street Journal*, July 25, 2011, p. A9.

[26] "Libya-Rebellion" *Middle East Reporter*, July 26, 2011.

[27] Dominique Soguel, "Qaddafi's Deadline to Bow Out Whooses Past" *Mail and Gaurdian*, July 27, 2011; Matthew Campbell and Ruth Sherlock, "A Brutal Home from Home for Qaddafi" *Sunday Times*, July 17, 2011, p. 36.

Efforts to get peace negotiations started continued into August without success. In retrospect, although the haphazard nature of the initiatives may have been unavoidable, by giving the regime the impression that it could play one side of the international coalition off against the other it reduced the chances that negotiations would succeed in ending the fighting. Given the regime's evident inability to accept the imminent peril they faced, however, it may well be that negotiations were never going to work anyway, even with greater coordination and had heavier-hitters than Khatib been doing the negotiating.

Special Forces and Glimmers of Progress

As negotiation efforts sputtered along, rebels had strengthened their positions in the Berber-populated Nafusah Mountains along the Tunisian border. The revolt there had started in late April, when a *katiba* took the border crossing between Wazen, Libya, and Dhiba, Tunisia, with little resistance from Qaddafi's forces.[28] Compared with other locations such as Misrata, the Tunisian border was more easily defended and offered the rebels easier access to outside supplies and other assistance. The townships there were also closer to Tripoli than Misrata was, and key oil pipelines that supplied the capital passed through the mountains. By July, rebel *kata'ib* controlled a half-dozen towns from Dhiba to Yafran, which was only 130 kilometers from Tripoli.

The continued attrition of Qaddafi's army by NATO and by the rebels elsewhere in the country had helped produce these advances, but another key factor was the direct aid now being provided to the *thuwwar* in the form of military equipment and special forces. It is now clear from official statements, news reporting, and other published sources that special forces from Britain, France, Italy, Qatar, and the UAE were on the ground at various locations across the country from the start of the conflict, and they became more and more engaged as the situation evolved. These

---

[28] David D. Kirkpatrick, "Western Libya Earns a Taste of Freedom as Rebels Loosen Qaddafi's Grip" *New York Times*, June 26, 2012, p. A12.

forces were never more than a few hundred, of which Europeans figured only a small portion, but they were enough to make a significant difference on the course of the war.[29]

Special forces played multiple roles. Before the intervention even started, they helped evacuate foreign nationals and focused on intelligence gathering – assessing not only the state of the regime forces but also the nature of the *thuwwar*, about which there were serious questions.[30] As the war progressed and contact with rebel fighters increased, however, special forces were training *thuwwar*, providing advice at the tactical and strategic level to *thuwwar* commanders, deconflicting NATO air strikes with *thuwwar* movements, providing intelligence to them, and ultimately fighting alongside them as they took Tripoli and tracked down Qaddafi afterward.[31] From the beginning of the conflict there were reports of special forces operating on the ground for targeting purposes.[32]

Qatar's role in building up the rebel army was particularly important. Qatar sent some 20,000 tons of weapons in at least eighteen separate arms shipments to specific rebel leaders, along with tens of millions of dollars in aid, as well as at least twelve ammunition shipments, via Sudan. Thirteen of the weapons shipments went directly to rebel leaders including the former jihadist Belhaj, bypassing the NTC, to its consternation. Qatar also trained the rebels in the use of the weapons it supplied. There were more than 100 Qatari advisors operating from Benghazi, Zintan, and eventually Tripoli, according to Qatari officials. These advisors were a

---

[29] "Accidental Heros" RUSI, September 2011; Julian Borger, Chris Stephen, and Richard Norton-Taylor, "Reversal of Rebel Fortunes That Led to Gates of the Capital" *Irish Times*, August 23, 2011, p. 10.

[30] "Accidental Heros"; Mark Mazzetti and Eric Schmitt, "C.I.A. Agents in Libya Aid Airstrikes and Meet Rebels" *New York Times*, March 30, 2011, p. A1.

[31] Thomas Harding, "Libya: SAS Leads Hunt for Gaddafi" *Daily Telegraph*, August 24, 2011.

[32] Nicholas Cecil and Nick Pisa, "SAS Using Lasers to Guide Missiles on to Key Targets" *Evening Standard*, March 21, 2011; "Heart Attack: RAF Bombs Gaddafi's Nerve Center" *Daily Star*, May 29, 2011, p. 6; Mark Mazzetti and Eric Schmitt, "Top Libyan Official Defects; Rebels Are Retreating: C.I.A. Spies Aiding Airstrikes and Assessing Qaddafi's Foes" *New York Times*, March 31, 2011, p. 1.

key link between NATO and the rebel forces, especially when it came to collecting information about potential targets on the ground.[33]

At first, NATO had refused to permit direct coordination with the rebels, but after accidentally bombing a *katiba* in early April, the alliance agreed to "deconfliction" between rebel movements and its strikes. Speaking with the Associated Press in June, one *katiba* commander said that in order to avoid getting hit, "we don't move unless we have very clear instructions from NATO."[34] (He was likely using the term NATO loosely to refer to European forces on the ground.) NATO also provided the rebels with transponders that gave allied aircraft a better idea of where the rebel forces were located, in order to deconflict air strikes with *thuwwar* movements and thus prevent casualties. In theory, deconfliction stopped just short of actually calling in strikes for the rebels, but in reality NATO wandered purposefully into the gray zone between the two.[35]

As one senior military officer explained, the rebels eventually learned where to go and not to go and would wait as NATO hit targets to clear a path for them to advance. This does not mean rebels were calling in air strikes, although the effect would have been similar; as the war progressed, special forces teams on the ground were doing this for the rebels, with greater and greater frequency, in a rough approximation of the "Afghan Model."[36] Rebels evidently had some mixed feelings about this. As one reported, "Now that we are with them [NATO], they control everything. They say when and where we can go; what we should or shouldn't do. Sometimes this is a good thing. Sometimes we feel they have different aims to our own."[37]

---

[33] Sam Dagher, Charles Levinson, and Margaret Coker, "Tiny Kingdom's Huge Role in Libya Draws Concern" *Wall Street Journal*, October 17, 2011, p. A1; Ian Blank, "Qatar Admits It Sent Troops to Support NTC Fighters" *Gaurdian*, October 27, 2011, p. 24.

[34] "Libyan Rebels Claim Breakout from Misrata" Associated Press Online, June 13, 2011.

[35] Mark Urban, "Inside Story of the UK's Secret Mission to Beat Gaddafi" BBC, January 19, 2012.

[36] Deborah Haynes, "Special Forces 'Played a Key Role' in Fight with Qadaffi" *Times*, September 23, 2011; Blank, "Qatar Admits It Sent Troops"; interview with senior U.S. military official, February 11, 2012.

[37] Anthony Loyd, "Gaddafi Laughs off Exile in Face of Rebel Attack on Key Town" *Times*, July 18, 2011, p. 29.

Egyptian forces were reported in the country from the start, arming and training rebels in the east.[38] In early April, there were reports that French forces were active in securing weapons sites in southern Libya.[39] On April 19, Britain announced that it would send a small military advisory team to Libya to "advise the NTC on how to improve their military organizational structures, communications and logistics."[40] France and Italy followed suit, with small numbers of military advisors to help the NTC.[41] The United States then pledged $25 million in nonlethal "drawdown" – in-stock supplies – to the rebels on April 26.[42]

In June, in a significant increase in its commitment, France airdropped weapons and ammunition along with humanitarian supplies to Misrata and the Nafusah Mountains. French aid included assault rifles, machine guns, rocket launchers, rocket-propelled grenades (RPGs), and Milan antitank missiles. Previous arms shipments to the *thuwwar* from Qatar and the UAE had gone primarily to Benghazi and from there only by boat, when possible to Misrata (sometimes putting naval vessels enforcing the arms embargo in a quandary).[43] At the end of the month, Britain also sent nonlethal supplies to help the military effort.[44] Small teams of French and British special forces were then deployed into the Nafusah Mountains to train the rebels in the use of these weapons and other equipment. Allied special forces also provided imagery to the rebels showing the locations of regime troops in the area and at least once gave the *thuwwar* telephone conversation intercepts that revealed the distress

---

[38] "Accidental Heros."
[39] "French Special Forces Carry Out Strike in Libya" *RIA Novosti*, April 7, 2011; "Accidental Heros."
[40] UK Ministry of Defence, "UK Military Liaison Advisory Team to be Sent to Libya" April 19, 2011.
[41] Alain Barluet, "Des conseillers militaires envoyés en Libye" *Le Figaro*, April 21, 2011, p. 5.
[42] "Obama Orders $25 Million in Aid to Libyan Rebels" April, 26, 2011.
[43] Philippe Gelie, "La France a parachuté des armes aux rebelles libyens" *Le Figaro*, June 28, 2011. http://www.lefigaro.fr/international/2011/06/28/01003-20110628ARTFIG00704-la-france-a-parachute-des-armes-aux-rebelles-libyens.php.
[44] David Jolly, "Britain Sends Supplies to Libyan Rebels" *New York Times*, June 30, 2011.

of regime commanders short on food, water, and ammunition.[45] Meanwhile, the UAE had established a small presence in Zawiyah in the west.[46] By the final phase of the operation, special forces from some countries were reportedly fighting alongside the *thuwwar*, albeit in very small numbers.[47] There were reports that in the run-up to the siege of Tripoli, French special forces helped the rebels cut the oil pipeline to a key refinery at Zawiya – an operation the British opted out of.[48]

The special forces not only provided rebel *kata'ib* with training and a link to the NATO operation, they also increased the rebels' ability to plan and coordinate their attacks strategically. At the beginning of the war, the *kata'ib* were spread out across the country and completely detached from one another, with no unified command and control to provide strategic direction to their attacks on regime forces. NATO and its partners provided technology to improve their communications and advice on how to coordinate their efforts across the theater. By early July, the *thuwwar* command had become much more unified.[49] In general, by providing the rebels with equipment, technology, intelligence, and advice and training, direct foreign assistance, even though small in size, had a significant impact on the ground. Results were not immediate, of course, and without the continued NATO air strikes they would probably not have been possible at all.

Taken alongside their earlier decisions to add helicopters and provide weapons for the rebels, the decision of the French and British to insert special forces was taken by many to be a clear violation of the UN civilian protection mandate. It is difficult to see how these additions could be

---

[45] Isabelle Lasserre, "Le rôle crucial mais discret des forces spéciales" *Le Figaro*, August 26, 2011, p. 6; Richard Norton-Taylor and Dominik Rushe, "Front: Libya: Rebels and NATO Planned Tripoli Assault Weeks Ago" *Gaurdian*, August 25, 2011, p. 8; Charles Levinson, Munreef Halawa, "Libyan Rebel Leader's Death Dims Advances" *Wall Street Journal*, July 29, 2011, p. A8.

[46] Portia Walker, "Qatari Military Advisers on the Ground, Helping Libyan Rebels Get into Shape" *Washington Post*, May 12, 2011.

[47] Urban, "Inside Story"; "Accidental Heros."

[48] Patrick Wintour and Nicholas Watt, "Cameron's War: Why PM Felt Gaddafi Had to Be Stopped" *Gaurdian*, October 3, 2011, p. 13.

[49] "Libya's Rebel Fighters Forge Unified Command" AFP, July 12, 2011.

covered under even a liberal interpretation of Paragraph 4 of Resolution 1973. British and French pressure for more action in general led to later allegations that British and French leaders had ulterior motives – especially commercial ones – for pushing their role in the intervention and were seeking to ensure that they came out of the war with solid relations with Libya's new authorities. This is plausible, but it cannot be supported from available public sources. Even if it were, that states should pursue a mix of commercial and other interests should hardly be surprising except to the most uninitiated in international affairs; it would not change the outcome of the war, except in the eyes of the most idealistic of observers. In any event, these operations were conducted in a strictly bilateral capacity, and insofar as they might be taken to be a breach of the UN mandate, they did not directly involve NATO, much less the United States.

Divisions in the Rebel Camp

The rebels' progress was almost stopped in its tracks by the divisions among the rebels themselves on July 28, when Commander Abdul Fattah Younes was killed in Benghazi, igniting internal violence and raising the possibility that the *thuwwar* might fall on each other in a bloody internecine struggle. Younes had been a key figure in the coup that brought Qaddafi to power, a member of his inner circle, and a one-time interior minister. When the revolts broke out, however, he defected and quickly established himself as an important rebel commander.[50]

It was difficult to say who killed Younes. Possibilities included death at the hands of Qaddafi loyalists, murder by untamed militias of Benghazi, retribution from Islamists for his repression of their revolt in Darnah in the 1990s, and execution by the rebel leadership themselves. Members of his tribe, the Obeidi, threatened violence if the killing were not

---

[50] Trevor Mostyn, "Obituary: Gen Abdel Fatah Younis: Military Leader and Gaddafi's Trusted Aide until He Defected to Libyan Rebel Forces" *Gaurdian*, August 1, 2011, p. 32.

thoroughly investigated. The situation worsened when, four days later, fighting broke out in Benghazi between *thuwwar* and alleged Qaddafi loyalists, killing seven.[51]

The assassination came as a surprise in Washington and disheartened observers at just the moment when it seemed progress was in sight. One thing the rebels had going for them so far was the fact that despite Libya's underlying regional, tribal, and ethnic diversity, the *thuwwar* had been relatively united in their common cause against Qaddafi. Now that unity appeared to be falling apart. This threatened the chances of a rebel victory and raised the specter of a Somalia scenario in which rebel chiefs fell upon each other in a broader conflagration. – just as Qaddafi had warned. To quell the internal tension, the rebel cabinet dissolved itself on August 9, but by mid-August, news media were still warning of an imminent fracture within the rebel camp that would undermine everything that had been accomplished.[52]

The Fall of Tripoli

As the rebels in Benghazi struggled with the fallout from Younes's killing, their compatriots in the Berber highlands began an advance on Tripoli. They pushed forward with unexpected speed. On August 15, driving eastward from the Nafusah Mountains, *kata'ib* seized Zawiyah, the oil refinery only a half hour by car from Tripoli.[53] A back and forth between Qaddafi forces lodged in the refinery and regime snipers perched on rooftops ensued for the next three days.[54] NATO began a more intensive bombing of Tripoli and the towns along the route there, degrading

---

[51] David D. Kirkpatrick, "Gun Battle Disrupts Rebel Base in Libya" *New York Times*, August 1, 2011, p. A4.

[52] Kareem Fahim, "Libyan Rebels Dissolve Cabinet Amid Discord" *New York Times*, August 9, p. A10; David D. Kirkpatrick and C.J. Chivers, "Internal Strife Threatens Cause of Libyan Rebels" *New York Times*, August 14, p. A1.

[53] Kareem Fahim, "Libya Rebels Threaten a Supply Line to the Capital" *New York Times*, August 15, 2011, p. A8.

[54] Kareem Fahim, "Refugees Flee Libya Oil City as Qaddafi's Forces Dig In" *New York Times*, August 18, 2011, p. A4; Kareem Fahim, "Libyan Rebels Gain Control of Key Oil Refinery as Qaddafi Forces Flee" *New York Times*, August 19, 2011, p. A6.

regime defenses. (See figure 7.1). Other measures were also afoot. For example, a small French special forces team departed Benghazi with *thuwwar* for Al Garaboli, deep in the regime-held territory. Operating under cover of night, they made their way ashore in small Zodiaks loaded with RPGs and light weapons, which they buried on the beach for later distribution to some twenty-five sleeper cells in Tripoli.[55]

The NTC had been working for several weeks to establish contacts in Tripoli itself and to encourage local underground committees to prepare for an uprising. They focused on areas where uprisings against Qaddafi had occurred and been suppressed in the early days of the revolt. They also shipped arms and troops from the west to Benghazi to build up strength along with the French and British contributions. Meanwhile, *thuwwar* had been infiltrating Tripoli, disguised as fishermen or by crossing into town from the mountains.

On Saturday, August 20, NATO further intensified its bombing of the capital. Five Paveway IV PGMs were dropped on the Baroni Center, an intelligence base for the regime. Tanks and artillery batteries were also hit.[56] Back in Washington, White House staff came into work after rumors that Qaddafi's son Saif al-Islam was about to make some kind of a big announcement – perhaps offering new terms for a peace deal. Nothing happened, however, and with all reporting suggesting the revolt in Tripoli had not started, staff went home. Suddenly, as night fell in Libya, officials checking Twitter in Washington noted a major uptick in chatter on clashes in the Libyan capital. According to one, Twitter was "all lit up" with reports of fighting there, even though the White House Situation Room

---

[55] Anthony Loyd, "The Secret Beach Rendezvous That Brought French Weapons to the Rebels" *Times*, September 10, 2011; Sean Rayment, "How the Special Forces Helped Bring Qaddafi to His Knees" *Telegraph*, August 28, 2011, http://www.telegraph.co.uk/news/worldnews/africaandindianocean/libya/8727076/How-the-special-forces-helped-bring-Gaddafi-to-his-knees.html; Natalie Nougayrède, "Des forces spéciales françaises, britanniques et arabes auprès de la rebellion" *Le Monde*, August 24, 2011, p. 4.

[56] Rayment, "How the Special Forces Helped."

had nothing yet to report because news of the assault had not hit the media yet.[57]

Rebel forces, joined by Qataris, met with very little resistance as they advanced on the capital. As the rebel *kata'ib* entered, multiple "shadow defections" occurred, as military commanders switched sides to allow the rebels to move into and capture the city.[58] Simultaneously, rebels in the east finally broke the standoff there by capturing Brega. NATO intensified its bombing of Qaddafi's compound, Bab al-Aziziya. By Monday, August 22, rebels were in control of the capital, despite ongoing skirmishes. The following day, *thuwwar* overran the compound itself. Qaddafi's apparatus of power was collapsing; his forces were in disarray.

The pace at which the rebels advanced took nearly everyone watching from Brussels, Naples, or Washington by surprise.[59] The expectation had been that the fight for Tripoli would be bloody and drawn out. Given the slow pace of the war to date and the fact that Qaddafi himself had chemical and other weapons at his disposal, the going assumption was that a siege of the capital would be bloody and could last as long as six months. When Tripoli was taken in a matter of a few days, observers were deeply relieved. NATO was saved from a potentially acrimonious debate over extending the mission and the U.S. administration escaped some tough choices about how far it was willing to go to win the war.

One major downside of the rapid fall of Tripoli, however, was that much of the planning that had been done for postconflict stabilization was now significantly less applicable than it would have been if the war had played out as expected.[60] The speed of the collapse combined with the stable postcollapse security situation and the rebels' objectives to foreign peacekeepers put an end to deliberations about the possibility of a postwar stabilization force.[61]

[57] Interview with senior White House official, February 13, 2012.
[58] Multiple news reports and interviews with White House officials, February 17, 2012.
[59] Multiple interviews with U.S. officials.
[60] Interviews with White House officials, February 17, 2012.
[61] Ibid.

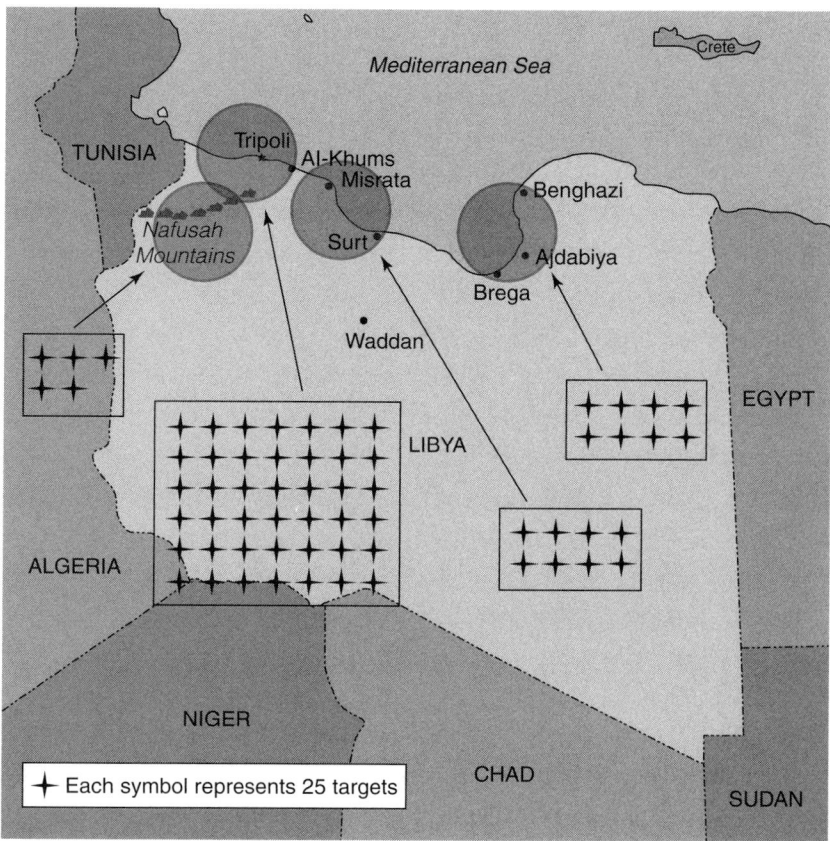

Figure 7.1 Libya's mid-northern coast/mid-western region was the most heavily targeted in the latter phase of Operation Unified Protector, July 18–October 23. *Source*: NATO, Operational Media Updates, April 18–October 23, 2011.

Although some leaders would later say the decision not to deploy postwar stabilization forces was a calculated strategy, it was in fact more a necessity produced by the conditions on the ground and the desires of most political leaders in the alliance, who had no interest at all in offering up troops for another potentially prolonged postwar deployment.

When to End It

On September 1, the Contact Group reconvened in Paris for a final meeting to mark the regime's downfall and build support for postwar reconstruction. In a reversal reflecting the new reality on the ground, Russia recognized the NTC. South Africa, however, was still blocking efforts at the UN to unfreeze Libya's overseas accounts so that the rebels could have access to the funds. Donilon was reportedly "obsessed" with the issue and by the fact that the rebels would be barred for so long from access to the funds that by any measure now rightly belonged to them. His attention helped overcome initial State Department concern that pressure to release the funds would create larger problems on the Security Council, which was now starting an acrimonious debate over how to respond to the war.[62] The South African government, under significant pressure, finally agreed to a release of $1.5 billion in frozen Libyan assets for the rebels. The funds were divided into three baskets: direct aid to the rebels, aid via intermediaries, and direct humanitarian aid to the Libyan population.[63]

The upshot of the Paris meeting, however, was that the postconflict strategy would be more hands off than had been the case in past NATO interventions. Neither NATO nor the UN would deploy ground forces for postconflict stabilization. Maintaining security and political stability was going to be up to the Libyans themselves.

On September 16, President Sarkozy and Prime Minister Cameron visited Tripoli. Libya was now moving toward postconflict transition, but with Qaddafi at large, tension was still high. Saif, whom *thuwwar* had claimed to have captured, soon appeared at Tripoli's Rixos Hotel, where foreign correspondents were holed up as disorder in the streets reigned. In a message on Syrian television, Qaddafi proclaimed

---

[62] In the White House, the funds were dubbed the Fishman Funds after the staffer who did the legwork to break them free. Interview with senior White House official, February 13, 2012.

[63] Interviews with White House officials.

he would not give up. "Let Libya be engulfed in flames. Libya will turn to hell," he said.⁶⁴ Meanwhile, the loyalist towns of Bani Walid and Sirte both refused to surrender.

The United States was nevertheless interested in seeing the operation brought to closure, in part to underscore the difference between this intervention and the Iraq and Afghanistan wars.⁶⁵ France, Britain, and other allies, however, were concerned that by shutting the operation down prematurely NATO risked seizing defeat from the jaws of victory. Despite Russia's belated recognition of the rebels, whom the Chinese now also supported, it would be almost impossible to get another UN Security Council resolution to intervene in the event further military measures were necessary, they argued.⁶⁶ Moreover, as long as Qaddafi was still at large, the possibility of further attacks on civilians was still a cause for concern. Allied leaders thus agreed to shut the operation down only after there was no credible threat to the civilian population and all of Qaddafi's remaining forces had returned to their barracks.

Meanwhile, the rebels had declared a unilateral ceasefire and offered negotiations for the surrender of the two final Qaddafi holdouts in Bani Walid – a stronghold of the Warfallah tribe that had supported Qaddafi during his rule – and Sirte, Qaddafi's hometown. NATO was meanwhile shifting its emphasis from strikes to surveillance. Speaking in Washington, General Ham explained that "collectively, Unified Protector is doing more collection, more surveillance and monitoring than they are doing strikes."⁶⁷ NATO air strikes did continue, however, and on September 11, the rebel *kata'ib* resumed operations to take the towns by force.

Progress was painfully slow. The holdouts managed to repulse one after another rebel attack, despite the fact that they were cut off entirely

---

⁶⁴ Federal News Service, "Highlights of U.S. Broadcast News Coverage of the Middle East from September 01, 2011."
⁶⁵ Interview with senior U.S. official, February 6, 2012.
⁶⁶ Interviews with allied officials, February 7, 2012.
⁶⁷ Remarks at Defense Writers Group Breakfast, Washington, DC, September 14, 2011. http://www.airforce-magazine.com/DWG/Documents/2011/September%202011/091411 ham.pdf.

Figure 7.2 Secretary Clinton meets Libyan soldiers at the steps of her C-17 military transport upon her arrival in Tripoli in Libya, October 18, 2011.
Source: State Department.

from the rest of the country and still under pressure from NATO air strikes. Rebels were eager to avoid a bloody end to the war with lots of civilian casualties, but rebel resolve, now that Tripoli was liberated, was also ebbing.[68] Defiantly, Qaddafi continued to issue statements predicting the imminent collapse of Libya's new government.[69] NATO was increasingly concerned with postconflict problems and improving situational awareness, especially regarding the status of Libya's chemical weapons stockpiles and man-portable air-defense systems (MANPADs).

In these circumstances, NATO agreed to a three-month extension of the operation on September 21. *Thuwwar* made several sorties into Sirte,

---

[68] Rod Nordland, "At Qaddafi Loyalists' Last Redoubts, a Struggle of Advances and Retreats" *New York Times*, September 18, 2011, p. A6.
[69] Arrai Television, September 20.

only to be repelled by Qaddafi's forces. Given that the rest of the country was under rebel control, General Jodice admitted he was "surprised by the tenacity of the pro-Qaddafi forces."[70] As at all the earlier stages in the operation, however, there was only so much NATO could do to increase the pressure without risking significant civilian casualties that might ruin what had so far been a very strong record in this regard.

Work on postwar reconstruction thus progressed under the cloud of the continued fighting in Sirte and Bani Walid. Secretary Clinton made the first major visit to Tripoli by an American official on October 18 (Figure 7.2). Her discussions focused not only on reconstruction but also on the U.S. effort to get control of Qaddafi's stockpiles of chemical weapons and MANPADs, lest they fall into the hands of Al-Qaeda and pose a threat to U.S. forces in Afghanistan or other theaters. Again, it was clear that the United States' postconflict role would, such as the U.S. role in the operation itself, be limited and focus on those areas where the United States had specific capabilities and saw specific interests.

On October 20, after several days of gradual rebel advances on Sirte, NATO planes spotted a convoy leaving the city. Before it was even two miles outside, a Predator that had been circling overhead fired a Hellfire missile that destroyed the leading vehicle. Two French Mirages then also attacked, scattering the convoy, and *Thuwwar* gave chase on the ground.[71] Qaddafi leapt from one of the cars into a nearby drainpipe,

---

[70] Eric Schmitt, "NATO Commander Says Resilience of the Qaddafi Loyalists Is Surprising" *New York Times*, October 11, p. A12.

[71] Marie Colvin, "Brutal Retribution" *Sunday Times*, October 23, 2011, pp. 23–25; Kareem Fahim, Anthony Shadid, and Rick Gladstone, "Violent End to an Era as Qaddafi Dies in Libya" *New York Times*, October 20, 2011, p. A1; "Rep. Rohrabacher Reiterates Call for Libya to Repay US for Military Intervention" *US Fed News*, November 25, 2011; Ben Farmer, "Gaddafi's Final Hours: Endgame in a Desert Drain, Eyewitness" *Sunday Telegraph*, October 23, 2011, pp. 20–21; "Libya to Be Declared Free as NATO Mission Set to End" AFP, October 21, 2011; Lolita C. Baldor and Bradley Klapper, "US Looks to Wrap Up Mission in Post-Gadhafi Libya" Associated Press, October 21, 2011; Alex Spillius, "Britain Admits RAF Teams Flew Armed Drones in Missions against Gaddafi" *Daily Telegraph*, July 27, 2012, p. 14; David Pugliese, "NATO's Secret War against Gadhafi" *Gazette*, February 21, 2012, p. A15.

where he attempted to hide. Nearby rebel fighters, however, converged on the spot and quickly pulled him out, beat him, and shot him in the head. Libyan leaders refused to confirm this account for obvious reasons, but later reports and the cell phone video that circulated immediately following his death suggest that, in the end, after forty-two years of dictatorship, Qaddafi was summarily executed by the *thuwwar*.

8 The Impact of the War and Its Implications

Libya after Qaddafi

Free of Qaddafi and with the war now over, the people of Libya rejoiced. Public services were gradually restored in most areas, and oil production recovered fairly quickly to near prewar levels. Uncertainty about the future nevertheless hung in the air. More than a million Libyans remained abroad in neighboring Tunisia or Egypt, unable – or fearful – to return. Libya was about to begin a long and difficult process of reconciliation with its past. It would do so under trying circumstances. The end of the Qaddafi regime was ultimately just an opening toward a richer and more meaningful kind of freedom that might allow Libya's new citizens to go about their lives with less fear and greater dignity. Realizing this future would be a major task. The NTC struggled to get its footing and suffered from continued apprehension about its basic legitimacy to govern, in no small part because so many of its members were either exiles with little connection to Libya or early defectors who only a year earlier had been regime loyalists. The NTC had been the face of the revolution to the outside world, but it was Libya's new government only by default. A new, more representative government of the people, however, would have to await elections and these would take several months to prepare.

Weak and fearful of alienating the population, the NTC proceeded with great caution on all fronts. This was not helpful, given the vast number of reconstruction and state-building tasks that loomed ahead.

Figure 8.1 Libyans celebrate their newfound freedom in Martyr's Square in Tripoli.
Source: NATO.

Initial hopes for rapid change began to fade in the face of Libya's daunting, though hardly uncommon, postconflict challenges. The spontaneous emergence of a myriad of small civil-society organizations across the country to deal with a range of problems offered some reason for optimism, but Libya had no formal institutions to work with. Qaddafi left behind a hollow state whose administrative and governing institutions barely functioned before the war, and were now half emptied of functionaries fearing retribution for ever having been part of that state. In addition to holding elections, Libya needed to write a constitution, set up a judicial system, and overhaul its security services. The citizens of the fledgling democracy had little or no experience with representative government and a deep-seated distrust of government in general, including political parties. They themselves would have to learn the responsibilities of citizenship.

Against the backdrop of these challenges, open disagreements broke out over the extent to which federalism and Islamic law would figure in the design of the new Libyan state. Meanwhile, concerns about Salafi extremists, relegated to the background during the intervention itself, resurfaced. Then there was the problem of the militias, which, after supplying the manpower for Qaddafi's overthrow, now controlled Libya's security. The postwar *kata'ib* were of varying size and in varying states of arms. To complicate matters, the proliferation of militias continued once the war was over, as groups sought to establish security in the absence of the state or, in the more ominous cases, to profit from that absence. Many simply patrolled the territory they had taken or defended during the war, waiting for the political situation to shake out and for an acceptable alternative to soldiering to present itself. Some skirmished over turf, especially in the south, where tribal conflicts over Saharan smuggling routes, suppressed under Qaddafi, broke out again. In most areas, these early skirmishes were not very harmful, but they underscored the inherent fragility of the security situation and the fact that the government in Tripoli lacked anything even approaching a monopoly on the legitimate use of force. Thus it could hardly be considered sovereign, despite the protestations of representatives of the Libyan government.

To make matters worse, the country was awash in small arms, machine guns, assault rifles, and RPGs that had been looted from regime casernes or introduced into the country from abroad during the war. Even more worrisome were some 20,000 SA-7 MANPADS estimated to have been in Qaddafi's possession before the war, which could pose a serious threat to civilian aircraft if they fell into the wrong hands. After the war, the United States committed $40 million to help secure them, but in February 2012, only 5,000 MANPADS were reported to have been secured. The hunt was ongoing when the attack on the Benghazi diplomatic facility occurred in September, as evidenced by the fact that one of the Americans killed there was a former U.S. Navy SEAL working as a contractor to track the weapons down.[1]

---

[1] "American Killed in Libya Was on Intel Mission to Track Weapons" ABC News, September 13, 2012. http://abcnews.go.com/Blotter/glen-doherty-navy-seal-killed-libya-intel-mission/story?id=17229037; C.J. Chivers, "How to Control Libya Missiles? Buy Them Up" *New York Times*, December 22, 2011, p. A1; Kate Brannen, "U.S. Still Hunting for Missing Libyan MANPADS" *Defense News*, February 2, 2012. http://www.defensenews.com/article/20120202/DEFREG02/302020009/U-S-Still-Hunting-Missing-Libyan-MANPADS.

Like all wars, the war in Libya also contributed to broader regional instability. With the home front quiet, some of Libya's more adventurous revolutionaries now decamped to Syria, where their newly honed skills could be offered up to the cause of overthrowing the Assad regime. In addition to experienced Islamic revolutionaries, Libya also became a source of weapons for anti-Assad forces. Mahdi al-Harati, for example, who was the Libyan-Irish leader of the Tripoli Brigade, one of the first rebel *kata'ib* to enter Tripoli in August, took off for Syria after a brief stint as a deputy to Belhaj. There, he formed the Liwa al-Ummah, composed largely of expatriate Syrians, and picked up the struggle against Assad. There were also many reports of arms from Libya making their way to the fight in Syria – at least one way of getting them out of Libya, quipped one U.S. official ironically.[2]

Weapons also flowed south and west across the Sahara as Qaddafi's Taureg mercenaries fled back to home turf, looting what they could of Libya's arms depots along the way. Taureg militias eventually entered eastern Niger and made their way into Mali, where they pushed the weak Malian state out of the north, creating a crisis in the southern capital of Bamako that led to a coup d'etat in March, 2012. The extremists groups closely linked to Al Qaeda in the Islamic Maghreb (AQIM) then crept into the vacuum in the north, imposed an extreme form of Sharia law, and started to attract jihadists from as far afield as South Asia. Alarm that Mali could become the "Afghanistan of Africa" generated pressure for another intervention to stem the extremist tide.[3] In January 2013, when the Malian capital Timbuktu appeared on the verge of takeover by AQIM linked forces, France intervened and took leadership of a coalition that included Britain, the United States and several other countries.

---

[2] Mary Fitzgerald, "The Syrian Rebels Libya Weapon" ForeignPolicy.com, August 9, 2012; conversation with U.S. official, August 19, 2012.

[3] "France's Hollande Calls for Mali Intervention, Clinton Says Nation Can't Fight Islamists Alone" Associated Press, September 26, 2012.

The presence of Al-Qaeda in the Islamic Maghreb (AQIM) was long-standing in the region before the Libyan uprising, but as the September 11, 2012, attack on the U.S. diplomatic facility in Benghazi showed, the inability of the new Libyan government to establish control over its own territory had opened new possibilities for Al-Qaeda or groups inspired by its message to make inroads. Qaddafi's claim that such forces would turn the country into the Somalia of the Mediterranean were wishful thinking on his part, but the threat would need to be dealt with adroitly if Libya was to sustain the inherent promise of the days that followed Qaddafi's demise.[4]

How Successful Was the Intervention?

The surreal but positive scene depicted at the opening of this book contrasts sharply with the descriptions of the attack on the U.S. compounds in Benghazi on September 11, 2012, in which four U.S. citizens, including U.S. ambassador Chris Stevens, were killed. A well-organized gang of assailants, some of whom appear to have had links to AQIM and other jihadi groups, took advantage of an outcry across the region against a scornful film that mocked the Prophet and had recently been released on the Internet by its maker, an Egyptian Coptic Christian based in the United States. The event was particularly tragic because Stevens, in his role as U.S. liaison with the NTC, had played an integral role in bringing the Libyans the very freedom without which his murder would probably not have occurred. Although it later became clear the attack had little to do with the incendiary video, at the time it seemed as if the positive effects of a billion dollars' worth of bombs, dropped, at no small political risk, to topple Qaddafi, had been suddenly erased as the pernicious views of one shady individual spiralled electronically around the world.

Serious issues were easily lost in the partisan firestorm that ensued. To some, the 9/11/12 attacks undermined the accomplishments of the

---

[4] Christopher S. Chivvis, "Libya's Downward Spiral" ForeignPolicy.com, September 13, 2012.

intervention and struck a blow to the whole idea of liberal intervention.[5] They certainly underscored the inherent difficulty of intervention and reminded the world that Libya was facing many of the challenges typical of postconflict countries. They ought not, however, obscure the record of what was actually accomplished by the initial intervention or skew our understanding of the broader implications of the Libya case, which is important for the United States and Europe as they grapple with the challenge of military intervention in an era of continued need, yet more limited resources.

To understand the implications of the intervention, we must first assess what it achieved. This requires looking not only at success with stated objectives, but at the cost of achieving them, what might have been done better, and how challenging a case Libya was in the first place.

Military and Political Objectives

When it comes to stated objectives, the operation has rightly been hailed as a success. In seven months of operations, the intervening powers maintained an arms embargo, facilitated humanitarian relief, created and sustained a no-fly zone, and helped protect Libya's civilian population from depredation at the hands of Qaddafi's forces. With Qaddafi dead, even some critics of the operation admitted it was a success. Senator McCain, for example, said magnanimously that the administration deserved "great credit" and that he thought the world was "a better place."[6]

Averting slaughter in Benghazi, the initial military objective, was accomplished quickly in the early days of Odyssey Dawn, before NATO was fully involved. U.S., French, and British air power swiftly destroyed

---

[5] E.g., Omer Taspinar, "The American Public and the Islamic World" *Today's Zaman Online*, September 16, 2012.

[6] Mark Landler, "For Obama, Some Vindication of His Much-Criticized Approach to War" *New York Times*, October 21, 2011, p. A16.

and repelled Qaddafi's tanks, thwarting what would surely have been a bloody assault on the city. Whether civilian losses would have numbered in the hundreds of thousands, as some U.S. officials claimed, is rather debatable, but there would surely have been large numbers of civilian casualties and probably gruesome murders. The immolation of some fifty *thuwwar* at the hands of retreating regime forces in a Tripoli warehouse offers a glimpse of what might have happened on a larger scale in Benghazi. Seven thousand perished in the massacre at Srebrenica during the Bosnian war, and the regime was easily capable of a slaughter on this scale. In the first two weeks of the revolt, when they were on the defensive, Qaddafi's forces were already estimated to have killed several hundred civilians.[7]

It will be many years before we know the extent to which the operation achieved its longer-term political objectives. More than two years after the revolution, Libya is still very unstable. While the technicals have receded from view on the streets of Tripoli, the *thuwwar* still cling to their weapons and are increasingly restless at the lack of progress toward realizing the revolution's ideals. This is of course in part because beyond ridding themselves of Qaddafi, rebels fought for different ideals. Meanwhile, nefarious groups have taken advantage of the situation to pursue their own interests.

Still, if uncertain, the situation is on many accounts better than it was when Qaddafi was there, and as long as Libya does not collapse into widespread internecine slaughter the intervention will have improved life for most Libyans. At a minimum, Libyans got the chance for a better future and this was an improvement over the status quo ante. Clearly, success will be judged even greater if Libya emerges on a par with its neighbors in Tunisia and Egypt, especially given that these countries had

---

[7] Decision on the "Prosecutor's Application Pursuant to Article 58 as to Muammar Mohammed Abu Minya GADDAFI, Saif Al-Islam GADDAFI and Abdullah AL-SENUSSI" Pre-Trial Chamber 1, International Criminal Court, ICC-01/11, June 27, 2011.

peaceful revolutions and more highly developed institutions to build upon.

The central strategic rationale U.S. administration officials emphasized in making the case for the intervention was that it would discourage conservative counterrevolutions against the uprisings in the Arab World, especially in Egypt and Tunisia. Success on this count is also difficult to judge and requires speculation and counterfactuals. Obviously, the intervention did not in a fell swoop guarantee the constitutional rights of the people of the region. This it could not have done, but it probably did have some limited positive impact on the Arab Spring, offering hope for protest movements and discouraging the region's more conservative regimes from brutal crackdowns on their citizens. President Assad might have suppressed his population earlier and even more violently had NATO not intervened, although the subsequent violence in Syria shows the limits of any such effect.

Relatively Low Costs

The intervention also achieved these goals at relatively low human and financial cost. Table 8.1 provides basic comparative statistics on the Libya and Kosovo interventions. Libya was significantly less intense than Kosovo but lasted much longer. According to the Pentagon, the estimated cost of Defense Department operations through September 30, 2011, was $1.1 billion.[8] This is much less than the cost of the Kosovo air war in real terms, which was $2.7 billion in 2011 dollars, not including the very substantial sums spent on postconflict peacekeeping. The British government said the war cost it 212 million pounds ($337 million), although some estimates ran much higher.[9] France spent approximately 350 million

---

[8] Kevin Baron, "For $1 Billion, One Dictator" *National Journal*, October 21, 2011.
[9] Nick Hopkins, "Libya Conflict May Cost UK £1.75bn" *Guardian*, September 25, 2011.

Table 8.1 *Libya and Kosovo in Comparative Perspective (Figures for Unified Protector only)*

	Kosovo	Libya (OUP)
Length of operation (days)	78	215
Total sorties	38,004[10]	26,500[11]
Strike sorties	19,484[12]	9,700[13]
Daily strike sorties	250	45
U.S. cost per strike sortie	$13,857	$11,340
Average number of sorties per day	~487	~123
Civilian deaths	~500[14]	~60
Cost of operations (billion 2011 dollars)	2.7	1.1
U.S. casualties	(2)[15]	0

euros ($502 million).[16] Needless to say, these amounts are a tiny fraction of the cost of the major multiyear conflicts in Iraq and Afghanistan. Compared to those, this was intervention on the cheap.

Available information indicates that civilian casualties from NATO operations were very limited. The UN International Commission of Inquiry on Libya investigated twenty NATO air strikes and found that in five of them, a total of sixty civilians died.[17] A *New York Times* on-the-ground examination of more than twenty-five air strike sites across Libya concluded that at least forty civilians and possibly more than seventy were

---

[10] Benjamin Lambeth, *NATO's Air War for Kosovo: A Strategic and Operational Assessment* (Santa Monica, CA: RAND Corporation, 2001), p. 61.

[11] NATO, "Operation Unified Protector: Final Mission Stats" November 2, 2011.

[12] Lambeth, *NATO's Air War*, p. 61.

[13] NATO, "Operation Unified Protector."

[14] Ivo H. Daalder and Michael E. O'Hanlon, *Winning Ugly: NATO's War to Save Kosovo* (Washington, DC: Brookings Institution, 2000), p. 240.

[15] The deaths of two U.S. Apache helicopter pilots in a training mission near Albania were the only U.S. casualties in Operation Allied Force. Steve Bowman, *Kosovo and Macedonia: U.S. and Allied Military Operations* (Washington, DC: Congressional Research Service, July 8, 2003), p. 3.

[16] French Senate, "Rapport générale no 107 (2011–2012)" November 17, 2011, section 2.

[17] UN Human Rights Council, "Report of the International Commission of Inquiry on Libya" A/HRC/19/68, March 2, 2012.

killed by NATO strikes.[18] In either case, despite the attention they were given in the press, these figures are very small relative to any other air campaign in recent history. Military losses were also limited to the F-15E that went down at the start of coalition operations in March and the UAE F-16 that crashed at Sigonella in April.[19]

In addition, by comparison with many prior interventions, the political costs were relatively low. Relations with dissenters within the Atlantic alliance were quickly patched up, and Germany became a supporter of the effort, even if it never deployed military forces. (German reticence, it should be noted, did have lingering negative effects on an already strained Franco-German relationship.) Russian diplomats sniped at NATO throughout, but there was no significant impact on other key issues in the U.S.–Russia relationship, such as missile defense cooperation and Russian accession to the WTO, both of which were more important to Russia than Libya.

Russia would later claim that NATO's liberal interpretation of the UN mandate was the reason for their unwillingness to agree to even a hortatory Security Council resolution against Syria's president Assad. NATO, and especially Britain and France, did relax their interpretation of the mandate over time, but unless the Russians are significantly more benighted than they appear they should have predicted that this was a possibility when they allowed Resolution 1973 to pass. Moreover, even if NATO had adopted a more conservative interpretation of the mandate, the Russians would almost certainly still have resisted military measures against Assad, given their much closer relationship with that regime. At worst, therefore, NATO's interpretation of the UN mandate may have made Security Council action in Syria a little more difficult, but Syria was always going to be a tougher case.

---

[18] C.J. Chivers and Eric Schmitt, "Libya's Civilian Toll: Denied by NATO" *New York Times*, December 18, 2011.

[19] "U.S. Fighter Jet Crashes in Rebel-Held Libya" Reuters, March 22, 2011; "NATO: UAE F-16 Crashes at Italian Airbase" Associated Press, April 27, 2011.

Related claims that the intervention came at the cost of killing R2P as a doctrine are also rather unfair. To a certain extent, if Russia, China, South Africa, and other countries raise objections to future Security Council Resolutions aimed at stopping humanitarian crises by referencing Libya, the claims will be true de facto. But this will be because these countries – and above all Russia and China – want to block the intervention for their own reasons, not because NATO used of R2P as an excuse for ousting Qaddafi. There is no evidence for claims that the United States and its allies duped other members of the Security Council into voting for a limited intervention when they fully intended to topple Qaddafi from the outset, or otherwise use R2P to pull the wool over the eyes of non-NATO states. To be sure, when the intervention started, the possibility that Qaddafi might fall as a result should have been clear to everyone. Security Council delegations in New York were well briefed on the resolution and understood its potential implications when they allowed it to pass. The multiple efforts to negotiate a settlement with Qaddafi are evidence of the intervening powers' genuine desire to see the war end differently than it did. Unfortunately, as Qaddafi rejected settlement efforts and leaders began to have concerns with NATO's staying power, it became harder and harder not to up the military pressure on the regime. Even then there was reluctance to do so.

As concerns the relationship between the operation in Libya and the collapse in Mali, it is important to distinguish between the impact of the war and the impact of the intervention itself. Too often in media reports, the situation in Mali and the growth of AQIM was blamed on the intervention, but Mali's Tuareg issue was long-standing. More accurately, Mali's collapse was only partially attributable to the civil war in Libya, a war in which NATO was involved, but did not cause.

In global terms, the intervention's impact on the strategic calculations of other despotic regimes is difficult to predict, as it cuts both ways. To avoid the tripwires that Qaddafi hit in March 2011, tyrants have reason to restrain their rhetoric and hold back from the most repressive measures against their people. This appears to have been the case in Syria, where

Assad for several months made an outward show of willingness to negotiate with protesters in his country. Even several months after the fighting had become serious, he refrained from inflammatory rhetoric or the use of fixed-wing aircraft against the rebels (although he did finally do so – and worse).

After Libya leaders who run athwart of international human rights standards may also seek closer alliances with China and Russia, who have the power to greatly retard Western military interventions. Such states may also increase their efforts to acquire technology that will better deter the deployment of Western airpower, including more sophisticated air-defense systems (preferably purchased from countries whose political weight can also deter intervention). The Libya intervention could even encourage them to develop weapons of mass destruction and demonstrate their willingness to use them to deter the West from seriously considering intervention in the first place – although such demonstrations would also risk the opposite effect.

Indeed, one of the more serious downsides of the Libya intervention is the fact that it occurred despite Qaddafi having renounced nuclear weapons, a fact that could well discourage other states such as Iran from doing the same. It is important to recognize such costs and remember them in the future. They do not, however, change a net positive assessment of what the intervention achieved.

How Difficult a Mission?

The achievements and relatively low cost of the operation should also be viewed in terms of the overall difficulty of the operation. Human and financial costs were relatively low in Libya in part because NATO had the good fortune of an adversary that was militarily weak, almost universally reviled, and proved tactically and strategically inept. Had Libya been farther from Europe, the cost and difficulty of the mission would have been much higher. Libya is a large country, but Qaddafi's infrastructure and the bulk of his military systems were located on the Mediterranean coast, within relatively easy striking distance of NATO air bases in Italy and Greece and the French aircraft carrier, *Charles de Gaulle*, which operated in a fairly permissive environment in the Mediterranean. Moreover, the sparse desert landscape made it easier to track and target regime forces whenever they moved outside of urban areas. Militarily, this was an air-sea campaign of a kind with which allies were broadly familiar; by contrast with counterinsurgency operations in Iraq and Afghanistan, there was no need to retool to learn a "new way of war."

Qaddafi's military capabilities were also middling at best, and his performance was inept. He possessed largely antiquated, even if lethal, Soviet weapons. On the surface he had a large army, but after years of mistreatment under his rule, its loyalty was always in question – and large numbers of defectors quickly filled the ranks of the *thuwwar*. Only the 32nd Brigade under the direct command of Qaddafi's son Khamis was reliable.

Qaddafi was also inept strategically. Had he pulled back his forces and made more credible offers of a ceasefire, he might have managed to halt the bombings and even split the alliance. Had he refrained from inflammatory and genocidal rhetoric at the outset, he might have avoided the intervention altogether. But he proved incapable of either. Whether this was a sign of the inherent fragility of his power or just being out of touch with reality is difficult to say. In either case, his willingness to continue attacking civilians throughout the war made it easier for NATO to stay within the remit of its Security Council mandate.

At the same time, Qaddafi had more drastic options at his disposal, but he chose not to use them. Terrorist attacks against U.S. or European interests might well have worked against him, as Milosevic's decision to intensify ethnic cleansing in Kosovo in 1999 did – but they could also have worked in Qaddafi's favor had they succeeded in breaking NATO's already troubled unity. Thankfully, there was no scorched-earth policy, no destruction of oil infrastructure on the scale of retreating Saddam forces in Iraq, and no use of his chemical weapons stocks. Such moves as these would have greatly raised the stakes and complicated the military and political management of the intervention.

The diplomatic context was also favorable. Despite their objections and lamentations, neither China nor Russia had a major interest in seeing Qaddafi remain in power. In this sense, the operation was easier even than Kosovo, where for much of the operation Russia's historical support for the Serbs complicated the picture, or Syria, a Russian client and customer for significant arms sales – including a sophisticated integrated air-defense system. Similarly, the progress of democratic revolutions in neighboring Tunisia and Egypt combined with the lack of major interest from these countries in disrupting Libya's domestic politics facilitated the effort.

The *thuwwar* themselves were also fairly unified in their objectives, highly motivated, and willing to accept outside support. The territorial base in Benghazi was a major advantage – one that Syria's rebels, for example, do not enjoy in their fight against Assad. Although tribal, regional, and other cleavages do exist in Libya, there was near unanimous opposition to Qaddafi's rule, and even when Younes was assassinated, the rebels managed to avoid internal rifts that would have wrecked their chances of victory. Libya was clearly not Bosnia, where, after years of murdering each other, ethnic groups (unsurprisingly) found it difficult to lay down their weapons, cohabitate, and govern together. With a less unified rebel movement, the chances the rebels might have fallen upon each other as the war dragged out would have been much greater.

All of these factors helped reduce cost of the war, and should be borne in mind when considering the feasibility of future operations. The underlying legitimacy of the war was perhaps the most important cost-reducing factor of all, however. Revulsion at Qaddafi was near universal; his actions were atrocious and widely agreed to be so. His morally reprehensible behavior was bad enough to get his regime unanimously ejected from its seat on the UN Human Rights Council. This was the foundation for a legitimacy that was then developed through diplomatic efforts that eventually resulted in UN Security Council sanction for the use of force against the regime. It made the coalition bigger, stronger, and better able to sustain the effort when the going got tough.

Room for Improvement

There was still room for improvement in some areas. Although this book is about the intervention rather than the postconflict reconstruction, it is clear now that more ought to have been done during and after the war to steer Libya toward a more durable peace even if doing so was very difficult. The unity the *thuwwar* displayed during the fight against Qaddafi did not endure after he was gone. The fissures evident when Younes was assassinated persisted and were in many ways compounded after the war, when security in Libya fell into the hands of a wide variety of armed groups with varying allegiances and often clashing agendas. Many of these groups were simply rebel *kata'ib* that stayed mobilized after the war, but some were in fact groups that formed after Tripoli fell, either out of fear of what the *thuwwar* might do to them (as in the case of towns perceived to have been insufficiently loyal to the cause) or for more nefarious purposes. The failure of the early Libyan government to address the problem by demobilizing these groups or bringing them under a centralized command structure would become the most severe impediment to postconflict stabilization – an impediment that would grow more and more serious over time. Just as the Libyans and NATO share responsibility for the success of the intervention, they should also share responsibility for this failure.

Although the absence of postconflict peacekeeping forces was as much a product of political constraints and the speed with which Tripoli fell as it was a well-considered strategy for postconflict reconstruction, it did reflect a current of thought skeptical about such deployments and statebuilding operations in general.[20] Noting the difficulties that the United States and its allies encountered in Iraq and Afghanistan, opponents of postconflict stabilization operations point to their high costs and the poor international record of sustaining them. They also argue that the presence of foreign troops increases the chances of a postwar insurgency,

---

[20] For example, Stephen Watts, Caroline Baxter, Molly Dunigan, and Christopher Rizzi, *The Uses and Limits of Small-Scale Military Interventions* (Santa Monica, CA: RAND Corporation, 2012).

because troops become an easy target for local groups that are dissatisfied with the peace. In addition, opponents claim that the trusteeship arrangements that have sometimes accompanied state-building operations in the past – for example in Bosnia, Kosovo, and Iraq – deprive local actors of ownership and thus encourage irresponsible behavior on the part of local elites, freeing them from the need to compromise and retarding the development of their own administrative skills and democratic culture.[21] In a similar vein, neoliberal economists often claim that a postwar international presence can skew incentives and have distortionary effects on the economy.[22]

Such arguments are grounded in sound reasoning and make sense up to a point. But Libya's difficult course since the end of the war suggests that there is real risk of overlearning the lessons of the past – and Iraq and Afghanistan in particular. The difficulties of a no-footprint approach have been glaring in Libya's postconflict period, when international actors, especially the United States, are severely limited in their ability to have any influence on a chaotic and dangerous postwar environment that they helped create – a situation that only became worse after Ambassador Stevens's death. Postwar planners were no doubt correct to eschew a major occupation force on the Iraq model, but there is a huge difference between the deployments in Iraq and Afghanistan, where more than 100,000 troops were sent in to fight extended counterinsurgencies, and complete absence of any foreign forces whatsoever in Libya. A more balanced approach could have involved some military footprint without violating the principle of local ownership. This would have increased the chances of stable recovery from the war. At a minimum, the failure to generate forces for postconflict stabilization speaks to the continued importance of efforts to develop postconflict capabilities in other countries and multilateral organizations, including the African Union, the EU, and the UN.

---

[21] Gerhard Knaus and Felix Martin, "Travails of the European Raj" *Journal of Democracy*, vol. 14, no. 3, (July 2003), pp. 60–74.
[22] Ted Galen Carpenter, "Another War of Choice" *National Interest*, March 18, 2011.

In any case, better planning for an immediate program of disarmament, demobilization, and reintegration would have put Libya on better footing once the fighting was over. In other cases where the light footprint is applied, it will be important to ensure not only that such a plan is in place but that the appropriate local actors have been fully convinced of its importance and have the capacity and will to carry it out. After the war, the El-Keib transitional government did not believe it had the authority to force the disarmament of the militias. In retrospect, however, the euphoria of victory may have provided the first transitional government with a better opportunity for rapid disarmament than was afforded the elected government that finally took the reins a year later, by which time the situation on the ground was already starting to sour.

Postwar planning was conducted by the allies throughout the operation, but in general, benefits would likely have been greater with better coordination and investment of resources. As is so often the case, allies had more immediate concerns to cope with as the war dragged on. Efforts to generate plans, build broad consensus for them, and develop native capabilities for executing these plans in the postwar environment could nevertheless have received more attention and resources. In August, the NTC did produce a constitutional declaration, but this was only a framework for Libya's democratic future, not a plan for overcoming its multiple and predictable postwar challenges. The lack of coordination between NTC efforts in Doha, UN efforts in New York, U.S. efforts in Washington, and the putative lead in London was in part the result of circumstance and personality, but it was a hindrance none the less. Similarly, more could have been done to develop the rebels' basic administrative and political capacities, not only in areas such as provision of public services but also in strategic communications, fiscal management, and on a more basic level, decision making, the lack of which plagued postwar Libya as leaders struggled with minimal bandwidth for the major tasks and decisions they urgently needed to undertake. Ideally, the decrepit state of Libya's institutions and its historical social, tribal, and regional fissures would have factored into planning for postconflict stabilization as soon as the prospect of intervention became real.

Another area in which some criticism is warranted is in the initial failure to appreciate fully how long Qaddafi might hold on to power. This diminished the impetus for consultation with Congress, which in turn reduced support on the Hill, complicated the White House's efforts to manage the intervention, and embroiled the Executive Branch in a debate over the War Powers Resolution. In France and Britain, leaders' expectations of a short war worked against the strategic patience necessary given the limits of their military capabilities and the political constraints under which they were operating.

There is, of course, ample precedent for leaders missing the mark in predicting how long an intervention will take or how stalwart a dictator will prove. In his scholarly work on the Kosovo conflict, Daalder himself criticized the Clinton administration for underestimating what it would take to get Milosevic to stand down. By the very complexity of what they seek to achieve and the human medium in which they are carried out, interventions – like all wars – will always be unpredictable. To expect perfect certainty about their outcomes – or even probabilities – beforehand is nearly impossible, and even if it were possible it would take far more time and resources than are normally available when the need to make a decision comes. At a minimum, however, leaders should recognize the possibility that things are highly unlikely to go as expected.

A final area in which more might have been done is in organizing the international community to negotiate a ceasefire. The possibility of a negotiated settlement was on the table throughout the conflict, and had things gone differently the war could have ended without Qaddafi's death. While it is unclear whether Qaddafi or his inner circle were ever close to accepting a negotiated deal, more probably could have been done to coordinate the multiple efforts to bring the conflict to a negotiated close, as the occasionally rancorous tone of official statements on the subject in July indicated. At the outset of future interventions, the leading governments should consider appointing and empowering an individual or group of sufficient stature to negotiate on its behalf. This will not, of course, ensure a negotiated settlement, but it should increase the chances thereof.

Whether a negotiated settlement was in fact the most desirable outcome in this particular case can be debated. A negotiated settlement would have had some obvious advantages, but having Qaddafi off the scene does as well. It would have been a big distraction and possibly disruptive if Qaddafi had remained alive and in the public eye after the war, but a negotiated settlement might have helped to deal with the difficult problem of reconciliation with the past, which continues to plague Libya today.

Implications for the Future

Shortcoming notwithstanding, the Libya intervention was a moderate success given what was achieved, how much it cost, and how challenging the operation was. It demonstrated that not all interventions need threaten national solvency and should help prevent a fatalistic mood about humanitarian crises or any overlearning of the lessons of Iraq and Afghanistan. It has important future implications for NATO, Europe, and the United States.

NATO after Libya

The Libya intervention took place at a time when the alliance was facing a daunting accumulation of challenges and a long-term erosion of confidence in its relevance on both sides of the Atlantic. A decade of war in Afghanistan had taken a serious toll on allied cohesion, political will, and public patience, not to mention military forces. The Iraq war had surfaced differences of strategic outlook both between the United States and key allies in Europe as well as among the Europeans themselves. Enlargement from fifteen to twenty-eight NATO members had increased the difficulty of building consensus and making decisions within the alliance. More recently, a global economic crisis and a near collapse of the Euro had forced European governments into deep defense cuts that threatened to exacerbate the capability gaps that NATO had been struggling to fix for years. In the United States, attention was shifting to Asia, a region in which NATO had never played a big role. Given the prospect of major defense spending cuts in the United States and the need to transform forces for the defense challenges of the new century, it is hardly surprising that questions about the durability of NATO, present in the best of times, were on the rise when the crisis broke out.

In these circumstances, NATO's relative success in Libya was a boon to the alliance. When Qaddafi fell and NATO operations over Libya ended, NATO leaders championed the operation as heralding a new, brighter future. Ambassador Daalder and Admiral Stavridis called it "NATO's success ... an extraordinary job, well done," hailing "an historic victory for the people of Libya who, with NATO's help, transformed their country from an international pariah into a nation with the potential to become a productive partner with the West."[23] Speaking in Tripoli, Secretary General Rasmussen said, "When the United Nations took the historic decision to protect you, NATO answered the call. We launched our operation faster than ever before.... We were effective, flexible and precise."[24] "There is no such thing as an opportune war," one senior U.S. military officer told us, "but it was a very opportune time for a war in NATO, because it showed that the alliance, without the U.S. standing at the helm, could do an operation, out of area, not in Europe."[25]

Credit for the intervention, however, should not go to NATO alone. The real victors were the *thuwwar*, who fought bravely and paid a price in

---

[23] Ivo H. Daalder and James G. Stavridis, "NATO's Success in Libya" *International Herald Tribune*, October 30, 2011.

[24] NATO Newsroom, "We Answered the Call – the End of Operation Unified Protector" October 31, 2011. http://www.nato.int/cps/en/natolive/news_80435.htm.

[25] Telephone interview with senior U.S. official, July 9, 2012.

blood that NATO did not and never would have. Without the rebel effort on the ground, Qaddafi would almost certainly not have fallen – in fact, the intervention would never have happened in the first place. They obviously deserve pride of place when apportioning credit.

That said, the *thuwwar* could never have won by themselves. Without NATO's intervention, their uprising would most likely have been snuffed out by Qaddafi's assault on Benghazi, and even if it had not, it would probably have become a low-level insurgency and dragged on for years. Without NATO's intervention, rebel forces would not have pushed the regime out of Misrata, and the uprisings in the Nafusah Mountains would have fizzled, had they started at all. NATO operations destroyed Qaddafi's capabilities to conduct major military offensives and terrorize his people from the air. At the same time, NATO cut off Qaddafi's supply lines from the outside world, making it nearly impossible for him to reequip his forces for further attacks. Aid to the rebels in the form of training, equipment, and intelligence allowed them both to coordinate their offensive strategically and to fight better tactically. Not least of all, NATO support boosted rebel morale and eroded the fighting spirit of Qaddafi's own forces. "I can't say we dislike or like NATO," said one *tha'ir* on the eastern front, but "without them we would have been finished."[26]

The intervention thus did not guarantee success, but it did create the strategic space in which rebels could develop, progress, and ultimately defeat the regime. This is an important conclusion, not least because in the aftermath of the intervention the significance of NATO's contribution was sometimes minimized by political leaders both in Libya and in NATO capitals in order to recognize the price the rebels paid in blood and to avoid delegitimizing the fragile postwar interim government. These may have been solid short-term rationales, and the *thuwwar* certainly deserved their credit, but in the longer term it is important that a more accurate narrative of the origins of the war emerge. An honest appreciation of the role of NATO and its

---

[26] Anthony Loyd, "Gaddafi Laughs Off Exile in Face of Rebel Attack on Key Town" *Times*, July 18, 2011, p. 29.

partners ought to serve as a foundation for strong and cooperative relations between Libya, Europe, and NATO in the future and a possible prophylactic against extremists that might seek to turn Libya against the West.

Despite NATO's accomplishments, after the war, there was much criticism of the alliance's performance and hand-wringing about its future. Allied capability shortfalls were a chief focus of such critiques. With the United States minimizing its role, allies had strained under the demands of sustained military operations, even against a relatively weak and politically inept enemy. Shortfalls in training and armaments, though long recognized, had suddenly become critical problems that participating militaries struggled to overcome. The United States had to strike a fine balance between keeping its role to a minimum and doing so little that it jeopardized operational effectiveness. Even after reducing the role of its fighter aircraft, therefore, the United States still flew more sorties and contributed more aircraft than any other ally, providing three-quarters of the ISR and tanker capacity, the vast majority of the capability used to destroy Qaddafi's air-defense system, much of the electronic warfare, the bulk of the strategists and targeteers, and the only armed drones.[27] All these capabilities were essential; without them the risks of military losses, civilian casualties, and general failure would have been an order of magnitude higher – so high as to have prohibited the operation.

Yet, NATO nations other than the United States did make important military contributions, demonstrating that NATO was more than just a political shell wrapped around the awesome military power of the United States. In the NATO phase of the operation, allies flew more than two-thirds of the overall sorties, 90 percent of the strike sorties, and managed a sustained contribution of about a hundred aircraft. Among them, France flew approximately one-third of the strike missions and the United Kingdom flew a little more than one-fifth, with Italy and Canada each coming in at around 10 percent. Belgium, Norway, and Denmark together accounted for another 22 percent. (Norway's share belies a very high operational tempo

[27] Daalder and Stavridis, "NATO's Victory in Libya."

IMPLICATIONS FOR THE FUTURE 191

for the shorter period during which it participated.) In Unified Protector, U.S. allies and partners destroyed 90 percent of the targets – a portion equal to the U.S. share in Kosovo. In Kosovo, many non-U.S. nations lacked precision-guided weapons, but in Libya nearly all the munitions had this capability.[28] Britain made significant contributions in ISR, although not without some difficulty. Greece and Italy contributed bases that significantly reduced the costs of the operation. Spain, Turkey, and the Netherlands all contributed additional air assets, while the majority of these countries, as well as Romania and Bulgaria, sent ships to the naval mission.[29] Several allies managed these contributions while simultaneously deploying significant forces in Afghanistan, as the French did in the case of Cote d'Ivoire.

As Secretary Gates emphasized in his controversial June speech in Brussels, the smaller allied militaries performed exceedingly well and overcame hurdles and shortfalls to make meaningful contributions to the civilian protection mission. Denmark, for example, provided strike aircraft and bunker busters that at one point in the operation were in short supply. Flying four F-16s from Sigonella air base (with six deployed), they dropped 930 bombs – 17 percent of the total munitions dropped in the campaign. These included conventional and laser-guided JDAMs as well as Paveways. On one occasion, the Danish bunker buster was even flown into a hole made by another bomb to destroy a multilevel bunker.[30] For its part, Belgium dropped 472 guided munitions in 620 sorties, and Norway dropped 588 guided munitions in 615 sorties.[31]

After capabilities, the lack of allied cohesion during the war also led some observers to predict a bleak future for the alliance. There is no question that cohesion could have been better. More than one policy maker interviewed for this book recalled having concerns at one time or

---

[28] Interview with senior U.S. official, February 6, 2012.
[29] Multiple sources.
[30] Bill Sweetman, "Reluctant Warriors" *Aviation Week & Space Technology*, January 2, 2012, p. 50.
[31] Christian F. Anrig, "The Belgian, Danish, Norwegian, and Dutch Experiences" in Karl P. Mueller, ed., *Precision and Purpose: Airpower in the Libyan Civil War*. Santa Monica, CA: RAND, forthcoming.

another about whether the whole thing would actually work. Only half the allies participated, and even fewer flew strike missions. The German abstention on the Security Council was a break with German foreign policy traditions. Although it took the lead in pushing for the intervention, France initially objected to using NATO for it. Turkey went back and forth. Poland opted out. Some allied political leaders wavered whereas others freelanced in an effort to bring the conflict to an end and seize the prize of peace. The underlying structural divisions within the alliance were less than over Iraq but greater than over Kosovo and, when viewed in light of the proximity of the operation to Europe and overall level of ambition, arguably greater than over Afghanistan, which is much farther away, much larger in scale, and therefore understandably controversial for most European publics. After the campaign, Secretary Clinton herself admitted having "periods of anguish and buyer's remorse," despite her satisfaction with the final outcome.[32]

Yet there is also a more positive story to tell behind these concerns, however legitimate they may be. The fact is that in spite of its internal discord and operations elsewhere in the world, the alliance still managed a generally successful seven-month operation, thereby showing greater flexibility than ever before. Even though Germany and others objected to the operation, they did not block it. That flexibility should help keep the alliance relevant. An alliance that marches in lock step on all the missions that matter to its members might be ideal, but in today's international environment it would be very difficult to realize. An alliance that acts only when all twenty-eight members agree on the strategy and policy alike would almost certainly never act at all.

Operation Unified Protector also demonstrated that NATO remained the best option for serious military action on behalf of the UN Security Council. The operation might have been conducted in a coalition-of-the-willing format, without drawing on NATO command structures, but it

---

[32] Joby Warrick, "Clinton's Efforts in Libyan War Called Vital" *Washington Post*, October 30, 2011, p. A1.

would have been more difficult. Further, integrating the Gulf partners and Sweden would have been more problematic given the lack of prior experience and the fact that the United States was not offering its command and control assets. Fewer partners would in turn have decreased the legitimacy of the operation and thus reduced the chances of success. As one officer explained, "If this had been a coalition to coalition transition, it would not have worked ... it was much simpler having existing structures, organization, people, all the standards that NATO brings, standards across the board, C2, weapons systems, etc. ... If you had done a transition to another entity you would have had to build it from scratch. The big strength of NATO is that it was there."[33]

The success of the intervention thus reminded leaders on both sides of the Atlantic that the alliance still had some utility. Success was reinforced by the fact that the underlying purpose of the intervention was broadly in line with the liberal democratic values that the alliance was originally forged to defend.

Looking ahead, a more difficult operation or an even larger role for countries other than the United States would obviously require improvements both in those capabilities that those countries contributed in Libya and especially in those capabilities that were lacking. A European contingent of twenty tanker aircraft would have made a very significant difference in Europe's contribution, for example. Pessimism is widespread about whether or not such improvements are within reach, given the secular downtrend in European defense spending and the possibility of further cuts resulting from the Euro crisis, but it should not be overdone.[34] France and Britain will purchase new aircraft, the only question is how long it will take and how far these purchases will go toward filling the gaps the operation revealed. Moreover, with European forces returning from Afghanistan, allies may find it easier to take on a greater role in a future operation such as Unified Protector or even a similar role in a more

---

[33] Ibid.
[34] Eric Schmitt, "NATO Sees Flaws in Air Campaign against Qaddafi" *New York Times*, April 14, 2012.

challenging scenario. France's decision to follow up its success in Libya with an intervention in Mali in 2013 – and its 2013 White Book on National Security – suggests that at a minimum, the will to take on a more significant role in international security is there. One can hope that the capabilities will not be too far behind.

The alliance will need to take concrete steps to build on its success. After all, while future interventions will be unique in their own ways, the prevailing political climate in Western capitals suggests that they will likely look more like the limited, air-dominant, broad coalition intervention in Libya than the multiyear U.S.-led ground force heavy operations in Afghanistan or Iraq.

Implications for Europe

After Libya, the outlook for the European Union's decade-long effort to build an EU alternative to NATO was rather gloomy. Toppling Qaddafi was exactly the kind of operation the EU had originally aspired to with its security and defense policy, but it had proven totally useless for this purpose. Ten years after its inception, the political and the military obstacles to realizing the EU's aspirations were thrown into stark relief.

As the crisis in Libya unfolded, the EU tried to find a role for itself, eventually developing plans to support UN humanitarian operations. Unfortunately, these never came to fruition. Planning took place in Rome, but in the end the initiative petered out when, after months of waiting, the UN failed to make a formal request for EU assistance and the EU planners had to pack up and go home. The divisions within Europe over the operation – as they were over stabilization deployments in Kosovo after recognition, in Iraq, and in other cases – were simply too great, especially with Germany opposed. As one European official pointed out in an interview for this book, a peculiar combination of British Euro-skepticism and Laborite pacifism made the EU's Vice President and High Representative Catherine Ashton the wrong person to push for an EU role, especially against the dogged Rasmussen.

Even had the EU found the political unity and leadership to pursue the EU option seriously, European capabilities gaps would have made an operation such as Unified Protector so much riskier that it would for all intents and purposes not have been possible. As the allies hashed out the lessons learned, some European officials would argue that the United States exaggerated Europe's shortfalls, perhaps in an effort to increase pressure on the alliance to purchase the Allied Ground Surveillance system that the United States was championing (and which was approved by the alliance in early 2012). These officials and experts recognized that the operation's ISR requirements had been provided in large part by the United States but suggested they had been so high because of the political requirement for very low civilian casualties and the information-rich environment in which the U.S. military had grown accustomed to operating in Iraq and Afghanistan. The implication was that the EU member states might have been able to make do without so much help from the United States, at least on ISR, had there been a greater political tolerance for civilian damage or had they been in charge, rather than the U.S. military. Such analysts also drew attention to the fact that initial French strikes against Benghazi took place prior to the destruction of Qaddafi's air defense by the United States, which they argue was less important than it was later made out to be by U.S. officials, given their knowledge of those defenses and ability to evade them with equipment such as the Rafale.

These arguments deserve a hearing, but they should not be taken too far. Very few European aircraft would really have been able to evade Qaddafi's air defenses without risk. It is also hard to see how the injunction to limit civilian deaths to the absolute minimum might have been relaxed, and European states were in no position to dictate a different conduct of operations for the U.S. military on which they relied so heavily.

Most seriously, perhaps, the Libya experience weakened one of the key rationales for developing EU military capabilities independent of NATO, namely that Europe needed a capacity for military action independent of the United States because the United States could not be counted on to support operations where U.S. interests were somewhat tangential yet European interests were intensely engaged. Libya demonstrated, to the contrary, that the United States is prepared, within NATO, to contribute enough capability to enable allied operations in situations where allies believe they have greater interests than the United States. It also demonstrated that the United States could do this without insisting on a dominant role.

Of course, the fact that the United States adopted this position in Libya is no guarantee it will do so again, but after Libya, justifying significant further investment in independent EU military capabilities would be more difficult, even as it underscores the need for greater European military capabilities at the national level.

If the implications of the experience were bad for the EU, the news was not all bad for Europe's national militaries, of which, after all, the EU and NATO are both comprised. French and British militaries were brought closer together. The defense cooperation treaties the two countries had signed in 2010 helped build momentum for the operation and were vindicated by the result. Although the tandem got off to a rough start, France and Britain eventually flew jointly crewed strike missions, and informal interviews in both services indicate an attitudinal change for the better as a result of the operation.[35] Working relationships between the French and British military and defense establishments grew stronger, improving the outlook for future cooperation, especially in North Africa and elsewhere on Europe's periphery.

The intervention also brought France closer to the alliance and vice versa. Unified Protector was the first NATO operation launched since France rejoined the NATO integrated military command structures at the Bucharest Summit in 2008, and France's decision (however tortured) not only to use NATO but to take a leading role in the operation was an important step closer to the alliance. The basic wisdom of the French reintegration into the NATO military command was affirmed. The broader

---

[35] Alastair Cameron, "The Channel Axis: France, the UK and NATO" in Adrian Johnson and Saqeb Mueen, eds., *Short War, Long Shadow*, RUSI Whitehall Report, 1–12.

exposure of the French military to NATO procedures increased their confidence therein. Somewhat ironically, given initial resistance to using NATO, Sarkozy would point to Libya during his subsequent election campaign to justify bringing France back into the NATO integrated military command.[36] France would not subsequently abandon its backing for the development of the EU's military capabilities, but the experience in Libya helped solidify the steps France has taken toward the alliance in recent years, validating to a large degree the 2008 French white paper on defense.

For Britain and France, the Libya operation was evidence of continued national relevance and strength at a time when doubts about that relevance were rising in the face of Europe's economic woes and deep cuts in already declining defense budgets. Success in Libya demonstrated that these challenges notwithstanding, there was still some fight left in "old" Europe. President Sarkozy and Prime Minister Cameron had shown that their countries could still play a critical and constructive role in global security. For its part, the United States had shown that it was willing to let them do so.

Lessons for the United States

The aspect of the Libya intervention that will likely be most remembered was President Obama's decision not only to limit the U.S. military role to airpower alone but to eschew the limelight and allow European allies – France and Britain in particular – to take the lead. Even if the reality was that the United States still did a great deal of the work behind the scenes – and in part because that was the reality – this decision was much criticized. It was a significant break from past U.S. practice, and even if polling suggested that many Republicans favored a similar formula for U.S. participation in the intervention, there was still a good deal of partisan criticism about "leading from behind."

---

[36] "La guerre de Libye et la tentation du 'storytelling' français" *Le Monde*, September 14, 2011, p. 24.

On one level, criticisms were of course a visceral reaction to the awkwardness of the phrase "leading from behind," coupled with a strong aversion to the idea that U.S. positions should be equivocal or nuanced in any way. But critics also voiced a number of more concrete objections to the approach. One of these was that if a mission is important enough to commit forces, the United States should do everything in its power to ensure success. In Libya, this would have meant keeping U.S. jets and bombers fully engaged in Unified Protector, firing more Tomahawks, sending in more drones, and possibly even inserting ground forces. As Senator McCain put it the day that Tripoli fell (notwithstanding his later, more magnanimous statements), "We regret that this success was so long in coming due to the failure of the United States to employ the full weight of our airpower."[37] Proponents of a more active role also argued that the reduced U.S. commitment signaled to other allies – especially in Eastern Europe – that it was acceptable to absent themselves from military operations. From this perspective, the risks restricting the U.S. role far outweighed the potential benefits. If the United States is prepared to wage war, critics argued, it should do so in such a way as to maximize the chances of success, even if that risks more blood and treasure.

Nevertheless, while the caveats the United States placed on its participation may have caused discomfort in some parts of Europe and increased operational risk to some degree, the approach reduced the political, military, and financial costs of toppling Qaddafi to U.S. taxpayers, enabled a broader coalition to participate in the war, and thus bolstered the legitimacy that was so crucial to success.

To begin with, it is unclear how much additional U.S. contribution – short of boots on the ground – would have accelerated Qaddafi's demise. The use of airpower was greatly constrained, after all. More U.S. ISR would have helped identify and strike more targets, and if the United

---

[37] "Statement by Senators McCain and Graham on End of the Qaddafi Regime in Libya" August 21, 2011.

States had added AC-130 gunships and provided more Predators it would likely have helped dislodge Qaddafi's forces from some positions more quickly, but it would not have accelerated the pace at which the *thuwwar* performance improved, which was an equally if not more important limiting factor.

The limited approach also reduced both the political risks and financial costs for a United States already severely stretched from the wars in Afghanistan and Iraq. Moreover, it tightened the screws on NATO allies and forced them to contribute more to achieving joint transatlantic security goals – a long-standing U.S. objective shared by Republican and Democratic administrations alike. The cost of Libya to the U.S. taxpayer was less than half the cost of the Kosovo air war and obviously several orders of magnitude less than the far longer wars in Afghanistan or Iraq. American troops were not placed in harm's way in Libya. Reducing costs entailed allowing other states to share the limelight and take credit for the operation's success; in so doing, they also risked taking more blame had it failed. Reducing the U.S. role may also have increased the legitimacy of the operation in a post-Iraq context.

The U.S. approach should furthermore encourage NATO allies to do more to maintain and strengthen their own military capabilities. President Obama's public statements limiting the U.S. role forced the allies to take the U.S. position seriously, as did the limited posture the United States eventually adopted in the theater itself. As long as the United States offers to cover all the military capabilities needed for alliance missions, the incentives for European parliaments to invest in sustaining, let alone improving, their own capabilities will always be limited. To be sure, limiting the U.S. role is not a sufficient condition for increasing European defense spending, but it can help. European experience in Libya has not had an impact on allied defense spending, but at a minimum it has stirred debate in European capitals about the wisdom of slashing defense budgets any further. As Sarkozy put it a few days after the fall of Tripoli, "President Obama has presented a new vision of American military involvement whose implication is that Europeans must assume more of their responsibilities."[38] When they do, this will ultimately strengthen NATO.

U.S. restraint, of course, will not be appropriate in all circumstances. In this case, it was possible because two key European allies – France and Britain – believed they had strong reasons for intervening, and because the operational difficulty was relatively low. Given a more challenging mission, further from Europe, the relative European role would necessarily diminish. While U.S. allies may eventually build military capabilities in areas that will allow them to play a similar role in a more demanding scenario, this will take years, and budgetary austerity might even mean they never do. For now, a repeat performance would only be possible in a case where European interests were again greater than U.S. interests and the military difficulty was low. The fact remains that the United States was the "indispensible nation" for these kinds of military operations. No other country – China, Russia, and India included – could have provided the capabilities that the United States did. The U.S. military was moreover able to provide these capabilities while heavily engaged in Afghanistan and in a war against Al-Qaeda in other far-flung parts of the world.

Notwithstanding these realities, the approach the United States took in this case should serve as a model for transatlantic security cooperation. In the future, the United States may sometimes find it difficult to commit the full power of its military to every NATO operation. Libya shows that it will not always need to. That the alliance can in some cases serve U.S. interests without a dominant U.S. role may be the single most important lesson of the Libya experience for the United States.

Libya and the Future of Liberal Intervention

The broadest lesson of the Libya case, however, is that limited military intervention can work, provided favorable conditions and limited objectives. In the wake of the major operations in Iraq and Afghanistan, the

---

[38] Nicolas Sarkozy, "19th Ambassadors' Conference: Speech by Nicolas Sarkozy, President of the Republic" Paris, August 31, 2011. As of May 8, 2012: http://www.franceonu.org/spip.php?article5730.

LIBYA AND THE FUTURE OF LIBERAL INTERVENTION 201

Figure 8.2 Free Libya graffiti in Tripoli, February 2013. Photo by author.

mood in the United States and Europe is again growing more insular and skeptical about intervention altogether. Many leaders have drawn the conclusion that military interventions will always be too costly to be worth it. Others have concluded meanwhile that intervention can never "work." But the Libya case demonstrates that even with a modest investment, intervention can sometimes help further the classical liberal values of human rights, representative government, and the rule of law. This is essential to recognize as leaders look ahead to a world in which budgets are tight, but globalization makes intervention sometimes unavoidable for moral and strategic reasons. This intervention did not guarantee a stable and democratic future for Libya, but it did stop a likely massacre, bolster perceptions of the west at a key moment in the region's history, and generally improve the economic and political outlook for most Libyans.

More specifically, Libya confirmed the value of what is sometimes referred to as the "Afghan Model," a military strategy in which precision airpower is coordinated by special forces on the ground to bring a decisive advantage to otherwise overmatched local rebel armies.[39] It did not show that it could work under all conditions, of course, or for all objectives. As discussed earlier in this chapter, several factors facilitated this intervention such as a relatively unified and motivated opposition.

Limited intervention will always be difficult for liberal democracies such as the United States, owing to the inherent tensions that arise from it. The use of force itself runs against the grain of the very same liberal political tradition that so highly values democracy and human rights and finds mass violence against civilians so abhorrent. As Stanley Hoffman observed in 1995, in the wake of the Rwanda massacre and amidst debate over whether or not to use force to end the war in Bosnia-Herzegovina, "The liberal vision has focused on one particular enemy: the Moloch of power, wherever found, either arbitrary and excessive at home or imperial and militaristic abroad." In other words, intense trepidation about power and the use of force are part of the DNA of liberal democracies. Hoffman pointed out, however, that there was another enemy to liberal values in today's world: "Not the violence that results in the clash of mighty powers or from the imposition of the power of the strong on the weak, but the violence that results from chaos from below."[40]

At home, the use of force raises liberal concerns about the growth of state power and, in the United States, the power of the executive branch in particular. The idea that any military action other than the strictly defensive inherently undermines republican forms of government is of ancient provenance, but it has perhaps been best expressed in postwar U.S. foreign policy by Senator Robert Taft in his critique of the Korean War in 1951.

---

[39] Richard B. Andres, Craig Wills, and Thomas Griffith Jr., "Winning with Allies: The Strategic Value of the Afghan Model" *International Security*, vol. 30, no. 3 (Winter 2005/06), pp. 124–160; Stephen Biddle, "Allies, Airpower, and Modern Warfare: The Afghan Model in Afghanistan and Iraq" *International Security*, vol. 30, no. 3, (Winter 2005/06) pp. 161–176. On Libya and the model, see Robert Farley, "Over the Horizon: Libya and the Afghan Model Revisited" *World Politics Review*, August 24, 2011.

[40] Stanley Hoffmann, "The Crisis of Liberal Internationalism" *Foreign Policy*, no. 98 (Spring 1995), pp. 159–177.

"More and more, as the world grows smaller," Taft wrote, "we are involved in the problems of foreign policy. If in the great field of foreign policy the president has the arbitrary and unlimited powers he now claims, then there is an end to freedom in the United States not only in the foreign field but in the great realm of domestic activity which necessarily follows any foreign commitments. The idea of freedom at home becomes very circumscribed indeed."[41] Such concerns are, it is worth noting, closely linked with concerns about the impact military interventions can have on national solvency, since interventions often turn out to be more expensive than expected and can generate upward pressure on the portion of national wealth that goes to the government. Such are precisely the concerns that have split the U.S. Republican party in recent years.

Heavy exertions of state power are also needed for postwar stabilization, and arguments for intervention thus often run into trouble with those currents of modern liberalism that are skeptical that state power can bring about meaningful change in human society. Contemporary neoliberal critics of intervention, for example, following in the footsteps of neoliberals such Friedrich Hayek, argue – not without some historical basis – that societies cannot simply be restructured from above; just as human nature would resist communist efforts at social engineering, so does it resist efforts by external powers to revamp existing institutions even in the name of liberal objectives.[42]

Liberal democratic leaders meanwhile confront the dilemma that while liberal ideals may be universal, decisions to intervene are always particular in nature. Liberal interventionists can easily become mired in a quandary when they choose to intervene, for example, to defend the rights of man in Libya but not in Syria, the Democratic Republic of

---

[41] Robert Taft, *A Foreign Policy for Americans* (New York: Doubleday, 1951), p. 23.
[42] Friedrich Hayek, *The Road to Serfdom* (Chicago: University of Chicago Press, 1944). For a leading contemporary neoliberal view of the Libya intervention, see Ted Galen Carpenter, "Another War of Choice" *National Interest*, March 18, 2011. For a discussion of the issue, see Christopher S. Chivvis, *The Monetary Conservative: Jacques Rueff and Twentieth Century Free Market Thought* (De Kalb: Northern Illinois University Press, 2010), chapter 4.

Congo, Darfur, or elsewhere that governments wantonly kill their people. This inconsistency in turn encourages the cynical view that liberal interventions are usually conspiracies that cloak selfish and sinister national interests. Given that history is replete with such examples – most recently Russia's 2008 invasion of Georgia, and some would argue, the 2003 U.S. invasion of Iraq – the concern is perhaps sometimes warranted. The motives for intervention will almost always need to include some degree of selfish national interest if political will is to be sustained and the operation is to be brought to fruition. But this does not mean that sinister motives always underlie interventions or that security and humanitarian motivations cannot and do not coexist. Indeed, most countries will be propelled forward toward intervention by a mix of both hard security interests and a desire to stand up for the values they believe in.

These genetic constraints on intervention will often force leaders who interevene to justify their actions with maximalist goals. Unfortunately, these are impossible to achieve with a limited use of force – indeed, they may be impossible to achieve with a maximum use of force. Limited intervention can only work when leaders exercise restraint and accept that the cost of doing a little good will likely be criticism for not having done more. America's foreign policy culture may make limited and nuanced policies hard to sell, but this does not mean that leaders should not try to do so. Limited interventions can achieve security objectives and further liberal goals, but countries like Libya should not be expected to become flourishing democracies overnight as a result.

In general, Libya should remain a positive, if smaller-scale, antidote to the sense of helplessness and cynicism about American power setting in after the deeply trying experiences of Iraq and Afghanistan, and this is a good thing. This was a small war, but one in which the United States ultimately managed to balance its long-standing providential impulse to bring freedom to others with a pragmatism born of the challenges and failures the country had faced in Iraq and Afghanistan. The balance struck respected America's Wilsonian tradition, while recognizing the inherent limits even a superpower faces when it tries to transform and remodel other nations. Libya should increase the chances that the United States and its allies will take action against other tyrants or in failing states in the future – though by no means should guarantee they will do so in every case or even in most.

Insofar as Libya gives encouragement to future interventions, the difficulties encountered in winning this small war should still inspire caution and reserve. Libya demonstrates that the light footprint can be moderately successful under certain circumstances and provided the objectives are limited. It does not tell us much about how useful the light footprint will be under significantly more challenging conditions, or when the objective is broader and more transformational, as was the case at the outset in Iraq and Afghanistan. The histories of those experiences are better guides here.

Liberal and cultural critics of military intervention who argue that democracy can never be introduced at the point of a spear may still be right in many contemporary cases, but this does not mean that military power does not have a role to play in toppling tyrants and saving people from atrocities and major humanitarian disasters. It is wrong to assume that the West's military superiority gives it the capability to refashion societies on its own model, but equally wrong to abrogate the responsibility to take the actions that we can take, however imperfect, to uphold the values in which our model is grounded. In Libya this is what was accomplished. The results are far from perfect and postwar stabilization has faltered, but ultimately the choice to intervene was the right one.

Appendix A Operation Unified Protector Participating Nations

STRIKER GROUP PLUS NAVAL OPS

Canada
Denmark
France
Italy
United States
United Kingdom

STRIKER GROUP – AIR OPERATIONS ONLY

Belgium
Norway

NON-NATO AIRPOWER CONTRIBUTORS

Jordan
Qatar
United Arab Emirates
Sweden

NO FLY ZONE PLUS NAVAL OPERATIONS

Greece
Netherlands
Spain
Turkey

NAVAL OPERATIONS

    Bulgaria
    Romania
    Turkey

NONPARTICIPATING NATO MEMBERS

    Albania
    Czech Republic
    Estonia
    Croatia
    Germany
    Hungary
    Iceland
    Luxembourg
    Latvia
    Lithuania
    Poland
    Portugal
    Slovakia
    Slovenia

Appendix B Operation Unified Protector Basing

AKROTIRI, CYPRUS

1 UK E3D Sentry (AWACS)[1]
1 UK Sentinel[2]
1 Nimrod R-1[3]

ARAXOS, GREECE

6 BE F-16[4]

SOUDA BAY, CRETE

16 FR Mirage[5] (redeployed from Corsica in April)
1 FR Atlantique[6]
6 NO F-16[7]

---

[1] Ministry of Defense, "Libya: Operation ELLAMY: Background Briefing." http://www.mod.uk/DefenceInternet/FactSheets/MilitaryOperations/LibyaOperationEllamyBackgroundBriefing.htm.
[2] Ibid.
[3] Ibid.
[4] Belgian Ministry of Defence. http://www.mil.be/def/subject/index.asp?LAN=fr&ID=1982.
[5] French Ministry of Defense, "L'opération Harmattan." http://www.defense.gouv.fr/operations/autres-operations/operation-harmattan-libye/dossier/l-operation-harmattan.
[6] Ibid.
[7] Office of the Norwegian Prime Minister, "Norway to Participate in Operations in Libya" Press Release no. 053–11, March 23, 2011.

6 QA Mirage 2000[8]
2 US RC-135 Rivet Joint[9]

AVIANO, ITALY

6 JOR F-16[10]
18 US F-16[11]
5 US EA-18G Growler[12]

SIGONELLA, ITALY

1 CA CP-140 Aurora[13]
6 DE F-16[14]
FR Harfang UAV[15]
5 FR Rafale[16]
8 SW Gripen (reduced to 5 on June 8)[17]
1 SW C-130 Hercules[18]
1 TUR KC-135 ("non-combat")[19]

---

[8] French Ministry of Defense, "L'opération Harmattan." http://www.defense.gouv.fr/operations/autres-operations/operation-harmattan-libye/dossier/l-operation-harmattan.

[9] Karl P. Mueller, ed., *Precision and Purpose: Airpower in the Libyan Civil War*. Santa Monica: RAND, 2013, Appendix B.

[10] Ibid.

[11] Ibid.

[12] Ibid.

[13] "Canadian Crews Home from Libya Mission" The Toronto Star, November 6, 2011, p. A7.

[14] Danish Ministry of Defense, "The Libya Operation." http://www.fmn.dk/eng/allabout/Pages/TheLibyaoperation.aspx.

[15] Martin Streetly, "France Deploys Harfang UAV over Libya" International Defence Review, IHS Global Limited, August 31, 2011.

[16] French Ministry of Defense, "L'opération Harmattan." http://www.defense.gouv.fr/operations/autres-operations/operation-harmattan-libye/dossier/l-operation-harmattan.

[17] "Swedish Gripens Deliver 37% of Libyan Reconnaissance" Defenseweb.com, August 8, 2011. http://www.defenceweb.co.za/index.php?option=com_content&view=article&id=17886:swedish-gripens-deliver-37-of-libyan-reconnaissance-reports&catid=35:Aerospace&Itemid=107.

[18] Ibid.

[19] Karl P. Mueller, ed., *Precision and Purpose: Airpower in the Libyan Civil War*. Santa Monica: RAND, 2013, Appendix B.

APPENDIX B

6 TUR F-16 ("non-combat")[20]
3 US RQ-4 Global Hawk UAV[21]
US MQ-1 Predator UAV[22]

TRAPANI, ITALY

4 IT Tornados[23]
4 IT Typhoon[24]
7 CA F-18[25]
2 CA CC-150 Polaris (refueling) or 2 CA CC-130 Hercules[26]
3 NATO E-3A Sentry[27]

DECIMOMANU, SARDINIA, ITALY

4 SP F-18[28]
1 SP B-707 refueling[29]
6 UAE F-16s[30] (later moved to Sigonella)
6 UAE Mirage 2000[31] (later moved to Sigonella)
6 NL F-16s[32]

---

[20] Ibid.
[21] Ibid.
[22] Ibid.
[23] Italian Ministry of Defense, "Continuano le missioni degli aerei e delle navi italiane nell 'ambito dell' operazione 'Unified Protector'" April 2, 2011. http://www.difesa.it/Operazioni_Militari/operazioni-internazionali_concluse/Libia-odissea-alba/News/2011-04/Pagine/missionideaereinaviUP.aspx.
[24] Ibid.
[25] Canadian Ministry of Defense, "Operation Mobile." http://www.comfec-cefcom.forces.gc.ca/pa-ap/ops/mobile/index-eng.asp.
[26] Ibid.
[27] Karl P. Mueller, ed., *Precision and Purpose: Airpower in the Libyan Civil War*. Santa Monica: RAND, 2013, Appendix B.
[28] Revista Española de Defensa, "Operacíon international en Libia" March, 2011. http://www.defensa.gob.es/en/Galerias/areasTematicas/misiones/fichero/Operacion-internacional-en-Libia.pdf.
[29] Ibid.
[30] AFP, "UAE Fighter Jets Arrive in Italy for Libya Operations" March 27, 2011.
[31] Ibid.
[32] Dutch Ministry of Defense, "F-16 Detachment Returns Home" November 9, 2011. http://www.defensie.nl/english/latest/news/2011/11/09/48190635/F_16_detachment_returns_home.

GIOIA DE COLLE, ITALY

16 UK Tornado GR.4[33]
10 UK Typhoon FGR.4[34]

AVORD, FRANCE

1 FR E-3F AWACS[35]

SOLENZARA, CORSICA, FRANCE

7 FR Rafale[36]
3 FR Mirage F1[37]

ISTRES, FRANCE

6 FR C-135[38]

MORON, SPAIN

15 US KC-135 Stratotanker (also based in the United Kingdom and France)[39]
4 US KC-10 Extender[40]

ROTA, SPAIN

1 US E-8C JSTARS[41]
2 US E-3B/C Sentry[42]

---

[33] "United Kingdom Defence and Security Report" Business Monitor International, April 2012.
[34] Ibid.
[35] French Ministry of Defense, "L'opération Harmattan." http://www.defense.gouv.fr/operations/autres-operations/operation-harmattan-libye/dossier/l-operation-harmattan.
[36] "Omni-potent jet" Flight International, June 14, 2011.
[37] Ibid.
[38] French Ministry of Defense, "L'opération Harmattan." http://www.defense.gouv.fr/operations/autres-operations/operation-harmattan-libye/dossier/l-operation-harmattan.
[39] Karl P. Mueller, ed., *Precision and Purpose: Airpower in the Libyan Civil War*. Santa Monica: RAND, 2013, Appendix B.
[40] Ibid.
[41] Ibid.
[42] Ibid.

APPENDIX B

BRIZE NORTON, UNITED KINGDOM

UK VC-10[43]
UK Tristar[44]

SEA-BASING

Charles de Gaulle (FR): *2 E-2C Hawkeye; 8 Rafale; 6 Super Étandard*
Tonnere (FR): *Tigre helicopter*
Giuseppe Garibaldi (IT): *4 AV-8B Harrier; SH-3D CSAR helicopter*
HMS *Ocean* (UK): *Apache helicopters*
USS *Bataan* (US): *AV-8B Harrier; CH-53 helicopter; V-22 Osprey*[45]

---

[43] Ministry of Defense, "Libya: Operation ELLAMY: Background Briefing." http://www.mod.uk/DefenceInternet/FactSheets/MilitaryOperations/LibyaOperationEllamyBackgroundBriefing.htm.

[44] Ibid.

[45] Kearsarge and Bataan ARG Public Affairs, "Kearsarge and Bataan Amphibious Ready Groups Complete Turnover" United States Navy, April 28, 2011.

Appendix C Regime Defections

FEBRUARY 20

- Dr. Ali Errishi, minister of immigration and expatriates, resigns and says that Gaddafi should step down.[1]
- Major General Suleiman Mahmoud defects.[2]
- Hussein Sadiq al Musrati, a "senior diplomat in China," steps down in an on-air interview with Al Jazeera and "call[s] on all diplomatic staff to resign."[3]
- Unidentified members of an army unit known as the "Thunderbolt squad" defect and say they have engaged in combat with Gaddafi's elite guards.[4]

FEBRUARY 21

- Justice Minister Mustafa Mohamed Abud Al Jalil resigns.[5]
- Deputy Permanent Representative to the UN Ibrahim O. Dabbashi leads twelve other members of Libya's UN mission in New York in renouncing Gaddafi.[6]

---

[1] The National Press Club, "Global Media Center: Dr. Ali Errishi." http://press.org/events/global-media-center-dr-ali-errishi.

[2] *Wall Street Journal* staff, "Defections from the Libyan Regime" *Dispatches* Weblog, entry posted February 23, 2011. http://blogs.wsj.com/dispatch/2011/02/23/defections-from-the-libyan-regime.

[3] Google, "AFP: Libyan Diplomat in China Resigns over Unrest: Report." http://www.google.com/hostednews/afp/article/ALeqM5gsfRzZOlaHX2n1PDDMG5pMt-5zyg?docId=CNG.6edc8c32f659a479171f46fdb59fcead.231.

[4] Reuters, "Libya Unrest Spreads to Tripoli as Benghazi Erupts." http://uk.reuters.com/article/2011/02/20/uk-libya-protests-idUKTRE71G0AW20110220.

[5] Reuters, "Libyan Minister Quits over Crackdown – Report." http://af.reuters.com/article/commoditiesNews/idAFLDE71K1PJ20110221.

[6] *The New York Times*, "Libya's U.N. Diplomats Break with Qaddafi." http://www.nytimes.com/2011/02/22/world/africa/22nations.html?_r=1.

APPENDIX C

- Ambassador to India Ali al-Essawi resigns.[7]
- Abdel Moneim al-Huny, permanent representative to the Arab League, resigns.[8]
- Two fighter jet pilots, one later identified as Col. Ali Faraj Alrabti, fly across the border into Malta, apparently after having been ordered to fire on protesters.[9]
- Libya's ambassador to Belgium (name unclear) resigns on Al Jazeera.[10]
- Saleh Ali Al Majbari and Jumaa Farris, counselors at the Libyan embassy in the United States, denounce Gaddafi and resign.[11]
- In Boston, Ali Richi, minister for immigration, denies he has resigned yet, but calls for all Libyan ambassadors to continue their work independently of the regime.[12]
- Unidentified members of the Libyan army are reported to be fighting forces loyal to Gaddafi.[13]
- Central Bank Governor Farhat Bengdara flies to Turkey, where he later announces his defection.[14]

FEBRUARY 22

- Interior Minister Abdel Fattah Younes al-Abidi resigns and urges the army to support protestors.[15]
- Ambassador to the United States Ali Aujali defects but says he will retain his post to serve the Libyan people.[16]

---

[7] RIA Novosti, "Libya's Ambassadors to India, Arab League Resign in Protest against Government." http://en.rian.ru/world/20110221/162698818.html.

[8] Ibid.

[9] *Times of Malta*, "Updated: Libyan Fighter Jets Arrive in Malta." http://www.timesofmalta.com/articles/view/20110221/local/two-libyan-fighter-jets-arrive-in-malta-two-helicopters-land.351349.

[10] *Global Arab Network*, "Libyan Ambassador to Belgium, Head of Mission to EU Resigns." http://www.english.globalarabnetwork.com/201102219940/Libya-Politics/libyan-ambassador-in-belgium-head-of-mission-to-eu-resigns.html.

[11] Al Jazeera staff, "Live Blog – Libya," *Live Blog – Libya* Welblog, entry posted February 21, 2011. http://blogs.aljazeera.com/blog/middle-east/live-blog-libya.

[12] Ibid.

[13] BBC News, "Muammar Gaddafi's State TV Appearance." http://www.bbc.co.uk/news/world-middle-east-12532795.

[14] Reuters, "Libyan Bankers Offer Support to Rebel Council." http://www.reuters.com/article/2011/07/16/us-libya-turkey-idUSTRE76F1G520110716.

[15] *Wall Street Journal* staff, "Defections from the Libyan Regime," *Dispatches* Weblog, entry posted February 23, 2011. http://blogs.wsj.com/dispatch/2011/02/23/defections-from-the-libyan-regime.

[16] Ibid.

- Ambassador to France Mohamed Salaheddine Zarem announces he backs the revolution.[17]
- Abdoulsalam El Qallali, Paris-based ambassador to UNESCO, backs the revolution without resigning.[18]
- Ambassador to Bangladesh Ahmed Attia Hamed Elimam resigns.[19]
- Staff of the Libyan consulate in Alexandria, Egypt, lower the national flag and join nearby antiregime protests.[20]
- Nuri al-Mismari, chief of state protocol and a Gaddafi ally for nearly forty years, resigns.[21]
- Two staff members of the embassy in Hungary join local antiregime protests. The embassy begins flying the old Libyan tricolor flag on March 21.[22]
- Staff at the Libyan embassy in Poland either resign or disavow links to Gaddafi (unclear).[23]

FEBRUARY 23

- Youssef Sawani, senior aid to Saif al-Islam Gaddafi, defects.[24]
- Ambassador to Australia no longer supports Gaddafi but stops short of formally resigning.[25]
- Ihab Al-Mismari, a counselor in Ottawa and son of the recently defected protocol chief, resigns.[26]

---

[17] Reuters, "Libyan Ambassadors in France back Revolt." http://af.reuters.com/article/libyaNews/idAFLDE71L1ZU20110222.

[18] Ibid.

[19] DNA, "Libya's Bangladesh Envoy Resigns." http://www.dnaindia.com/world/report_libya-s-bangladesh-envoy-resigns_1511579.

[20] Reuters, "Staff of Libyan Consulate in Egypt Lower Flag." http://www.reuters.com/article/2011/02/22/libya-protests-egypt-flag-idUSLDE71L1OJ20110222.

[21] Reuters, "Factbox: Diplomats Desert Libya's Gaddafi." http://www.reuters.com/article/2011/02/23/us-libya-diplomacy-defection-idUSTRE71M4DS20110223.

[22] Index, "Tüntettek Líbia budapesti követségénél." http://galeria.index.hu/kulfold/2011/02/22/tuntettek_libia_budapesti_kovetsegenel/?current_image_num=7&image_size=l;%20http://daemon.indapass.hu/http/session_request?redirect_to=http%3A%2F%2Findex.hu%2Fkulfold%2F2011%2F02%2F18%2Flazongas_az_arab_vilagban%2Fa_lazadok_zaszloja_leng_a_budapesti_kovetsegen%2F&partner_id=bloghu.

[23] Al Jazeera, "Libyan Diplomats Defect en masse." http://www.aljazeera.com/news/africa/2011/02/201122275739377867.html.

[24] Al Jazeera, "Gaddafi Defiant as State Teeters." http://www.aljazeera.com/news/africa/2011/02/20112235434767487.html.

[25] *The Age*, "Australia Recognises Libyan Rebels." http://www.theage.com.au/national/libyan-embassys-stance-on-upheaval-unclear-20110222-1b42p.html.

[26] *Oman Tribute*, "Benghazi Residents Destroy Mercenaries' Barrack." http://www.omantribune.com/index.php?page=news&id=85675&heading=Middle%20East.

APPENDIX C

- Omran Zwed, cultural counselor to Australia, declares: "We represent the Libyan people and no longer the Libyan regime."[27]
- Led by counselor Osama Ahmed, staff at the embassy in Malaysia condemn crackdown and raise pre-Gaddafi flag.[28]
- Salaheddin M. El Bishari, ambassador to Indonesia, formally resigns and simultaneously quits his role as envoy to Singapore, Brunei, and ASEAN.[29]

FEBRUARY 24

- Top security official and Gaddafi cousin, Ahmed Gadhaf al-Dam, travels to Cairo and defects.[30]
- Rumors circulate that several provincial governors have stayed in Libya and defected to the opposition.[31]

FEBRUARY 25

- Abdul-Rahman al-Abbar, prosecutor general, resigns and joins opposition.[32]
- Mohamed Amer Bayou, Gaddafi spokesman, resigns.[33]
- The Libyan delegation to the Arab League in Cairo renounces links to Gaddafi and says it now represents the people.[34]
- Reports surface that the entire Libyan embassy in New Delhi has defected.[35]

---

[27] Reuters, "Factbox: Diplomats Desert Libya's Gaddafi." http://www.reuters.com/article/2011/02/23/us-libya-diplomacy-defection-idUSTRE71M4DS20110223.

[28] Ibid.

[29] *The Jakarta Post*, "Libyan Ambassador to RI Quits in Protest." http://www.thejakartapost.com/news/2011/02/23/libyan-ambassador-ri-quits-protest.html.

[30] Al Jazeera staff, "Live Blog – Libya Feb 24," *Live Blog – Libya* Welblog, entry posted February 24, 2011. http://blogs.aljazeera.com/blog/africa/live-blog-libya-feb-24.

[31] BBC News, "BBC News – Libya protests/ Gaddafi embattled by opposition gains." http://www.bbc.co.uk/news/world-africa-12564104.

[32] Reuters, "Libya's Prosecutor General Says Joins Opposition." http://www.reuters.com/article/2011/02/25/libya-prosecutor-idUSWEB186120110225.

[33] Asharq Alawsat, "Libyan Officials Abandon Gaddafi Regime en masse." http://www.asharq-e.com/news.asp?id=24296.

[34] *The Guardian staff*, "Libya in Turmoil – Friday 25 February." *Middle East Live* Weblog. Entry posted February 25, 2011. http://www.guardian.co.uk/world/blog/2011/feb/25/libya-turmoil-gaddafi-live.

[35] Ibid.

- Abdurrahman Mohamed Shalgham, ambassador to the UN, denounces Gaddafi in a speech at the UN headquarters.[36]
- The resignation of the entire Libyan mission to the UN in Geneva is followed by the resignations of most representatives in New York.[37]
- Ali Ibrahim Emdored, ambassador to Portugal, resigns in protest.[38]

FEBRUARY 26

- Issa Ashur, ambassador to Somalia, calls on Gaddafi to step down.[39]
- Sad Mujbir, ambassador to Iran, calls on Gaddafi to step down.[40]

MARCH 1

- Embassy in Malta defects.[41]
- Brigadier General Musa'ed Ghaidan Al Mansouri, head of the Al Wahat Security Directorate, defects.[42]
- Brigadier General Hasan Ibrahim Al Qarawi defects.[43]
- Brigadier General Dawood Issa Al Qafsi defects, claims he is bringing many other officers with him.[44]

MARCH 3

- Saad Bakar, the second ranking Libyan diplomat in Namibia, defects.[45]

---

[36] NPR, "Libyan Ambassador Denounces Gadhafi at U.N." http://www.npr.org/blogs/thetwo-way/2011/02/25/134069630/libyan-ambassador-denounces-gadhafi-at-u-n.

[37] *The Guardian* staff, "Libya in Turmoil – Friday 25 February." *News Blog* Weblog. Entry posted February 25, 2011. http://www.guardian.co.uk/world/blog/2011/feb/25/gaddafi-libya-live-blog#l block-1.

[38] *The Jerusalem Post*, "Libyan Ambassador to Portugal Quits in Protest." http://www.jpost.com/Headlines/Article.aspx?id=209872.

[39] BBC News, "As It Happened: Libya Revolt on Saturday." http://news.bbc.co.uk/2/hi/programmes/9408497.stm.

[40] Ibid.

[41] *Times of Malta*, "Jubilation as Pre-Gaddafi Flag Is Raised on Libyan Embassy." http://www.timesofmalta.com/articles/view/20110301/local/old-libyan-flag-taken-into-libyan-embassy.352598.

[42] http://blogs.aljazeera.net/live/africa/live-blog-libya-march-1.

[43] Ibid.

[44] Ibid.

[45] *The Namibian*, "Libyan Diplomats in Namibia Defect." http://www.namibian.com.na/index.php?id=28&tx_ttnews%5Btt_news%5D=86190&no_cache=1.

MARCH 8

- The Libyan embassy in the Netherlands makes no official statement but raises the pre-Gaddafi national flag.[46]

MARCH 11

- The Libyan embassy in Switzerland defects.[47]

MARCH 13

- Colonel Ali Atiyya, a pilot based out of Miteega Air Base in Tripoli, defects.[48]

MARCH 20

- Minister of Foreign Affairs Moussa Koussa defects to Britain.[49]

APRIL 7

- Minister of Energy Omar Fathi bin Shatwan flees to Malta, claims other members of Qaddafi's inner circle also want to defect but fear for their lives.[50]

MAY 11

- Faraj Saeed al-Aribi, Libya's consul in Cairo, quits his post to join the rebels.[51]

---

[46] NOS, "Vlag revolutie op consulaat Libië." http://nos.nl/artikel/224201-vlag-revolutie-op-consulaat-libie.html.

[47] Swissinfo, "Libyan Embassy Cuts Ties to Gaddafi Regime." http://www.swissinfo.ch/eng/news_digest/Libyan_embassy_cuts_ties_to_Gaddafi_regime.html?cid=29706010.

[48] Al-Jazeera, Video of Col 'Attiya Announcing His Defection, March 13, 2011. http://www.youtube.com/watch?v=cflBa7DSVzU.

[49] *The Telegraph*, "Libyan Foreign Minister Moussa Koussa Defects to Britain." http://www.telegraph.co.uk/news/worldnews/africaandindianocean/libya/8417350/Libyan-foreign-minister-Moussa-Koussa-defects-to-Britain.html.

[50] *The Guardian*, "Muammar Gaddafi's Former Energy Minister Flees to Malta." http://www.guardian.co.uk/world/2011/apr/07/shatwan-flees-libya-malta.

[51] Reuters, "Libyan Consul in Cairo Joins Rebel Ranks – TV." http://af.reuters.com/article/egyptNews/idAFLDE74A2JO20110511.

MAY 12

- Ammar Bilqasem, air force brigadier and military attaché in the UAE, quits his post to join the rebel ranks.[52]

MID-MAY

- Shukri Ghanem, oil minister, defects. He is later found dead in the Danube River in Vienna in April 2012.[53]

MAY 26

- Al Hadi Hadeiba, ambassador to EU and Benelux countries, defects.[54]

MAY 30

- Five unspecified generals (including Gen. Melud Massoud Halasa and Yahmet Salah), two colonels, and a major from the Libyan army turn up in Italy, saying they have defected and joined the rebels.[55]
- Reported 120 officers join these generals in defecting.[56]

JUNE 5

- Al-Amin Manfur, labor minister, defects while at a Geneva meeting of the International Labor Organization and announces support for the NTC.[57]

JUNE 9

- An unspecified general defects to Tunisia, taking ten other ranking officers with him.[58]

---

[52] Al Arabiya News, "Libyan Military Attaché in UAE Defects to Rebels as NATO Pounds Qaddafi Compound." http://english.alarabiya.net/articles/2011/05/12/148802.html.

[53] BBC News, "Libya ex-Minister Shukri Ghanem Dead in Danube River." http://www.bbc.co.uk/news/world-europe-17889660.

[54] Reuters, "Libya's Ambassador to EU Defects – EU." http://af.reuters.com/article/libyaNews/idAFLDE74P2FO20110526.

[55] Huffington Post, "5 Libyan Army Generals Defect." http://www.huffingtonpost.com/2011/05/30/5-libyan-army-generals-defect_n_868768.html.

[56] Reuters, "Over 100 Libyan Army Members Defect from Gaddafi." http://www.reuters.com/article/2011/05/30/us-libya-officers-idUSTRE74T41820110530.

[57] *The New York Times*, "Qaddafi Compound Is Pounded in Day Raid." http://www.nytimes.com/2011/06/08/world/africa/08tripoli.html?_r=1.

[58] *Times of Malta*, "Libyan General among Refugees in Tunisia." http://www.timesofmalta.com/articles/view/20110609/world/libyan-general-among-refugees-in-tunisia.369808.

APPENDIX C

JUNE 13

- Longtime Gaddafi supporter Sassi Garada defects and is rumored to be in either England or Switzerland.[59]

JUNE 16

- Ibrahim Wafi, brigadier general, air marshal, and defense attaché to Portugal, defects.[60]

JUNE 20

- Brigadier General Fouad El Idrissi defects along with thirty-four followers.[61]

JUNE 26

- The Libyan national football team defects while in Mali for a match, later traveling to Tunisia.[62]

JULY 4

- An unspecified group of officers defects and joins rebels in a strategic western town of Yefren as NATO steps up bombing.[63]

AUGUST 15

- Interior Minister Nasser al-Mabroud Abdullah, who had been appointed in the wake of his predecessor al-Abidi's defection, flies to Egypt to defect.[64]

---

[59] The Huffington Post, "Sassi Garada, Gaddafi Insider, Reportedly Defects." http://www.huffingtonpost.com/2011/06/13/sassi-garada-defects-gaddafi-insider-flees_n_876181.html.

[60] http://www.youtube.com/watch?v=H-j7Zs–pjw Not verified, but likely authentic.

[61] http://www.youtube.com/watch?v=0IRbNXvAJic Not verified, but likely authentic.

[62] CBS News, "Libya's National Football Team Defects." http://www.cbsnews.com/2100-202_162-20074459.html.

[63] Al Arabiya News, "More Qaddafi Officers Defect as NATO Steps Up Airstrikes." http://www.alarabiya.net/articles/2011/07/05/156133.html.

[64] The Guardian, "Libya's Interior Minister Flies to Egypt in Apparent Defection." http://www.guardian.co.uk/world/2011/aug/15/libya-interior-minister-cairo-egypt.

AUGUST 19

- Abdel Salam Jalloud, former Libyan prime minister who was sacked by Gaddafi in the 1990s, flees to rebel-held Zintan to join the opposition.[65]

AUGUST 20

- Omran Abukraa, Libya's relatively recently appointed oil minister, does not return from a trip to Tunisia.[66]

AUGUST 21

- Baghdadi Mahmudi, secretary of the General People's Committee (prime minister), escapes to Tunisia; extradited back to Libya to face trial in 2012.[67]

AUGUST 22

- Ambassador to Namibia Salem Mohamed Krayem and the rest of embassy staff declare loyalty to revolution.[68]
- Embassy in Japan begins flying the rebel flag.[69]
- Embassy in Ethiopia begins flying the rebel flag under the direction of Ambassador Ali Awidan.[70]

LATE AUGUST

- Most of Libya's 165 diplomatic missions now back the NTC.[71]

---

[65] *The Telegraph*, "Libya: Former Prime Minister Defects, Dealing Col Gaddafi Another Blow." http://www.telegraph.co.uk/news/worldnews/africaandindianocean/libya/871272.6/Libya-former-prime-minister-defects-dealing-Col-Gaddafi-another-blow.html.

[66] Reuters, "Oil Minister Does not Return to Libya-Tunisia: Source." http://uk.reuters.com/article/2011/08/20/us-libya-minister-oil-idUKTRE77J0WV20110820.

[67] Reuters, "Libyan PM in Hotel in Southern Tunisia: Sources." http://www.reuters.com/article/2011/08/22/us-libya-pm-tunisia-idUSTRE77L2K820110822.

[68] *The Namibian*, "Libyan Diplomats in Namibia Defect." http://www.namibian.com.na/index.php?id=28&tx_ttnews%5Btt_news%5D=86190&no_cache=1.

[69] Huffington Post, "'Die, Gadhafi': Libya's Embassies Abroad Defect." http://www.huffingtonpost.com/huff-wires/20110824/libyan-embassies-defect.

[70] Ibid.

[71] Inquirer, "'Die, Gadhafi': Libyan Embassies in Manila, Other Countries Defect." http://globalnation.inquirer.net/10211/die-gadhafi-libyas-embassies-abroad-defect.

Appendix D Contact Group

(As of London Meeting, March 29, 2011)

COUNTRIES

- Albania
- Belgium
- Bulgaria
- Canada
- Croatia
- Czech Republic
- Denmark
- Estonia
- France
- Germany
- Greece
- Hungary
- Iceland
- Italy
- Iraq
- Jordan
- Kuwait
- Latvia
- Lebanon
- Lithuania
- Luxembourg
- Malta
- Morocco
- Netherlands
- Norway
- Poland
- Portugal
- Qatar
- Romania

Slovakia
Slovenia
Spain
Sweden
Tunisia
Turkey
United Arab Emirates
United Kingdom
United States of America

ORGANIZATIONS

Arab League
European Union
North Atlantic Treaty Organization
Organization of the Islamic Conference
United Nations

OBSERVERS

Australia
Holy See
World Bank

Bibliography

Ackerman, Bruce, "Obama's Unconstitutional War" ForeignPolicy.com, March 24, 2011.

Anderson, Jon Lee, "King of Kings: The Last Days of Muammar Qaddafi" *New Yorker*, November 7, 2011, vol. 87, no. 35.

Andres, Richard B., Craig Wills, and Thomas Griffith, Jr., "Winning with Allies: The Strategic Value of the Afghan Model" *International Security*, vol. 30, no. 3 (Winter 2005/06).

Annan, Kofi, "Intervention" Ditchley Foundation Lecture XXXV, June 26, 1998. http://www.ditchley.co.uk/page/173/lecture-xxxv.htm.

Anrig, Christian F., "Allied Air Power over Libya" *Air and Space Power Journal* (Winter 2011).

Arrai Television, September 20.

Ashdown, Paddy, "It Is Time for Europe to Back a No-Fly Zone in Libya" *Financial Times*, March 13, 2011.

Bandow, Doug, "Libya: Costs Outweigh Benefits" *National Interest*, October 21, 2011.

Baron, Kevin, "For $1 Billion, One Dictator" *National Journal*, October 21, 2011. http://www.nationaljournal.com/for-1-billion-one-dictator-muammar-el-qaddafi-20111020.

Bass, Gary J., "How Doing the Right Thing Can Go So Wrong" *Washington Post*, April 10, 2011.

"Battle for Libya: Key Moments" Al Jazeera, August 23, 2011. http://www.aljazeera.com/indepth/spotlight/libya/2011/08/20118219127303432.html

Beaumont, Peter and Martin Chulov, "Libyan Protesters Risk 'Suicide' by Army Hands" *Guardian*, February 19, 2011. http://www.guardian.co.uk/world/2011/feb/19/libyan-protesters-gaddafi-suicide-army.

Beaumont, Peter and Chris McGreal, "Front: Libya: Military: Gaddafi's Jets Slow Rebel Advance on Sirte" *Guardian*, March 8.

Belasco, Amy, *The Cost of Iraq, Afghanistan, and Other Global War on Terror Operations since 9/11*. Washington, DC: Congressional Research Service, RL33110, March 29, 2011.

Bennhold, Katrin, "France Tries to Re-Seize Its Lost Momentum" *International Herald Tribune*, February 24, 2011.

Biddle, Stephen, "Allies, Airpower, and Modern Warfare: The Afghan Model in Afghanistan and Iraq" *International Security*, vol. 30, no. 3 (Winter 2005/06).

Biddle, Stephen, "What Bombs Can't Do in Libya" *Washington Post*, March 26, 2011.

Billah, Zakarya Moukine, "Libye: Une Opposition Disparate et Déstructurée" *Le Monde*, February 23, 2011. http://www.lemonde.fr/afrique/article/2011/02/23/libye-une-opposition-disparate-et-destructuree_1484272_3212.html.

Blank, Ian, "Qatar Admits It Sent Troops to Support NTC Fighters" *Guardian*, October 27, 2011.

Bolton, John, "Obama Wobbly on Libya" BostonHerald.com, April 21, 2011.

Boot, Max, "Planning for a Post-Qaddafi Libya" *New York Times*, March 22, 2011.

Borger, Julian, Chris Stephen, and Richard Norton-Taylor, "Reversal of Rebel Fortunes That Led to Gates of the Capital" *Irish Times*, August 23, 2011.

Bourcier, Nicolas, "Benghazi: Les Insurgés se dotent d'un gouvernement" *Le Monde*, March 8, 2011.

Bourcier, Nicolas, "Libre soldats de Libye" *Le Monde*, March 10, 2011.

Bowman, Steve, *Kosovo and Macedonia: U.S. and Allied Military Operations*. Washington, DC: Congressional Research Service, IB10027, July 8, 2003.

Boyes, Roger, "Hesitant Obama Made Up His Mind Thanks to European Resolve" *Times*, March 18.

Burns, John F., "Qaddafi Compound Is Pounded in Day Raid" *New York Times*, June 7, 2011.

Calabresi, Massimo, "Susan Rice: A Voice for Intervention" *Time Magazine*, March 24, 2011.

"Cameron: UK Working on 'No-Fly Zone' Plan for Libya" BBC News, February 28, 2011. http://www.bbc.co.uk/news/uk-politics-12598674.

Carpenter, Ted Galen, "Another War of Choice" *National Interest*, March 18, 2011.

Chivers, C.J., "Libyan Rebels Don't Really Add Up to an Army" *New York Times*, April 7, 2011.

Chivers, C.J., "Problems with Logistics, Coordination and Rivalries Hamper Libya's Rebels" *New York Times*, July 21, 2011.

Chivers, C.J., "Taking Airport, Rebels in Libya Loosen Noose" *New York Times*, May 12, 2011.

Chivers, C.J. and Eric Schmitt, "Libya's Civilian Toll: Denied by NATO" *New York Times*, December 18, 2011.

Chivvis, Christopher S., *The Monetary Conservative: Jacques Rueff and Twentieth Century Free Market Thought*. De Kalb: Northern Illinois University Press, 2010.

Chivvis, Christopher S., "Libya's Downward Spiral" Foreignpolicy.com, September 13, 2012.

Chorin, Ethan, *Exit the Colonel: The Hidden History of the Libyan Revolution*. New York: Public Affairs, 2012.

Clapper, James, "Hearing to Receive Testimony on the Current and Future Worldwide Threats to the National Security of the United States." U.S. Senate Committee on Armed Services, March 10, 2011. http://armed-services.senate.gov/Transcripts/2011/03%20March/11–11%20-%203–10–11.pdf.

Clark, Wesley K., "Gen. Wesley Clark Says Libya Doesn't Meet the Test for U.S. Military Action" *Washington Post*, March 11, 2011.

Clemons, Steve, "Libya: Huge Win for Libyans, a Win for Obama, Challenges Next" *Atlantic*, August 22, 2011.

Clinton, Hillary, "Testimony on the 2012 State and USAID Budget Request." U.S. House of Representatives, Appropriations Committee, Washington, DC, March 10, 2011. http://appropriations.house.gov/_files/031011TestimonyofSecretaryofStateHillaryClinton.pdf.

Coates, Sam, "A Lonely War for Cameron … But Now He Knows His Comrades in Arms" *Times*, September 10, 2011.

Cody, Edward, "France, Britain Want NATO to Fight Harder against Qaddafi's Forces" *Washington Post*, April 12, 2011. http://www.washington

post.com/world/france-wants-nato-to-fight-harder-against-gaddafis-forces/2011/04/12/AFN8pxOD_story.html.

Colter, Irwin and Jared Genser, "Libya and the Responsibility to Protect" *International Herald Tribune*, February 28, 2011. http://www.nytimes.com/2011/03/01/opinion/01iht-edcotler01.html?scp=205&sq=Libya&st=nyt.

"Comments by Secretary Robert Gates, Secretary of Defense and General James Cartwright, Vice Chairman of the Joint Chiefs of Staff." Washington, DC, Thursday, April 21, 2011. http://www.jcs.mil/speech.aspx?ID=1589.

"Confused in Libya" *Washington Post*, March 23, 2011.

Cooper, Helene, "Obama and Merkel Tell Qaddafi to Go" *New York Times*, June 7, 2012. http://www.nytimes.com/2011/06/08/world/africa/08prexy.html?_r=1&ref=libya.

Cooper, Helene and Mark Lander, "Following U.S. Sanctions, U.N. Security Council to Meet on Libya" *New York Times*, February 26, 2011. http://www.nytimes.com/2011/02/27/world/africa/27diplomacy.html?pagewanted=1&sq=Libya&st=nyt&scp=177.

Cooper, Helene and Mark Lander, "U.S. Imposes Sanctions on Libya in Wake of Crackdown" *New York Times*, February 25, 2011.

Cooper, Helene and Steven Lee Myers, "Shift by Clinton Helped Persuade President to Take a Harder Line" *New York Times*, March 19, 2011.

Cooper, Robert "The New Liberal Imperialism" Observer.co.uk, April 7, 2002.

Daalder, Ivo, "Libya – A NATO Success Story" Atlantic Council of the United States, Washington, DC, November 7, 2011. http://nato.usmission.gov/sp110711.html.

Daalder, Ivo and James Steinberg, "The Future of Preemption" *American Interest* (Winter 2005). http://www.the-american-interest.com/article.cfm?piece=35.

Daalder, Ivo H. and Michael E. O'Hanlon, *Winning Ugly: NATO's War to Save Kosovo*. Washington, DC: Brookings Institution, 2000.

Daalder, Ivo H. and James G. Stavridis, "NATO's Victory in Libya" *Foreign Affairs*, vol. 91, no. 2 (March/April 2012).

Dagher, Sam, Charles Levinson, and Margaret Coker, "Tiny Kingdom's Huge Role in Libya Draws Concern" *Wall Street Journal*, October 17, 2011.

"Debate Builds Steam: West Considers No-Fly Zone for Libya" *Der Spiegel*, March 8, 2011. http://www.spiegel.de/international/world/0,1518,749678,00.html.

Decision on the "Prosecutor's Application Pursuant to Article 58 as to Muammar Mohammed Abu Minya GADDAFI, Saif Al-Islam GADDAFI and Abdullah AL-SENUSSI" Pre-TrialChamber 1, International Criminal Court, ICC-01/11, June 27, 2011.

"Denmark Running Out of Libya Bombs" *Politiken*, June 9, 2011. http://politiken.dk/newsinenglish/ECE1303431/denmark-running-out-of-libya-bombs/.

Densmore, Robert, "French Pilots over Libya Decline US Intel; Clearance Just Too Slow" AOL Defense, September 21, 2011. http://defense.aol.com/2011/09/21/french-pilots-over-libya-decline-us-intel-clearance-just-too-sl/.

"Des hélicoptères français participent aux frappes" France2.fr, June 4, 2011. http://info.france2.fr/monde/des-helicopteres-francais-participent-aux-frappes-69065831.html.

DeYoung, Karen and Joby Warrick, "U.S., Allies Step Up Pressure on Libya" *Washington Post*, March 1, 2011.

Dobbins, James, John G. McGinn, Keith Crane, Seth G. Jones, Rollie Lal, Andrew Rathmell, Rachel M. Swanger, and Anga Timilsina, *America's Role in Nation-Building: From Germany to Iraq*. Santa Monica, CA: RAND Corporation, 2003.

Dobbins, James, Seth G. Jones, Keith Crane, Andrew Rathmell, Brett Steele, Richard Teltschik, and Anga Timilsina, *The UN's Role in Nation-Building: From the Congo to Iraq*. Santa Monica, CA: RAND Corporation, 2005.

Dobbins, James, Seth G. Jones, Keith Crane, Beth Cole DeGrasse, *The Beginners Guide to Nation-Building*. Santa Monica, CA: RAND Corporation, 2007.

Dobbins, James, Seth G. Jones, Keith Crane, Christopher S. Chivvis, Andrew Radin, F. Stephen Larrabee, Nora Bensahel, Brooke K. Stearns, and Benjamin W. Goldsmith, *Europe's Role in Nation-Building: From the Balkans to the Congo*. Santa Monica, CA: RAND Corporation, 2008.

Douthat, Ross, "A Very Liberal Intervention" *New York Times*, March 21, 2011.

Douthat, Ross, "Libya: The End and the Beginning" New York Times Blogs, August 24, 2011.

Drezner, Daniel W., "Does Obama Have a Grand Strategy?" *Foreign Affairs*, vol. 30, no. 3 (May-June 2011).

Drezner, Daniel W., "Why Libya Is Not a Template for Future Military Statecraft" ForeignPolicy.com, August 25, 2011. http://drezner.foreignpo

licy.com/posts/2011/08/25/why_libya_is_not_a_template_for_military_statecraft.

Dubik, James M., "Finish the Job" *New York Times*, April 26, 2011.

Erlanger, Steven, "Libya's Dark Lesson for NATO" *New York Times*, September 4, 2011.

Erlanger, Steven, Elisabeth Bulmiller, and David D. Kirkpatrick, "Europeans Press Libya Showdown" *International Herald Tribune*, March 19, 2011.

"Europe's Leaders Fear Libya Could Become Next Afghanistan" *Der Spiegel*, March 14, 2011. http://www.spiegel.de/international/world/0,1518,750852,00.html.

Fahim, Kareem, "Libyan Rebels Dissolve Cabinet Amid Discord" *New York Times*, August 9, 2011.

Fahim, Kareem, "Libya Rebels Threaten a Supply Line to the Capital" *New York Times*, August 15, 2011.

Fahim, Kareem, "Refugees Flee Libya Oil City As Qaddafi's Forces Dig In" *New York Times*, August 18, 2011.

Fahim, Kareem, "Libyan Rebels Gain Control of Key Oil Refinery as Qaddafi Forces Flee" *New York Times*, August 19, 2011.

Fahim, Kareem and David D. Kirkpatrick, "Qaddafi's Grip on the Capital Tightens as Revolt Grows" *New York Times*, February 23, 2011.

Fahim, Kareem, and David D. Kirkpatrick, "Qaddafi's Forces Hit Back at Rebels" *New York Times*, March 1, 2011.

Fahim, Kareem and David D. Kirkpatrick, "Rebels Face Onslaught by Loyalists in Libya" *International Herald Tribune*, March 9, 2011.

Farmer, Ben, "Inside Benghazi's Training Camps" *Telegraph*, April 24, 2011. http://www.telegraph.co.uk/news/worldnews/africaandindianocean/libya/8469896/Libya-Inside-Benghazis-rebel-training-camps.html.

Federal News Service, "Highlights of U.S. Broadcast News Coverage of the Middle East from September 01, 2011."

Filkins, Dexter, "Flaws in U.S. War Left Hundreds of Civilians Dead" *New York Times*, July 21, 2002.

Freedom House, *Freedom in the World 2010*. Washington, DC. http://www.freedomhouse.org/report/freedom-world/2010/libya.

"French Fighter Jets Fly Over Country" Radio France Internationale (Paris), March 19, 2011.

BIBLIOGRAPHY

Garamone, Jim, "Roughead: Ships Were Ready for Odyssey Dawn" American Forces Press Service, March 23, 2011. http://www.defense.gov/news/newsarticle.aspx?id=63272.

Gates, Robert, U.S. House of Representatives, "Hearing of the Defense Subcommittee of the House Appropriations Committee, U.S. Department of Defense Budget Review" Washington, DC, March 2, 2011.

Gates, Robert, Speech at the United States Military Academy (West Point, NY), February 25, 2011. http://www.defense.gov/speeches/speech.aspx?speechid=1539.

Gelb, Leslie H., "Don't Use U.S. Force in Libya" The Daily Beast, March 8, 2011.

Gelb, Leslie H., "How Libya Saps America's Power" Daily Beast, April 17, 2011.

Gelie, Philippe, "La France a parachuté des armes aux rebelles libyens" Le Figaro, June 28, 2011. http://www.lefigaro.fr/international/2011/06/28/01003-20110628ARTFIG00704-la-france-a-parachute-des-armes-aux-rebelles-libyens.php.

Gerecht, Reuel Marc, and Mark Dubowitz, "Obama, American Liberator?" *Washington Post*, September 2, 2011.

Gertler, Jeremiah, "Operation Odyssey Dawn (Libya): Background and Issues for Congress" Congressional Research Service, R41725, March 30, 2011.

Gordon, Philip, "The Democratic Wave in the Arab World: Transatlantic Perspectives" Remarks at the EU Washington Forum, Sofitel Lafayette Square Hotel, Washington, DC, October 27, 2011. http://www.state.gov/p/eur/rls/rm/2011/176472.htm.

Gros, Philippe, "De Odyssey Dawn à Unified Protector: Bilan transitoire, perspectives et premiers enseignements de l'engagement en Libye" Note de la Fondation pour la Recherche Stratégique, April 21, 2011. http://www.frstrategie.org/barreFRS/publications/notes/2011/201104.pdf.

Guibert, Nathalie, "Près de deux mois de frappes intensives pour les hélicoptère" *Le Monde*, July 27, 2011.

Haas, Richard, "The U.S. Should Keep Out of Libya" *Wall Street Journal*, March 8, 2011.

Haas, Richard, "Prepared Statement by Richard N. Haas" *United States Senate Committee on Foreign Relations*, First Session, 112th Congress, April 6, 2011.

Haas, Richard, "But Plan to Put Boots on the Ground" *Financial Times*, August 23, 2011.

Harding, Thomas, "Libya: Navy Running Short of Tomahawk Missiles" *Telegraph*, March 23, 2011. http://www.telegraph.co.uk/news/worldnews/africaandindianocean/libya/8400079/Libya-Navy-running-short-of-Tomahawk-missiles.html.

Harding, Thomas, "Libya: SAS Leads Hunt for Gaddafi" *Daily Telegraph*, August 24, 2011.

Harding, Thomas, "Future RAF Missions under Threat if Libyan Intervention Continues" *Telegraph*, June 20, 2012. http://www.telegraph.co.uk/news/uknews/defence/8588125/Future-RAF-missions-under-threat-if-Libyan-intervention-continues.html.

Hastings, Michael, "Inside Obama's War Room" *Rolling Stone*, October 27, 2011.

Hayek, Friedrich, *The Road to Serfdom*. Chicago: University of Chicago Press, 1944.

Haynes, Deborah, "Special Forces 'Played a Key Role' in Fight with Qaddafi" *Times*, September 23, 2011.

Heilbrunn, Jacob, "Samantha and Her Subjects" *National Interest*, (May-June, 2011).

Hill, Evan, "The Day the Katiba Fell" Al Jazeera, March 1, 2011. http://www.aljazeera.com/indepth/spotlight/libya/2011/08/20118219127303432.html.

Hoffmann, Stanley, "The Crisis of Liberal Internationalism" *Foreign Policy*, No. 98 (Spring 1995).

Hopkins, Nick, "Libya Conflict May Cost UK £1.75bn" *Guardian*, September 25, 2011. http://www.guardian.co.uk/politics/2011/sep/25/libya-conflict-uk-defence-bill.

Ignatius, David, "Acting as Police Chief" *Washington Post*, March 29, 2011.

Ignatius, David, "Drone Attacks in Libya a Mistake" Washington Post, April 21, 2011. http://www.washingtonpost.com/blogs/post-partisan/post/drone-attacks-in-libya-a-mistake/2011/03/04/AFtZrRKE_blog.html.

Indyk, Martin S., Kenneth G. Liberthal, and Michael E. O'Hanlon, *Bending History: Barack Obama's Foreign Policy*. Washington, DC: Brookings Institution Press, 2012.

International Commission on Intervention and State Sovereignty, *Report on the Responsibility to Protect*. December 2001. http://responsibilitytoprotect.org/ICISS%20Report.pdf.

International Institute for Strategic Studies, "NATO Steps Up the Pace in Libya" *Strategic Comments*, August 24, 2011.

"Intervention in Libya at Odds with UN Resolution – Russia's Lavrov" *RIA Novosti*, March 28, 2011. http://en.rian.ru/russia/20110328/163245789.html.

Irish, John and Doherty, Regan E., "Libyan Conflict Brings French-Qatari Ties to the Fore" Reuters, April 13, 2011.

Johnson, Adrian and Saqeb Mueen, eds., *Short War, Long Shadow: The Political and Military Legacies of the 2011 Libya Campaign*. London: Royal United Services Institute (RUSI), Whitehall Report, 1–12.

Joint and Coalition Operational Analysis, "Libya: Operation Odyssey Dawn (OOD)" September 21, 2011.

Kagan, Robert, "To the Shores of Tripoli" *Weekly Standard*, vol. 16, no. 47, September 5, 2011.

Kennedy, Alison, "Norway to End Libyan Fighter Contributions" *Foreigner*, (Oslo), June 12, 2011. http://theforeigner.no/pages/news/norway-to-end-libyan-fighter-contributions/.

Kirkpatrick, David D., "Errant Missile Hit Civilian Home in Libya, NATO Says" *New York Times*, June 19, 2012.

Kirkpatrick, David D., "Gun Battle Disrupts Rebel Base in Libya" *New York Times*, August 1, 2011.

Kirkpatrick, David D., "Libyan Rebels Trumpet Coordination in Attacks" *New York Times*, June 17, 2012.

Kirkpatrick, David D., "NATO Says It Mistakenly Hit Rebels Again" *New York Times*, June 19, 2012.

Kirkpatrick, David D., "Western Libya Earns a Taste of Freedom as Rebels Loosen Qaddafi's Grip" *New York Times*, June 26, 2012.

Kirkpatrick, David D., and C. J. Chivers, "Internal Strife Threatens Cause of Libyan Rebels" *New York Times*, August 13, 2011.

Kirkup, James, "Navy Chief: Britain Cannot Keep Up Its Role in Libya Air War Due to Cuts" *Telegraph*, June 13, 2011. http://www.telegraph.co.uk/news/worldnews/africaandindianocean/libya/8573849/Navy-chief-Britain-cannot-keep-up-its-role-in-Libya-air-war-due-to-cuts.html.

Knaus, Gerhard, and Felix Martin, "Travails of the European Raj" *Journal of Democracy*, vol. 14, no. 3, (July 2003).

Krauthammer, Charles, "The Obama Doctrine: Leading from Behind" *Washington Post*, April 28, 2011.

Lambeth, Benjamin, *Air Power Against Terror: America's Conduct of Operation Enduring Freedom*. Santa Monica, CA: RAND Corporation,

2001. http://www.rand.org/content/dam/rand/pubs/monographs/2006/RAND_MG166–1.pdf.

Lambeth, Benjamin, *NATO's Air War for Kosovo: A Strategic and Operational Assessment*. Santa Monica, CA: RAND Corporation, 2001. http://www.rand.org/pubs/monograph_reports/MR1365.html.

Lander, Mark, "U.S. Condemns Libyan Tumult but Makes No Threats" *New York Times*, February 23, 2011.

Lander, Mark and Dan Bilefsky, "Specter of Rebel Rout Helps Shift U.S. Policy on Libya" *New York Times*, March 17, 2011.

Lasserre, Isabelle, "Le rôle crucial mais discret des forces spéciales" *Le Monde*, August 26, 2011.

Leiby, Richard and Muhammad Mansour, "Arab League Asks U.N. for No-Fly Zone over Libya" *Washington Post*, March 12, 2011. http://www.washingtonpost.com/world/arab-league-asks-un-for-no-fly-zone-over-libya/2011/03/12/ABoie0R_story.html.

Leparmentier, Arnaud and Philippe Ricard, "Libye: L'Europe écarte pour l'instant l'option militarie" *Le Monde*, March 13, 2011.

Levinson, Charles and Munreef Halawa, "Libyan Rebel Leader's Death Dims Advances" *Wall Street Journal*, July 29, 2011.

Lewis, William, "Libya: Dream vs. Reality" *Mediterranean Quarterly*, vol. 22, no. 3, (Summer 2011).

Li, Gary, "Libyan Rebels' Weapons Deficit" International Institute for Strategic Studies, Experts Commentary, March 8, 2011. http://www.iiss.org/whats-new/iiss-experts-commentary/libyan-rebels-weapons-deficit/.

"Libya: UK Apache Attack Helicopters Launch First Strikes" *Telegraph*, June 4, 2011. http://www.telegraph.co.uk/news/worldnews/africaandindianocean/libya/8556202/Libya-UK-Apache-attack-helicopters-launch-first-strikes.html.

"Libya: UK Apache Helicopters Used in NATO Attacks" BBC News, June 4, 2011. http://www.bbc.co.uk/news/uk-13651736.

"Libya Jails Russia, Ukraine, Belarus 'Mercenaries'" *Agence France Press*, June 4, 2012.

"Libya Unrest: Scores Killed in Benghazi 'Massacre'" BBC News, February 20, 2011. http://www.bbc.co.uk/news/world-africa-12517327.

"Libya and the War Powers Act" *New York Times*, June 16, 2011. http://www.nytimes.com/2011/06/17/opinion/17fri1.html.

"Libyan Rebels and Their Arab Spring Armament" Al Jazeera, July 18, 2011. http://www.aljazeera.com/programmes/faultlines/2011/07/2011718132823320628.html.

"Libye: Kadhafi prend le risque d'encourager une guerre civile" *Le Monde*, February 22, 2011. http://www.lemonde.fr/afrique/article/2011/02/22/libye-kadhafi-prend-le-risque-d-encourager-une-guerre-civile_1483828_3212.html.

"Libye: Une opposition disparate et déstructurée" *Le Monde*, February 23, 2011. http://www.lemonde.fr/afrique/article/2011/02/23/libye-une-opposition-disparate-et-destructuree_1484272_3212.html.

"Live Blog–Libya Feb 22" Al Jazeera, February 22, 2011. http://blogs.aljazeera.net/africa/2011/02/22/live-blog-libya-feb-22.

Lizza, Ryan, "The Consequentialist: How the Arab Spring Remade Obama's Foreign Policy" *New Yorker*, May 2, 2011. http://www.newyorker.com/reporting/2011/05/02/110502fa_fact_lizza.

Lobe, Jim, "US Neo-Cons Urge Libya Intervention" Al Jazeera, February 27, 2011.

"L'opposition libyenne demande l'aide de l'Europe" *Le Monde*, March 10, 2011. http://www.lemonde.fr/afrique/article/2011/03/10/direct-bataille-diplomatique-entre-kadhafi-et-l-opposition_1490863_3212.html.

Loyd, Anthony, "The Secret Beach Rendezvous that Brought French Weapons to the Rebels" *Times*, September 10, 2011.

Mazzetti, Mark and Eric Schmitt, "C.I.A. Agents in Libya Aid Airstrikes and Meet Rebels" *New York Times*, March 30, 2011.

McGreal, Chris, "Libya: Rebel Training Camp" *Guardian*, April 8, 2011.

Mead, Walter Russell, "W Gets a Third Term in the Middle East" The American Interest Blog, August 22, 2011. http://blogs.the-american-interest.com/wrm/2011/08/22/w-gets-a-third-term-in-the-middle-east/.

Menon, Rajan, "Breaking the State" *National Interest* (May-June 2011).

Morris, Nigel and David Usborne, "Cameron Frustrated with Obama's Refusal to Act" *Independent*, March 13, 2011.

Moseley, Lieutenant General T. Michael, USAF, "Operation Iraqi Freedom–By the Numbers" Shaw AFB, S.C., Assessment and Analysis Division, Headquarters U.S. Central Command Air Forces, April 30, 2003.

Mostyn, Trevor, "Obituary: Gen Abdel Fatah Younis: Military Leader and Gaddafi's Trusted Aide until He Defected to Libyan Rebel Forces" *Guardian*, August 1, 2011.

"Mr. Obama Speaks on Libya" *Washington Post*, March 29, 2011.

Mueller, Karl, ed., *Precision and Purpose: Airpower in the Libyan Civil War*. Santa Monica, CA: RAND Corporation, forthcoming.

Mulholland, Hélène, "Libya Crisis: EU Agrees Sanctions as UK Warns of 'Day Of Reckoning' for Gaddafi" *Guardian*, February 28, 2011. http://www.guardian.co.uk/world/2011/feb/28/libya-crisis-eu-sanctions-day-reckoning-gaddafi.

Myers, Steven Lee, "$1 Billion Is Pledged to Support Libya Rebels" *New York Times*, June 10, 2011.

n+1, "A Solution from Hell: The Perils of Humanitarian Intervention" Slate.com, August 17, 2011. http://www.slate.com/articles/arts/culturebox/2011/08/a_solution_from_hell.html.

Nordland, Rod, "Arms Said to Reach Libyan Rebels" *International Herald Tribune*, April 18, 2011.

Nordland, Rod, "At Qaddafi Loyalists' Last Redoubts, a Struggle of Advances and Retreats" *New York Times*, September 18, 2011.

Norton-Taylor, Richard and Dominik Rushe, "Front: Libya: Rebels and NATO Planned Tripoli Assault Weeks Ago" *Guardian*, August 25, 2011.

NATO, "Statement on Libya Following the Working Lunch of NATO Ministers of Foreign Affairs with Non–NATO Contributors to Operation Unified Protector" Brussels, April 14, 2011. http://www.nato.int/cps/en/natolive/official_texts_72544.htm.

"NATO: UAE F-16 Crashes at Italian Airbase" Associated Press, April 27, 2011. http://www.airforcetimes.com/news/2011/04/ap-uae-f16-crash-in-italy-042811/.

NATO Newsroom, "We Answered the Call – the End of Operation Unified Protector" Brussels, October 31, 2011. http://www.nato.int/cps/en/natolive/news_80435.htm.

NATO Press Office, "NATO Defence Ministers Will Discuss Situation in Libya and Longer Term Prospects in Middle East" Brussels, March 7, 2011. http://www.nato.int/cps/en/natolive/news_71277.htm.

NATO Press Office, "NATO Ready to Support International Efforts on Libya" Brussels, March 11, 2011. http://www.nato.int/cps/en/natolive/news_71446.htm.

NATO Press Office, "Press Briefing on Libya" Brussels, April 19, 2011. http://www.nato.int/nato_static/assets/audio/audio_2011_04/20110419_110419a.mp3.

NATO Press Office, "Operation Unified Protector Final Mission Stats" Brussels, November 2, 2011. http://www.nato.int/nato_static/assets/pdf/pdf_2011_11/20111108_111107-factsheet_up_factsfigures_en.pdf.

"NATO Says Lost U.S. Unmanned Helicopter in Libya" Reuters, June 21, 2011. http://www.reuters.com/article/2011/06/21/us-libya-nato-helicopter-idUSTRE75K1OO20110621.

Nougayrède, Natalie, "M. Sarkozy cherche à corriger l'image de la France en saluant la vague démocratique arabe" *Le Monde*, March 1, 2011.

Nougayrède, Natalie, "Recit: Comment la France a-t-elle décidé d'intervenir en Libye?" *Le Monde*, April 19, 2011.

Nougayrède, Natalie, "La guerre de Libya met à l'épreuve le lien transatlantique" *Le Monde*, May 24, 2011.

Nougayrède, Natalie, "Des forces spéciales françaises, britanniques et arabes auprès de la rebellion" *Le Monde*, August 24, 2011.

Obama, Barack, David Cameron, and Nicolas Sarkozy, "Libya's Pathway to Peace" *International Herald Tribune*, April 15, 2011. http://www.nytimes.com/2011/04/15/opinion/15iht-edlibya15.html.

"Obama Orders $25 Million in Aid to Libyan Rebels" AFP, April, 26, 2011.

O'Hanlon, Michael, "Libya and the Obama Doctrine" foreignaffairs.com, August 31, 2011.

"On ne s'improvise pas diplomate" *Le Monde*, February 23, 2011.

Osborn, Andrew, "Libya: Col Gaddafi has 'suicide plan' to blow up Tripoli" *Telegraph*, July 14, 2011. http://www.telegraph.co.uk/news/worldnews/africaandindianocean/libya/8636883/Libya-Col-Gaddafi-has-suicide-plan-to-blow-up-Tripoli.html.

Ourdan, Rémy, "A Ras Lanouf, les rebelles en déroute" *Le Monde*, March 12, 2011.

Ourdan, Rémy "Les raids aériens, terreur des 'chabab' insurgés" *Le Monde*, March 13, 2011.

Pack, Jason, ed., *The 2011 Libyan Uprisings and the Struggle for the Post-Qaddafi Future*. New York: Palgrave, 2013.

Pape, Robert A., "When Duty Calls: A Pragmatic Standard of Humanitarian Intervention" *International Security*, vol. 37, no. 1 (Summer 2012).

Pargeter, Alison, *Libya: The Rise and Fall of Qaddafi*. New Haven: Yale University Press, 2012.

Parliament of the United Kingdom, *Defence Committee – Ninth Report: Operations in Libya*. January 25, 2012, chapter 4. http://www.publications.parliament.uk/pa/cm201012/cmselect/cmdfence/950/95002.htm.

Pollack, Kenneth M., "Libya Escalation Inevitable" nationalinterest.org, May 6, 2011. http://nationalinterest.org/commentary/libya-escalation-inevitable-5259.

Posner, Eric A., "Outside the Law" ForeignPolicy.com, October 25, 2011. http://www.foreignpolicy.com/articles/2011/10/25/libya_international_law_qaddafi_nato.

Rayment, Sean, "How the Special Forces Helped Bring Qaddafi to His Knees" *Telegraph*, August 28, 2011. http://www.telegraph.co.uk/news/worldnews/africaandindianocean/libya/8727076/How-the-special forces-helped-bring-Gaddafi-to-his-knees.html.

Reisner, Hiram, "Brzezinski: Libya Action Isn't War, but Necessary Intervention" Newsmax, March 24, 2011.

"Révoltes arabes: répression brutale en Libye, à Bahreïn et au Yémen" *Le Monde*, February 20, 2011.

Rice, Susan E., "The Genocide in Darfur: America Must Do More to Fulfill the Responsibility to Protect" *Opportunity08*, Brookings Institution, 2007. http://www.brookings.edu/research/papers/2007/10/~/media/Research/Files/Papers/2007/10/24darfur%20rice%20Opp08/PB_Darfur_Rice.PDF.

"Rice to Take Lessons from Rwanda Genocide" *All Things Considered*, NPR, February 23, 2009.

Ripley, Tim, "Power Brokers, Qatar and the U.A.E. Take Center Stage" Jane's Intelligence Review, December 21, 2011.

Risen, Clay, "Obama's Non-Doctrine Doctrine" New York Times Blogs, August 26, 2011.

Romney, Mitt, "Mission Muddle in Libya" The National Review Online, April 21, 2011.

Rowland, Jacky, "French Contact with Libyans over Gaddafi" Al Jazeera, July 12, 2011. http://www.aljazeera.com/news/africa/2011/07/201171214412794693.html.

Royal United Services Institute, *Accidental Heroes: Britain, France and the Libya Operation*. London, September 2011. http://www.rusi.org/downloads/assets/RUSIInterimLibyaReport.pdf.

Russian Ministry of Foreign Affairs, "Transcript of Replies by Russian Minister of Foreign Affairs Sergey Lavrov to Media Questions at Press Conference Following Russia–NATO Council Meeting" Berlin, April 15, 2011. http://

BIBLIOGRAPHY

www.mid.ru/bdomp/brp_4.nsf/e78a48070f128a7b43256999005bcbb3/e75a0b6dad683042c32578770022e0a8!OpenDocument.

Russian Ministry of Foreign Affairs, "Russian Foreign Minister Sergey Lavrov Interview" *Vesti 24*, Moscow, July 7, 2011. http://www.mid.ru/bdomp/brp_4.nsf/e78a48070f128a7b43256999005bcbb3/2fa3ca1205302976c32578c70051b17b!OpenDocument.

Sanger, David E. and Thom Shanker, "Gates Warns of Risks of a No-Flight Zone" *New York Times*, March 3, 2011.

Sanger, David E. and Thom Shanker, *Confront and Conceal*. New York: Crown Publishers, 2012, p. 340.

Sarkozy, Nicolas, Speech at the 19th Ambassadors' Conference, Paris, August 31, 2011. http://www.franceonu.org/spip.php?article5730.

Saunders, Doug, "Rebels Rely on Teens to Fill Ranks" *Globe and Mail*, July 11, 2011.

"Saving Lives in Libya" *Washington Post*, April 28, 2011.

Schmitt, Eric, "NATO Air War in Libya Faces Daunting Task" *New York Times*, May 25, 2011.

Schmitt, Eric, "NATO Commander Says Resilience of the Qaddafi Loyalists Is Surprising" *New York Times*, October 11, 2011.

Shadid, Anthony, "Clashes in Libya Worsen as Army Crushes Dissent" *New York Times*, February 18, 2011.

Shadid, Anthony and Kareem Fahim, "Rebels in Libya Strain to Forge a Unified Front" *New York Times*, March 9, 2011.

Shadid, Anthony and David D. Kirkpatrick, "Libyan Rebels Defiant but in Disarray, as Qaddafi's Forces Gain Momentum" *New York Times*, March 11, 2011.

Shanker, Thom and John F. Burns, "Nations Bombing Libya Ask for Help Amid Strain" *New York Times*, June 9, 2011.

Shipman, Tim, "Cameron Backs Sarkozy Calls for Libya Air Strikes" *Daily Mail*, March 11, 2011.

Slaughter, Anne-Marie, "Fiddling While Libya Burns" *New York Times*, March 13, 2011.

Slaughter, Anne-Marie, "Why the Libya Sceptics Were Proven Wrong" *Financial Times*, August 25, 2011.

So, Jimmy, "Kerry: A Libyan No-Fly Zone Is Not Intervention" CBS News, March 6, 2011. http://www.cbsnews.com/stories/2011/03/06/ftn/main20039797.shtml.

Speaker John A. Boehner Letter to the President Obama on Military Action in Libya, March 23, 2011. http://www.speaker.gov/UploadedFiles/POTUSLetter_032311.pdf.

Squires, Nick, "Libya: Italy Demands Investigation into Whether NATO Warship Ignored Refugees" *Telegraph*, August 5, 2011. http://www.telegraph.co.uk/news/worldnews/africaandindianocean/libya/8684942/Libya-Italy-demands-investigation-into-whether-Nato-warship-ignored-refugees.html.

Starkey, Jerome, "It's a Mad Max Conflict" *Times*, May 14, 2001.

Steltzenmüller, Constanze, "Gates Was Far Too Nice about NATO's Failings" *Financial Times*, June 16, 2011.

Stewart, Rory and Gerald Knaus, *Can Intervention Work?* New York: Norton, 2011.

Stolberg, Sheryl Gay, "Still Crusading, but Now on the Inside" *New York Times*, March 30, 2011.

Strauss, Delphine, "Turkey Attacks France on Libya 'Crusade'" *Financial Times*, March 24, 2011. http://www.ft.com/cms/s/0/fe514f9c-5631-11e0-8de9-00144feab49a.html#axzz1qXP3P89x.

"Sur fond de critiques, Nicolas Sarkozy demande des sanctions contre la Libye" *Le Monde*, February 23, 2011. http://www.lemonde.fr/politique/article/2011/02/23/sur-fond-de-critiques-nicolas-sarkozy-demande-des-sanctions-contre-la-libye_1484003_823448.html.

Sweetman, Bill, "Reluctant Warriors" *Aviation Week & Space Technology*, January 2, 2012.

Taft, Robert, *A Foreign Policy for Americans*. New York: Doubleday, 1951.

Talmon, Stefan, "Recognition of the Libyan National Transitional Council" *American Society of International Law: Insights*, vol. 15, no. 16 (June 16, 2011).

Tapper, Jake, "Where Is Mitt Romney on Libya?" ABC News, October 20, 2011. http://abcnews.go.com/blogs/politics/2011/10/where-is-mitt-romney-on-libya/.

Taspinar, Omer, "The American Public and the Islamic World" Today's Zaman Online, September 16, 2012.

"Time Is on Gadhafi's Side" *Der Spiegel*, March 3, 2011. http://www.spiegel.de/international/world/0,1518,748863,00.html.

Tomasky, Michael, "Obama's True Claim to Fame" Daily Beast, August 23, 2011.

Traynor, Ian, "Turkey and France Clash over Libya Air Campaign" *Guardian*, March 24, 2011. http://www.guardian.co.uk/world/2011/mar/24/turkey-france-clash-libya-campaign.

UN Human Rights Council, *Report of the International Commission of Inquiry on Libya*. A/HRC/19/68, March 2, 2012.

U.S. Defense Department, "U.S. Casualty Status" as of February 28, 2012.

U.S. Defense Department, Office of the Assistant Secretary of Defense, Public Affairs, "DOD News Briefing with Vice Adm. Gortney from the Pentagon on Libya Operation Odyssey Dawn" Washington, DC, March 19, 2011. http://www.defense.gov/transcripts/transcript.aspx?transcriptid=4786.

U.S. Defense Department, Office of the Assistant Secretary of Defense, Public Affairs, "DoD News Briefing with Adm. Locklear via Teleconference from USS Mount Whitney" Washington, DC, March 22, 2011. http://www.defense.gov/transcripts/transcript.aspx?transcriptid=4793

U.S. Defense Department, Office of the Assistant Secretary of Defense, Public Affairs, "DOD News Briefing with Rear Adm. Hueber via Telephone from USS Mount Whitney" Washington, DC, March 23, 2011. http://www.defense.gov/transcripts/transcript.aspx?transcriptid=4794

U.S. Defense Department, Office of the Assistant Secretary of Defense, Public Affairs, "DOD News Briefing with Vice Adm. Gortney from the Pentagon on Libya Operation Odyssey Dawn" Washington, DC, March 28, 2011. http://www.defense.gov/transcripts/transcript.aspx?transcriptid=4803.

U.S. Defense Department, Office of the Assistant Secretary of Defense, Public Affairs, "The Security and Defense Agenda (Future of NATO), As Delivered by Secretary of Defense Robert M. Gates, Brussels, Belgium, Friday, June 10, 2011." http://www.defense.gov/speeches/speech.aspx?speechid=1581.

U.S. Defense Department, Office of the Assistant Secretary of Defense, Public Affairs, "DOD News Briefing with Secretary Gates and Adm. Mullen from the Pentagon" Washington, DC, March 1, 2011. http://www.defense.gov/transcripts/transcript.aspx?transcriptid=4777.

U.S. Defense Department, Office of the Assistant Secretary of Defense, Public Affairs, "Media Availability with Secretary Gates at the NATO Defense Ministers Meeting from Brussels, Belgium" Washington, DC,

March 10, 2011. http://www.defense.gov/transcripts/transcript.aspx?transcriptid=4783.

U.S. Department of State, Undersecretary for Public Diplomacy and Public Affairs, "Teleconference Background Briefing on North Atlantic Council (NAC) Discussions on Libya" Washington, DC, March 24, 2011. http://www.state.gov/r/pa/prs/ps/2011/03/159100.htm.

"U.S. Fighter Jet Crashes in Rebel-Held Libya" Reuters, March 22, 2011. http://www.reuters.com/article/2011/03/22/us-libya-usa-crash-idUSTRE72L20E20110322.

"U.S.: Hundreds of Civilian Deaths in Iraq Were Preventable" Press Release for the report, *Off Target: The Conduct of War and Civilian Casualties in Iraq*. Human Rights Watch, Washington, DC, December 12, 2003. http://www.hrw.org/news/2003/12/12/us-hundreds-civilian-deaths-iraq-were-preventable.

U.S. Mission to NATO, "Remarks to the Press on Libya and Operation Unified Protector, Ambassador Ivo Daalder" September 8, 2011. http://nato.usmission.gov/libya-oup-90811.html.

U.S. Mission to the United Nations, "Remarks by Ambassador Susan E. Rice, U.S. Permanent Representative to the United Nations, at the Security Council Stakeout on Libya" New York, NY, March 16, 2011. http://usun.state.gov/briefing/statements/2011/179644.htm.

U.S. Senator John McCain, Press Office, "Statement by Senators McCain and Lieberman Regarding the Situation in Libya" Washington, DC, March 4, 2011. http://mccain.senate.gov/public/index.cfm?FuseAction=PressOffice.PressReleases&ContentRecord_id=826d50c1-d891-a303-ca02-c6714dd50c30&Region_id=&Issue_id=.

U.S. Senator John McCain, Press Office, "Statement by Senators McCain and Graham on End of the Qaddafi Regime in Libya" August 21, 2011. http://mccain.senate.gov/public/index.cfm?ContentRecord_id=ef07da62-0100-107e-d7ac-08531bd793e5&FuseAction=PressOffice.PressReleases.

"US Sends 'Time to Go' Message to Gaddafi" Al Jazeera, July 19, 2011. http://www.aljazeera.com/news/africa/2011/07/2011718233615749270.html.

UN Human Rights Council, *Report of the International Commission of Inquiry on Libya*. A/HRC/19/68, March 2, 2012.

United Nations Security Council, Press Statement on Libya, SC/10180, February 22, 2011. http://www.un.org/News/Press/docs/2011/sc10180.doc.htm.

United Nations Security Council Resolution 1970 (2011), February 26, 2011. http://www.un.org/ga/search/view_doc.asp?symbol=S/RES/1970%20%282011%29.

Valentino, Benjamin A., "The True Costs of Humanitarian Intervention" *Foreign Affairs*, vol. 90, no. 6 (November-December 2011).

Vandevalle, Diederik, *History of Modern Libya*. New York: Cambridge University Press, 2012.

Van Genugten, Saskia, "Libya after Gadhafi" *Survival*, vol. 53, no. 3, (June-July 2011).

Walker, Portia, "Qatari Military Advisers on the Ground, Helping Libyan Rebels Get into Shape" *Washington Post*, May 12, 2011.

Watt, Nicholas and Patrick Wintour, "Libya No-Fly Zone Call by France Fails to Get David Cameron's Backing" *Guardian*, February 23, 2011.

Watts, Stephen, Caroline Baxter, Molly Dunigan, and Christopher Rizzi, *The Uses and Limits of Small-Scale Military Interventions*. Santa Monica, CA: RAND, 2012.

Weaver, Matthew, "Muammar Gaddafi Condemns Tunisia Uprising" *Guardian*, January 16, 2011.

Weisberg, Jacob, "What Is Obama's Foreign Policy?" *Slate*, May 24, 2011.

Western, Jon, and Joshua S. Goldstein, "Humanitarian Intervention Comes of Age" *Foreign Affairs*, vol. 90, no. 6 (November–December 2011).

White House, Office of the Press Secretary, "Remarks by the President on a New Beginning" Cairo University, Cairo, June 4, 2009. http://www.whitehouse.gov/the-press-office/remarks-president-cairo-university-6-04-09.

White House, Office of the Press Secretary, "Press Conference by the President" L'Aquila, Italy, July 10, 2009.

White House, Office of the Press Secretary, "Remarks by the President on Libya" February 23, 2011. http://www.whitehouse.gov/blog/2011/02/23/president-obama-speaks-turmoil-libya-violence-must-stop.

White House, Office of the Press Secretary, "Readout of President Obama's Calls with President Sarkozy of France, Prime Minister Cameron of the United Kingdom and Prime Minister Berlusconi of Italy" February 24, 2011.

White House, Office of the Press Secretary, "Readout of President Obama's meeting with His National Security Team on Libya" Washington, DC, March 15, 2011. http://www.whitehouse.gov/the-press-office/2011/03/15/readout-president-obamas-meeting-his-national-security-team-libya.

White House, Office of the Press Secretary, "Remarks by the President on the Situation in Libya" Washington, DC, March 18, 2011. http://www.whitehouse.gov/the-press-office/2011/03/18/remarks-president-situation-libya.

White House, Office of the Press Secretary, "Remarks by the President in Address to the Nation on Libya" March 28, 2011. http://www.whitehouse.gov/the-press-office/2011/03/28/remarks-president-address-nation-libya.

Will, George F., "Obama's Illegal War" *Washington Post*, May 29, 2011.

Wolfowitz, Paul, "America's Opportunity in Libya" *Wall Street Journal*, November 3, 2011.

"World Cannot Stand Aside from Libya, says Cameron" BBC News, March 8, 2011. http://www.bbc.co.uk/news/uk-12680280.

Worth, Robert F., "On Libya's Revolutionary Road" *New York Times Magazine*, March 30, 2011.

Zakaria, Fareed, "A Doctrine We Don't Need" *Washington Post*, July 7, 2011.

Zakaria, Fareed, "A New Era in U.S. Foreign Policy" CNN.com, August 23, 2011.

Index

A Problem from Hell, 10, 51
A-10 warthog, 111
A-130 Flying Fortress, 111
Abrams, Elliott, 49
Abu Dhabi, 131, 132, 133
Acheson, Dean, 13
Afghan Model, 156, 201, 202, 225, 226
Afghanistan, xiii, xv, 2, 4, 6, 10, 15, 18, 31, 40, 42, 44, 45, 46, 47, 59, 62, 63, 65, 78, 84, 111, 134, 144, 167, 172, 177, 181, 184, 187, 191, 192, 193, 194, 195, 199, 200, 202, 204, 205, 226, 230
Ajdabiya, 53, 101, 103, 104, 127
Al-Jazeera, 99, 219
Al-Qaeda, 30, 45, 47, 118, 152, 167, 173, 200
Al-Qaeda in the Islamic Maghreb (AQIM), 173, 179
al-Thani, Hamad Bin Khalifa, 79
Anders Fogh Rasmussen, 34
Angela Merkel, 34
Arab League, 3, 27, 36, 41, 53, 55, 56, 60, 90, 99, 215, 217, 224, 234
Arab Spring, 9, 19, 40, 52, 106, 234, 235
Ashdown, Paddy, 7

Bab al-Azizya, 1
Bahrain, 10, 31, 52, 54
Baida, 26
Baker, James, 7
Balkans, 5, 63, 229
Belgium, 41, 74, 85, 89, 100, 114, 136, 137, 190, 191, 207, 215, 223, 241
Ben Ali, Zine al-Abidine, 23

Benghazi, 1, 3, 25, 26, 27, 31, 33, 53, 56, 58, 63, 69, 79, 80, 81, 84, 85, 86, 90, 94, 101, 103, 105, 106, 107, 108, 116, 117, 120, 130, 144, 149, 155, 157, 159, 160, 161, 171, 173, 174, 182, 189, 195, 214, 216, 226, 230, 234
Berlusconi, Silvio, 29, 69, 74
Biddle, Stephen, 202, 226
Biden, Joe, 38, 48, 65
Blinken, Tony, 65
Boehner, John, 91, 140, 142, 239
Bolton, John, 8
Bosnia-Herzegovina, 4
Bouchard, Charles, 98, 120
Brazil, 60
Brega, 33, 53, 86, 101, 103, 104, 110, 117, 127, 128, 129, 139, 162
Britain, 4
Brzezinski, Zbigniew, 8
Bush, George W., 44

Cairo, 20, 29, 151, 217, 219, 243
Cameron, David, 28, 29, 30, 34, 35, 37, 39, 42, 48, 60, 66, 77, 103, 107, 112, 118, 124, 158, 164, 196, 197, 227, 235, 237, 239, 243, 244
Canada, 41, 89, 100, 137, 190, 207, 223
Cardillo, Robert, 56
Central Intelligence Agency (CIA), 22, 45
China, 37, 59, 61, 116, 165
Chirac, Jacques, 36, 76
Chollet, Derek, xvi, 143, 152
Chou En Lai, 14
Clark, Wesley, 6

245

Clinton Administration, 4, 43, 49, 186
Clinton, Hillary, xi, 48, 55, 66, 67, 69, 78, 79, 142, 166, 167, 192
Congress, U.S., viii, 1, 10, 23, 31, 38, 43, 47, 48, 49, 55, 56, 80, 81, 89, 91, 139, 140, 141, 142, 143, 161, 186, 227, 230, 231
Contact Group, viii, ix, 78, 125, 131, 143, 152, 164, 223
Controversies Over Libya, 6
Cretz, Gene, 143, 152
Cyrenaica, 21, 25

Daalder, Ivo, xvi, 71, 72, 97, 99, 100, 125, 177, 186, 188, 190, 228, 242
Dabbashi, Ibrahim al-, 27
Darfur, 50, 204, 238
Davutoglu, Ahmet, 73, 78
Deauville, 131, 149
Defense Department, vii, 44, 55, 57, 67, 68, 81, 84, 86, 88, 89, 121, 137, 140, 141, 176, 241
Denmark, 89, 100, 119, 136, 190, 191, 207, 223, 229
Doha, 131, 144, 185
Donilon, Tom, 8, 37, 38, 48, 49, 57, 143, 164
Douthat, Ross, 8
Drezner, Daniel, 12
Dubik, James, 9

Egypt, 6, 7, 19, 20, 21, 22, 25, 27, 31, 52, 87, 93, 169, 175, 182, 216, 221
Eisenhower, Dwight, 18
Erlanger, Steven, 10, 99, 230
European Union (EU), xvii, 5, 23, 30, 31, 35, 36, 41, 62, 72, 73, 75, 125, 184, 194, 195, 196, 197, 215, 220, 224, 231, 236

Fazzan, 21
Fillon, François, 36
Fox, Liam, 112
France, xi, 3, 4, 5, 14, 27, 28, 29, 30, 32, 34, 35, 36, 37, 40, 42, 51, 52, 53, 55, 58, 60, 61, 62, 66, 68, 69, 70, 71, 73, 75, 75, 76, 77, 78, 79, 80, 83, 86, 87, 88, 89, 99, 100, 104, 109, 111, 112, 114, 116, 119, 124, 125, 126, 127, 128, 129, 134, 137, 149, 151, 152, 154, 157, 158, 159, 161, 165, 167, 172, 174, 176, 177, 178, 181, 186, 190, 192, 193, 195, 196, 197, 200, 207, 212, 216, 223, 226, 227, 229, 230, 231, 234, 235, 237, 238, 240, 243

Gates, Robert, 18, 29, 38, 40, 41, 44, 45, 46, 47, 48, 50, 54, 56, 57, 58, 67, 69, 114, 121, 136, 137, 191, 228, 231, 239, 240, 241
Gelb, Leslie, 10
Germany, 40, 42, 60, 61, 62, 72, 75, 83, 84, 87, 111, 112, 134, 136, 178, 192, 194, 208, 223, 229
Ghoga, Abdel Hafix, 32
Gordon, Philip, xvi, 72, 231
Graham, Lindsey, 141, 198, 242
Green Book, 22

Haass, Richard, 9
Hague, William, 37
Ham, Carter, 88, 116, 165
Hayek, Friedrich, 203
Hoffman, Stanley, 202
Human Rights Watch, 49, 102, 242
Hussein, Saddam, 18

Idriss I, 21
International Criminal Court (ICC), xvii, 23, 30, 150, 175, 229
Iraq, xiii, xv, 2, 4, 5, 10, 15, 18, 20, 22, 31, 44, 46, 50, 52, 59, 62, 65, 75, 86, 112, 144, 177, 181, 184, 187, 192, 194, 195, 199, 202, 204, 205, 223, 226, 229, 242
ISR issues, 111, 112, 113, 114, 116, 190, 191, 195, 198
Istanbul, 71, 131, 133, 152
Italy, 30, 58, 69, 72, 76, 88, 89, 98, 100, 112, 120, 121, 139, 153, 154, 157, 181, 190, 207, 210, 211, 220, 223, 240, 243

Jalil, Mustafa Abdel, 27, 32, 153, 214
Jibril, Mahmoud, 32
Jodice, Ralph, 98, 137, 167
Joint Forces Command Naples, 98
Jordan, 31, 79, 98, 99, 100, 207, 223
Juppé, Alain, 36, 60, 76, 78, 101, 102, 125, 151

Kagan, Robert, 11
kata 'ib, 80, 86, 95, 96, 102, 106, 107, 123, 126, 128, 130, 147, 154, 156, 158, 160, 162, 165, 171, 172, 183
Kennan, George, 13
Kerry, John, 142
Khamis brigade, 104, 109, 181
Khatib, Abdel al-, 152, 153
Kissinger, Henry, 7
Koh, Harold, 140
Kosovo, xii, xiii, 4, 5, 43, 49, 66, 76, 97, 100, 110, 139, 144, 176, 177, 181, 182, 186, 191, 192, 194, 199, 226, 228, 234
Krauthammer, Charles, 9
Kucinich, Dennis, 140
Kuwait, 100, 132, 223

Lavrov, Sergey, 118, 233, 238
Le Monde, 36
liberal intervention, xv, 174
Libya, vii, viii, ix, x, xi, xii, xiii, xiv, xv, 1, 3, 4, 5, 6, 7, 8, 9, 10, 11, 12, 13, 15, 19, 21, 22, 25, 26, 27, 28, 29, 30, 31, 33, 34, 35, 37, 38, 39, 40, 41, 42, 43, 44, 45, 46, 47, 49, 50, 51, 52, 53, 54, 58, 59, 60, 61, 63, 64, 66, 67, 72, 73, 74, 76, 77, 78, 79, 80, 81, 83, 85, 86, 87, 88, 89, 90, 91, 93, 94, 97, 98, 99, 100, 101, 102, 103, 104, 105, 107, 108, 109, 111, 112, 114, 117, 118, 119, 120, 121, 123, 124, 125, 127, 128, 130, 131, 132, 133, 134, 135, 136, 137, 139, 140, 141, 142, 143, 144, 145, 147, 149, 150, 151, 152, 153, 154, 155, 156, 157, 158, 159, 160, 161, 163, 164, 166, 167, 169, 170, 171, 172, 173, 174, 175, 177, 178, 180, 182, 183, 185, 187, 188, 190, 191, 193, 194, 195, 197, 198, 199, 200, 201, 202, 203, 205, 214, 215, 216, 217, 218, 219, 220, 221, 222, 225, 226, 227, 228, 229, 230, 231, 232, 233, 234, 235, 236, 237, 238, 239, 240, 241, 242, 243, 244
Libyan Islamic Fighting Group (LIFG), 45, 46
Lieberman, Joe, 37, 38, 141, 242
Lizza, Ryan, 9
Locklear, Samuel, 81, 85, 88, 98, 116, 241

London, 70, 100, 131, 185, 223, 238

Mali, crisis, 172, 179
Malinowski, Tom, 49
Man Portable Air Defense Systems (MANPADS), 171, 172
Margelov, Mikhail, 149, 150
McCain, John, 37, 38, 141, 142, 174, 198, 242
McDonough, Denis, 38
Mead, Walter Russell, 13
Medvedev, Dmitri, 61
Merkel, Angela, 42, 138, 228
MI6, 37, 45
Michèle Alliot-Marie, 36
Middle East, 4, 13, 18, 19, 28, 31, 40, 43, 46, 108, 131, 142, 149, 151, 153, 165, 217, 230, 235, 236
military intervention, 3, 4, 6, 8, 16, 41, 44, 124, 172, 174, 205
Misrata, x, 26, 33, 84, 85, 95, 102, 103, 104, 105, 107, 108, 117, 119, 120, 122, 123, 129, 130, 147, 154, 156, 157, 189
Moussa, Amr, 36, 90, 219
Mubarak, Hosni, 20, 25, 36
Mullen, Michael, 46, 57, 67, 241
munitions stocks, 135

National Security Council (NSC), 50, 51
National Transitional Council (NTC), 32, 33, 94, 103, 107, 131, 132, 133, 146, 153, 155, 156, 157, 161, 164, 169, 173, 185, 220, 222, 226
NATO, viii, xiii, xiv, 3, 5, 6, 9, 10, 11, 18, 32, 34, 36, 39, 40, 41, 49, 61, 62, 63, 69, 71, 71, 72, 73, 74, 77, 78, 81, 86, 88, 89, 92, 96, 97, 98, 99, 100, 101, 102, 103, 104, 105, 109, 110, 111, 112, 114, 115, 117, 118, 119, 120, 121, 123, 124, 125, 126, 127, 128, 129, 130, 131, 136, 137, 139, 148, 150, 152, 154, 155, 156, 158, 159, 160, 161, 162, 163, 164, 165, 166, 167, 170, 174, 176, 177, 178, 179, 180, 181, 188, 189, 190, 192, 193, 194, 195, 196, 199, 220, 221, 227, 228, 230, 232, 233, 236, 238, 239, 240, 241, 242
  defense ministerial, 134
  defense ministerial, informal, 32
  Foreign Ministerial, 117

NATO, (cont.)
 France's reintegration into military command structures, 75
Netherlands, 89, 119, 191, 207, 219, 223
New Yorker, 1, 9, 59, 225, 235
Nicolas Sarkozy, 29
no-fly zone, 3, 7, 27, 28, 32, 33, 34, 35, 37, 38, 39, 41, 42, 44, 47, 48, 50, 51, 54, 56, 58, 60, 65, 77, 80, 83, 90, 97, 99, 119, 136, 174, 225, 227, 234, 239, 243
North Atlantic Council (NAC), 39, 76, 77, 78, 97, 120, 165, 242
Norway, 74, 84, 87, 89, 100, 119, 135, 136, 190, 191, 207, 223, 233

O'Hanlon, Michael, 12
Obama Administration, 3
Obama, Barak, 3, 7, 8, 9, 10, 11, 12, 13, 18, 19, 20, 29, 30, 31, 35, 36, 38, 39, 42, 43, 44, 48, 49, 50, 51, 52, 53, 54, 56, 57, 58, 59, 60, 61, 64, 65, 66, 68, 69, 70, 75, 77, 90, 91, 92, 93, 103, 104, 116, 118, 121, 138, 140, 141, 142, 143, 145, 148, 149, 157, 164, 174, 176, 178, 197, 199, 200, 225, 226, 227, 228, 229, 231, 232, 233, 235, 237, 238, 239, 240, 243
Obeidi tribe, 159
Odyssey Dawn, viii, 79, 80, 81, 82, 83, 86, 87, 88, 89, 94, 94, 98, 101, 111, 174, 231, 233, 241

Pan Am Flight 103, 22
Pentagon, xv, 32, 46, 66, 81, 86, 89, 145, 176, 241
Poggio-Renatico, 98, 113
Poland, 27, 40, 75, 111, 136, 192, 208, 216, 223
Pollack, Ken, 238
Power, Samantha, 10, 51, 57, 67, 84, 87, 99, 119, 127, 141, 149, 153, 225, 231, 233
Predator UAV, 121, 141, 167
prudent planning, 39, 40, 98

Qaddafi, Muammar, viii, xiii, xiv, 1, 2, 3, 5, 6, 7, 8, 10, 14, 21, 22, 23, 25, 26, 27, 28, 29, 30, 32, 33, 34, 35, 36, 37, 38, 39, 40, 41, 43, 44, 45, 47, 49, 52, 53, 54, 55, 56, 57, 58, 61, 63, 64, 65, 67, 68, 69, 70, 71, 78, 80, 81, 83, 85, 86, 90, 93, 94, 96, 99, 100, 101, 102, 103, 104, 106, 107, 108, 109, 110, 111, 112, 114, 116, 117, 118, 119, 120, 121, 123, 124, 125, 126, 129, 130, 131, 132, 133, 134, 135, 137, 138, 140, 143, 144, 145, 147, 148, 149, 150, 151, 152, 153, 154, 155, 156, 158, 159, 160, 161, 162, 164, 165, 166, 167, 169, 171, 172, 173, 174, 175, 179, 180, 181, 182, 183, 186, 187, 188, 189, 190, 193, 194, 195, 198, 214, 215, 216, 217, 218, 219, 220, 221, 222, 225, 226, 227, 228, 230, 232, 233, 235, 236, 237, 238, 239, 242, 243
 death of, 167
Qaddafi, Saif, 27, 150, 151, 161, 164, 175, 216, 229
Qasr Bu Hadi, battle of (1915), 102
Qatar, 77, 79, 86, 89, 98, 99, 100, 108, 132, 154, 155, 156, 157, 207, 223, 226, 243

Rafale, 69, 70, 80, 89
Ras Lanuf, 33, 53
Rasmussen, Anders Fogh, 39, 40, 72, 77, 188, 194
Reid, Harry, 142
Responsibility to Protect (R2P), 50, 63
Rice, Susan, 50, 59, 60, 67, 69, 103, 226, 238, 242
Richards, David, 37
Rickets, Peter, 37
Rome, 131, 132, 143, 194
Rommel, Erwin, 79
Romney, Mitt, 9, 238, 240
Rompuy, Herman Van, 35
Rubio, Marco, 141
Russia, xiv, 27, 32, 59, 60, 61, 62, 69, 102, 109, 118, 145, 149, 150, 164, 165, 178, 180, 182, 200, 204, 233, 234, 238
Rwanda, 38, 49, 50, 51, 58, 202, 238

Sarkozy, Nicolas, 30, 34, 35, 36, 38, 42, 48, 60, 66, 69, 73, 75, 77, 99, 103, 118, 124, 132, 151, 164, 197, 199, 200, 237, 239, 240
Saudi-Arabia, 19, 22, 54
Sigonella Air Base, 178, 191
Sirte, 1, 26, 34, 79, 101, 129, 165, 166, 167, 226
Slaughter, Anne-Marie, 7
Somalia, 4

INDEX

South Africa, 60, 63, 148, 164
special forces, 126, 154, 155, 156, 157, 158, 161, 238
Srebrenica, 175
Stavridis, James, 39, 97, 98, 100, 188, 190, 228
Stevens, Chris, 107, 173, 184
Strategic Defence Review (U.K.), 37
striker group, 100, 119, 135
Syria, xiv, 10, 61, 80, 92, 150, 172, 178, 179, 182, 203

Taft, Robert, 202
targeteers, 113, 114, 190
Tarhouni, Ali, 132
Terbil, Fathi, 25
Thani, Hamad Bin Khalifa al-, 77, 108
thuwwar, 30, 45, 47, 96, 99, 101, 102, 103, 104, 106, 107, 110, 122, 126, 128, 131, 132, 138, 145, 147, 153, 154, 155, 156, 157, 158, 160, 161, 162, 164, 168, 175, 181, 182, 183, 188, 189, 199
Tigre helicopter, xi, 127
Tobruk, 26
Tomasky, Michael, 12
Tripoli, viii, x, xi, xvi, 2, 10, 11, 26, 27, 29, 33, 46, 53, 73, 80, 83, 85, 86, 96, 102, 104, 105, 117, 118, 126, 129, 135, 137, 139, 143, 145, 147, 148, 149, 150, 151, 153, 154, 155, 158, 160, 161, 162, 164, 166, 170, 171, 172, 175, 183, 188, 198, 199, 201, 214, 219, 233, 236, 237
Tripolitania, 21, 26
Truman, Harry, 13
Tunisia, 7, 19, 20, 21, 23, 25, 31, 35, 38, 52, 87, 93, 94, 152, 154, 169, 175, 176, 182, 220, 221, 222, 224, 243
Turkey, 40, 72, 73, 76, 77, 103, 112, 119, 145, 191, 192, 207, 208, 215, 224, 240
Twitter, 14, 88, 161

UN Security Council, vii, xviii, 3, 6, 7, 28, 29, 30, 38, 42, 50, 51, 58, 59, 60, 61, 63, 64, 68, 69, 84, 96, 97, 100, 107, 126, 164, 165, 178, 179, 181, 182, 192, 228, 242
UN Security Council Resolution 1970, 30, 34, 38, 41, 48, 87, 116, 132, 150, 242
UN Security Council Resolution 1973, vii, 3, 59, 60, 64, 72, 74, 78, 84, 90, 100, 116, 126, 159, 178

OP-4, 100
Unified Protector, ix, xvii, 96, 99, 101, 118, 120, 163, 165, 177, 188, 191, 193, 195, 196, 198, 207, 209, 231, 236, 242
United Arab Emirates (UAE), 55, 77, 79, 89, 98, 99, 132, 154, 157, 158, 178, 211, 220, 236
United Kingdom, 3, 27, 29, 30, 32, 34, 35, 36, 37, 39, 40, 41, 42, 52, 53, 55, 58, 60, 62, 68, 71, 72, 77, 78, 79, 81, 83, 86, 87, 88, 89, 91, 100, 112, 124, 125, 126, 127, 128, 134, 135, 137, 143, 154, 157, 158, 159, 161, 165, 167, 174, 176, 178, 186, 191, 193, 194, 196, 197, 200, 207, 219, 224, 227, 233, 237, 238
United Nations, vii, xviii, 3, 4, 6, 7, 24, 27, 28, 29, 30, 35, 41, 42, 48, 50, 51, 58, 59, 60, 61, 63, 64, 66, 67, 72, 73, 80, 84, 97, 103, 107, 118, 120, 125, 131, 132, 134, 152, 158, 159, 164, 165, 177, 178, 182, 185, 188, 192, 194, 214, 218, 224, 233, 241, 242

Vandewalle, Dierdrik, 21

War Powers Act, 124, 139, 141, 186, 234
War Powers Resolution, 141
Washington Post, 8
Westerwelle, Guido, 62
White House, 9, 10, 12, 14, 20, 29, 30, 38, 39, 43, 45, 48, 49, 50, 52, 54, 56, 57, 58, 59, 64, 66, 71, 91, 93, 134, 138, 139, 140, 141, 142, 143, 144, 145, 147, 152, 161, 162, 164, 186, 243
Wikileaks, 23
Will, George, 10, 140, 144, 243
Wolfowitz, Paul, 11
Woodward, Margaret, 93

Younes, Abdel Fattah, 101, 159, 160, 182, 183, 215

Zakaria, Fareed, 11
Zawiyah, 33, 53, 117, 147, 158, 160
Zine al-Abidine Ben Ali, 20
Zuma, Jacob, 60, 148, 150